1, 2, AND 3 JOHN

New Testament Series

NEW INTERNATIONAL BIBLICAL COMMENTARY

WITHDRAWN

1, 2, AND 3 JOHN

THOMAS F. JOHNSON

Based on the New International Version

HENDRICKSON
PUBLISHERS

PATERNOSTER
PRESS

Original Hendrickson Publishers edition 1993

First published jointly 1995, in the United States by Hendrickson
Publishers, and in the United Kingdom by the Paternoster Press,
P. O. Box 300, Carlisle, Cumbria CA3 0QS

Printed in the United States of America

Library of Congress Cataloging-in-Publication Data

Johnson, Thomas Floyd
    1, 2, and 3 John /   Thomas F. Johnson.
      p.   cm. — (New International biblical commentary; 17)
    Includes bibliographical references and indexes.
    1. Bible.   N.T.   Epistles of John—Commentaries. I. Bible.   N.T.
Epistles of John. English. New International. 1993. II. Title.
III. Title: First, Second, and Third John. IV. Series.
BS2805.3.J646 1993
227'.94077—dc20   93–24717
                                        CIP

ISBN 0–943575–75–3

British Library Cataloguing in Publication Data

Johnson, Thomas F.
    1, 2, and 3 John. – (New International Biblical Commmentary
    Series; Vol. 17)
    I. Title   II. Series
227.907

ISBN 0–85364–671–6

Table of Contents

2 John

3 John

Foreword

New International Biblical Commentary

Although it does not appear on the standard best-seller lists, the Bible continues to outsell all other books. And in spite of growing secularism in the West, there are no signs that interest in its message is abating. Quite to the contrary, more and more men and women are turning to its pages for insight and guidance in the midst of the ever-increasing complexity of modern life.

This renewed interest in Scripture is found both outside and inside the church. It is found among people in Asia and Africa as well as in Europe and North America; indeed, as one moves outside of the traditionally Christian countries, interest in the Bible seems to quicken. Believers associated with the traditional Catholic and Protestant churches manifest the same eagerness for the Word that is found in the newer evangelical churches and fellowships.

We wish to encourage and, indeed, strengthen this world-wide movement of lay Bible study by offering this new commentary series. Although we hope that pastors and teachers will find these volumes helpful in both understanding and communicating the Word of God, we do not write primarily for them. Our aim is to provide for the benefit of every Bible reader reliable guides to the books of the Bible—representing the best of contemporary scholarship presented in a form that does not require formal theological education to understand.

The conviction of editor and authors alike is that the Bible belongs to the people and not merely to the academy. The message of the Bible is too important to be locked up in erudite and esoteric essays and monographs written only for the eyes of theological specialists. Although exact scholarship has its place in the service of Christ, those who share in the teaching office of the church have a responsibility to make the results of their research accessible to the Christian community at large. Thus, the Bible scholars who join in the presentation of this series write with these broader concerns in view.

A wide range of modern translations is available to the contemporary Bible student. Most of them are very good and much to be preferred—for understanding, if not always for beauty—to the older King James Version (the so-called Authorized Version of the Bible). The Revised Standard Version has become the standard English translation in many seminaries and colleges and represents the best of modern Protestant scholarship. It is also available in a slightly altered "common Bible" edition with the Catholic imprimatur, and the New Revised Standard Version appeared in 1989. In addition, the New American Bible is a fresh translation that represents the best of post–Vatican II Roman Catholic biblical scholarship and is in a more contemporary idiom than that of the RSV.

The New Jerusalem Bible, based on the work of French Catholic scholars but vividly rendered into English by a team of British translators, is perhaps the most literary of the recent translations, while the New English Bible is a monument to modern British Protestant research. The Good News Bible is probably the most accessible translation for the person who has little exposure to the Christian tradition or who speaks and reads English as a second language. Each of these is, in its own way, excellent and will be consulted with profit by the serious student of Scripture. Perhaps most will wish to have several versions to read, both for variety and for clarity of understanding—though it should be pointed out that no one of them is by any means flawless or to be received as the last word on any given point. Otherwise, there would be no need for a commentary series like this one!

We have chosen to use the New International Version as the basis for this series, not because it is necessarily the best translation available but because it is becoming increasingly used by lay Bible students and pastors. It is the product of an international team of "evangelical" Bible scholars who have sought to translate the Hebrew and Greek documents of the original into "clear and natural English . . . idiomatic [and] . . . contemporary but not dated," suitable for "young and old, highly educated and less well educated, ministers and laymen [sic]." As the translators themselves confess in their preface, this version is not perfect.

However, it is as good as any of the others mentioned above and more popular than most of them.

Each volume will contain an introductory chapter detailing the background of the book and its author, important themes, and other helpful information. Then, each section of the book will be expounded as a whole, accompanied by a series of notes on items in the text that need further clarification or more detailed explanation. Appended to the end of each volume will be a bibliographical guide for further study.

Our new series is offered with the prayer that it may be an instrument of authentic renewal and advancement in the worldwide Christian community and a means of commending the faith of the people who lived in biblical times and of those who seek to live by the Bible today.

W. WARD GASQUE

Preface

This commentary has been fifteen years in the thinking and four years in the writing. I became interested in the letters of John as a graduate student in the late 1970s at Duke University, under the mentorship of D. Moody Smith. His insightful exposition of the Johannine literature and his interest in their historical and cultural setting stimulated my dissertation research into the unusually antithetical language of the epistles of John. The social science categories of social conflict and sect helped me understand this phenomenon, though social science "explanation" was and is only one helpful lens through which to view NT documents. For the next ten years I taught the Gospel and letters of John in college and in seminary, along with other NT subjects, including my first love, New Testament theology. The passion for theology came from a student assistantship of two years at Fuller Seminary with the late George Eldon Ladd. I received the generous offer to write this commentary the day after I had been chosen as president of Sioux Falls College. That was more than four years ago. I owe W. Ward Gasque, Patrick Alexander, Phil Frank, and the other editorial staff at Hendrickson Publishers my gratitude not only for their confidence in me as an author but also for their patience as I worked on this wonderful project during summers, "spring breaks," and holidays.

The only way to make good sense of the letters of John is to understand that the Elder, as the writer calls himself, wrote nearly every verse with one eye on his opponents, the false teachers, who had incited a schism within the community. This violation of community was a violation of love, the distinctive Johannine "new commandment" (John 13:34). The secessionists not only broke the love command but rejected Jesus, as the Elder and the loyal Johannine Christians understood him. This failure of truth and love, and the Elder's passionate response to it, penetrates every passage of these epistles. I have left the full understanding of these matters to the Introduction and to the exposition of the text itself.

It is difficult to overstate the debt which all interpreters of the Johannine literature owe to Raymond E. Brown, S.S. For more than thirty years, first in his two-volume Anchor Bible Commentary on the Gospel of John, and then in his Anchor Bible Commentary of the Epistles of John, and in a host of other writings on these books, Ray Brown has been the master teacher from whom all students of the Gospel and letters of John have learned. That he is frequently cited in the Additional Notes of this commentary, in agreement and in disagreement with my conclusions, is evidence of my personal debt to his thorough research, careful thinking, and profound scholarship.

Special thanks are due to my college for allowing me the time to work on this book, to my assistant Rita Jerke for her help in its completion, and to my wife, Michele, and to my family, Jason, Amy, Sarah, and Diane, for their continual encouragement to get it done!

October 1992

Abbreviations

AB	Anchor Bible (series)
ACNT	Augsburg Commentary on the New Testament (series)
act.	active
AnBib	Analecta Biblica
aor.	aorist
AV	Authorized Version
BAGD	W. Bauer, W. F. Arndt, F. W. Gingrich, and F. Danker, *A Greek-English Lexicon of the New Testament and Other Early Christian Literature*, 2d ed., Chicago: University of Chicago Press, 1979
BJRL	*Bulletin of the John Rylands Library*
BST	Bible Speaks Today (series)
c.	*circa*, about
cf.	compare
chap./chaps.	chapter/chapters
Clem.	Clement
Did.	Didache
Diogn.	Diognetus
diss.	dissertation
ed./eds.	edited by, editor/editors
e.g.	for example
esp.	especially
et al.	and others
f./ff.	and the following
fr.	from
Gk.	Greek
Hb.	Hebrew
Herm. *Man.*	Shepherd of Hermas, *Mandates*
HNTC	Harper's New Testament Commentaries (series)

HTKNT	Herder's Theologische Kommentar zum Neuen Testament (series)
ICC	International Critical Commentary (series)
IDB	*Interpreter's Dictionary of the Bible*
i.e.	that is
Int	*Interpretation*
ISBE	*International Standard Bible Encyclopedia*
IVPNTC	InterVarsity Press New Testament Commentary (series)
JBL	*Journal of Biblical Literature*
JTS	*Journal of Theological Studies*
KJV	King James Version
lit.	literal, literally
LXX	Septuagint
Macc.	Maccabees
MNTC	Moffatt New Testament Commentary (series)
MS/MSS	manuscript/manuscripts
n.	note
NASB	New American Standard Bible
NCBC	New Century Bible Commentary (series)
NEB	New English Bible
Nestle	Nestle-Aland Greek New Testament, 26th ed.
NICNT	New International Commentary on the New Testament (series)
NIDNTT	*New International Dictionary of New Testament Theology*
NIV	New International Version
NovT	*Novum Testamentum*
NRSV	New Revised Standard Version
NT	New Testament
NTM	New Testament Message (series)
NTS	*New Testament Studies*
OT	Old Testament
p./pp.	page/pages
pass.	passive
perf.	perfect
pl.	plural
pres.	present
ptcp.	participle

rev.	revised
RevExp	*Review and Expositor*
RSV	Revised Standard Version
SBLDS	Society of Biblical Literature Dissertation Series
SBT	Studies in Biblical Theology
Spec. Laws	*Special Laws*
TC	Tyndale Commentaries (series)
T. Dan	Testament of Dan
TDNT	*Theological Dictionary of the New Testament*
TEV	Today's English Version
UBS	United Bible Societies, *Greek New Testament*, 3d ed.
v./vv.	verse/verses
vol./vols.	volume/volumes
ZNW	*Zeitschrift für die neutestamentliche Wissenschaft*
ZThK	*Zeitschrift für Theologie und Kirche*
1QH	Thanksgiving Hymns, Dead Sea Scrolls
1QM	War Scroll, Dead Sea Scrolls
1QS	Manual of Discipline, Dead Sea Scrolls
4QFlor	Florilegium, Dead Sea Scrolls

Introduction

The letters of John in the New Testament are treasured for their memorable teaching on love and forgiveness, yet they were written in the midst of one of the fiercest conflicts in first-century Christianity. The same author who wrote, ". . . God is love" (1 John 4:8); ". . . since God so loved us, we also ought to love one another" (1 John 4:11); "We love because he first loved us" (1 John 4:19); also wrote ". . . many antichrists have come . . . They went out from us, but they did not really belong to us" (1 John 2:18–19); ". . . we know who the children of God are and who the children of the devil are" (1 John 3:10), and "Many false prophets have gone out into the world. . . . This is the spirit of antichrist" (1 John 4:1, 3).

On the one hand, the author can assure his readers that "If we confess our sins, he is faithful and just and will forgive us our sins" (1 John 1:9). On the other hand, he warns that "Many deceivers, who do not acknowledge Jesus Christ as coming in the flesh, have gone out into the world. Any such person is the deceiver and the antichrist . . . Do not take him into your house or welcome him" (2 John 7, 10).

In 3 John the author commends Gaius for showing love and hospitality to strangers (3 John 5–8), but Diotrephes, we learn, refuses to welcome them: "He also stops those who want to do so and puts them out of the church" (3 John 10). Clearly, what is going on in the Johannine epistles is not all sweetness and light! There is a real conflict raging, evidence of which exists in all three letters, and it is this controversy that has called forth these passionate epistles.

The Author

If these three writings, known as the letters of John, are all from the same person, and the preponderance of evidence indicates that they are,[1] then we may call their author "the Elder" (Gk. *ho presbyteros*), for that is the only name he ever gives himself

(2 John 1; 3 John 1). The order in which he wrote the letters is impossible to determine, though 1 John appears to be a general writing (it is a "letter" or "epistle" only in the broadest sense of these terms; see the discussion of genre below) intended for several churches in the author's purview. Consequently, it provides a good background for examining the concerns raised in the other, more focused letters. Second John is written to a specific congregation and refers to matters discussed in 1 John (e.g., the dual emphases on love and truth, vv. 1–6, and the reference to "the deceivers" who deny the humanity of Jesus, v. 7). Third John is a letter to an individual. It shares the vocabulary of love and truth with the other epistles. In 3 John the Elder mentions a letter that he wrote to the church (v. 9), but it is not possible to know if he is referring to 1 John, 2 John, or another letter.

Did the Elder also write the Gospel of John? Despite the extensive similarities between the letters and the Gospel, the differences, though not overwhelming, are significant,[2] and this question should probably be answered in the negative. According to its own testimony, the Fourth Gospel was written by someone called "the disciple whom Jesus loved" (John 21:20, 24; cf. John 13:23; 19:26; 20:2; 21:7). Yet John 21:24 and other passages in the Gospel contain indications that the original Gospel of this beloved disciple had been edited, at least in minor ways, before it reached its present form. For example, 21:24c ("we know that his testimony is true") can be the words only of someone other than the author. The context implies that this beloved disciple has at long last died (John 21:20–23). This same understanding of "we" may also apply in 1:14 ("we have seen his glory"), in 1:16 ("from the fullness of his grace we have all received"), and in 3:11 ("we speak of what we know, and we testify to what we have seen, but still you people do not accept our testimony"). Since the entire Gospel appears to come to a natural conclusion at 20:31, chapter 21 is probably an epilogue from the "we" of 21:24.

Who is the "we"? It is, most naturally, the followers of the beloved disciple,[3] his own disciples, who became or who are already the leaders of the Johannine community. The letters, especially 2 and 3 John, are incontrovertible evidence for the existence of the Johannine community. Whether this community should be called a "school" or contained a "school" is another matter.[4] After the death of the beloved disciple, they edited and copied the Fourth Gospel, which their founder and teacher had written, probably over many years, as a summary of his teaching and a theological interpretation of the Christ event.

The Elder of the Johannine epistles was probably one of the "we," a disciple of the beloved disciple, who has taken from him the mantle of authority for at least a portion of his community, though it becomes clear in the letters that not all in the community accept this authority. In this sense, one could argue that the final forms of the Gospel and the letters do come from the same hand, though it would be more accurate to say that they come from the same community or circle. The Elder closely identifies with his mentor and counts himself as part of the founding, eyewitness generation through his association with those who were eyewitnesses and with "that which was from the beginning" (1 John 1:1–3; 2:7, 24; 3:11; 2 John 5–6). The same "we" who spoke in the Gospel of John speaks anew in the prologue of the first epistle. It is not clear whether the Elder was himself an eyewitness, as 1 John 1:1–3 seems to imply, or whether he simply counts himself in solidarity with the original disciples of the Lord.[5]

That is as far as the internal evidence from the Gospel and the letters of John can take us. What about the external evidence, the testimony of tradition? After all, the titles of the Johannine writings arose from the belief that they were written by the apostle John, the son of Zebedee, beloved disciple of Jesus. The earliest certain quotation of the letters of John is in Polycarp's letter to the Philippians (c. A.D. 130), though he does not mention any author. Toward the end of the second century, about A.D. 180, Irenaeus, bishop of Lyons, quotes from 1 and 2 John, as well as the Gospel, and attributes them to "John, the disciple of the Lord," whom he believes is the beloved disciple and probably thinks of as John, the apostle, the son of Zebedee, though he never calls him this. He says that John wrote the Gospel in Ephesus during the reign of Trajan (A.D. 98–117; *Against Heresies* 3.3.4).

Irenaeus' reasons for believing this do not appear to be well founded. When he was a child in Asia Minor, he had heard Polycarp, who had told of his association with "John" and other eyewitnesses (in Eusebius, *Eccl. Hist.* 5. 20. 4). But this John may not have been the apostle, and Polycarp never mentions his own relationship with John. In fact, there were two Johns known in the early second century, the apostle and "the elder John." Papias (c. A.D. 150) calls this latter John, "the disciple of the Lord" and "a living and surviving voice," and he distinguishes him from the apostle John, who has died (in Eusebius, *Eccl. Hist.* 3.39.3f). Irenaeus could well have confused the two Johns. Though some have tried to connect this John the Elder to the Elder of 1–3 John,[6] there is nothing in the tradition which does so. The external evidence does not provide additional clues to the identity of our Elder, unless, of course, Papias' John the Elder is the Elder of 2 John 1 and 3 John 1.[7]

In summary, it is best to understand all the letters of John as written by one person, the Elder, a disciple of "the disciple whom Jesus loved," one of the "we" who edited and circulated the Fourth Gospel and perhaps an eyewitness to some part of Jesus' ministry (though the language of 1 John 1:1–3 does not require this). He had succeeded the "beloved disciple" as leader of the community and had assumed pastoral responsibility for a number of churches which were united by the common tradition of the Gospel of John.[8]

The Readers, the Date, and the Provenance

Who were the first recipients of the Johannine epistles? They were Christians who looked back to the disciple whom Jesus loved as their founder and teacher (John 21:20–24). Further, it is likely that this Johannine community, circle,[9] or "school" preserved the written witness of the Beloved Disciple, their tradition about Jesus, in what we know as the Gospel of John. It had been written, though perhaps not yet in final form,[10] about a decade or so before these letters. Accepting the traditional date for the Gospel at A.D. 80–90, the letters of John may be dated about A.D. 90–100.

If the book of Revelation, with its letters to the seven churches, also comes from this community, as it almost certainly does, then we can say that at the time the Johannine epistles were written the author and his readers lived in the Roman province of Asia (modern Turkey). More specifically, early Christian tradition places them in and around the great Roman city of Ephesus (Eusebius, *Eccl. Hist.* 3.1.1; Irenaeus, *Against Heresies* 3.1.2).[11] Second and Third John imply that the writer and his readers are at some distance from one another, so that travel is not easy, and the provision of hospitality is necessary.

The recipients also appear to meet together in house churches. Early Christians, lacking official meeting places such as church buildings, often met in homes (Acts 2:46; 5:42; 8:3; 12:12; 16:15, 40; 17:5–7; 18:7; Rom. 16:5; 1 Cor. 16:19; Col. 4:15; Phlm. 2). Second John is written to such a congregation, which the author calls "the chosen lady and her children," as he calls his own church "the children of your chosen sister" (2 John 1, 13). Third John, written to the Elder's "dear friend," Gaius, mentions the author's home church (3 John 6) and the house church of Diotrephes (vv. 9–10). Gaius probably belongs to another assembly nearby. It is not clear how these churches are organized. The Elder understands them to be under his pastoral authority, but that authority is being challenged, both by those who have left the community and by some who remain.

The Historical Setting and Occasion

What was happening in these churches? This community came into existence through the Beloved Disciple's witness to the life, teaching, and miraculous signs of Jesus (John 21:20–24; cf. 19:35). He wrote the Fourth Gospel "that you may believe that Jesus is the Christ, the Son of God, and that by believing you may have life in his name" (John 20:31). But these Johannine Christians had been persecuted and rejected, as Jesus said they would be, by those who did not accept their message about Jesus as the divine Son of God and Messiah. The authorities had expelled them from the synagogues, and they had become separated from their homes, families, and spiritual roots (John 16:2; cf. John 9:22, 34–35; 12:42). Though they felt that the world hated them (1 John 3:13), they took comfort in the knowledge that it had hated Jesus, their master, before them (John 15:18–20).[12]

Now, some years after the writing of the Gospel,[13] another crisis has arisen. We learn from 1 John 2:19 that a schism, a church split, has divided the Johannine community. A large and influential group has left the original fellowship. The author calls them "liars" (1 John 1:6; 2:4, 22; 4:20), "deceivers" (1 John 2:26; 3:7; 2 John 7), "antichrists" (1 John 2:18, 22; 4:3; 2 John 7), "children of the devil" (3:10), "murderers" (3:15), and "false prophets" (4:1). The issues appear to have been doctrinal (Christology and pneumatology), ethical (love and sin), spiritual (the claims of the opponents for a mystical and intimate relationship with God), and political (struggles over the Elder's authority). It is difficult to reconstruct the entire controversy, since we are able to infer the views of the opponents only through the writings of the Elder.[14]

Doctrine: Christ and the Spirit

The secessionists, while affirming the deity of Christ, denied his humanity. They rejected the incarnation, that "the Word became flesh and made his dwelling among us" (John 1:14a). Specifically, the writer says, they cannot "acknowledge that Jesus Christ has come in the flesh" (1 John 4:2; 2 John 7).

This is the same as denying "Jesus," the human name for Christ (1 John 4:3). Literally, 1 John 4:3 says, "And every spirit that does not confess *the Jesus* is not from God." In the same way, 1 John 2:22 should be read with the emphasis on the name "Jesus." The schismatics deny that the flesh-and-blood man, Jesus, is the divine Christ. To do so is to deny not only the Son but the Father as well, since, in Fourth Gospel terms, Jesus is "the way and the truth and the life," through whom alone one comes to the Father (John 14:6). Similarly, in 1 John 5:1, to be "born of God" one must believe that "*Jesus* is the Christ," while in 1 John 5:5, to "overcome the world" one must believe that "*Jesus* is the Son of God." Acknowledging *Jesus* as the Son of God is also the way to mutual indwelling with God (1 John 4:15). In each instance the emphasis falls on the subject, the human "Jesus," not on the predicated title. To underscore their faulty Christology even further, the Elder (2 John 1; 3 John 1), accentuates "the blood of Jesus" and his sacrificial death on the cross (1 John 1:7; 2:2; 4:10; 5:6–8).

The secessionists found this Christology impossible, because they were docetists (Gk. *dokeō*, "to seem, or appear"). They believed that the divine Christ, the eternal Son of God, only appeared or seemed to be human, when he came to this world to be its Savior. They emphasized "his glory, the glory of the One and Only, who came from the Father" (John 1:14b). As part of a wider gnostic cultural movement, which dualistically separated spirit as good and matter as evil and asserted salvation by esoteric knowledge (Gk. *gnōsis),* the Elder's opponents could not integrate the fact of Jesus' fully human historical existence into their assumed and entirely spiritual concept of God. They were like Cerinthus and his followers, possible contemporaries of our Johannine Christians, who separated Jesus and the Christ (a possible textual variant of 1 John 4:3 may refer to this; see the discussion in R. Brown, *Epistles*, pp. 494–96). They thought that the divine, spiritual Christ descended on Jesus at his baptism but left him before the suffering of the cross (Irenaeus, *Against Heresies* 1.26.1).[15]

While it is not a major issue, as Christology is, the doctrine of the Spirit was also a matter of disagreement for the Elder and his opponents.[16] Just as in Old Testament conflicts over true and false prophets (1 Kgs. 22:1–28; Jer. 23:9–40; Ezek. 13:1–23; cf. Amos 7:10–17), both sides in the Johannine conflict claimed to speak by the Spirit (1 John 4:1-3) and to know what the Spirit says (1 John 5:6). They claimed to have a special "anointing" from God (1 John 2:20, 27, likely a reference to the Holy Spirit; see the commentary on these verses). But the opponents were saying that the Spirit had left the Johannine Christians still loyal to the Elder, or that they had a false, or "counterfeit," anointing (2:27). The Elder counseled his "dear children" not to listen to "those who are trying to lead you astray" (2:26). The Spirit, or the Spirit's anointing, has not left them, and it is genuine. In fact, because they have this anointing, the faithful Christians do not need anyone to teach them, especially the schismatics (2:27).

On the attack, the Elder claimed that God gave *us* his Spirit (1 John 3:24; 4:13), not them. Their "spirit" is not to be believed. They, the heretics, are "false prophets" who "have gone out into the world" (4:1; cf. 2:19; 2 John 7). They "do not acknowledge Jesus," and they are "not from God." On the contrary, they represent the eschatological "spirit of antichrist" (4:3). "They are from the world"; whereas "we are from God" (4:4–6). We have "the Spirit of truth"; they have "the spirit of error" (4:6).[17] Since all sides claimed charismatic inspiration, this disagreement over the Spirit could not be resolved, except by doctrinal (in this instance, christological) test: who confesses the incarnate Jesus Christ (1 John 4:2; cf. 1 Thess. 5:19–21; 2 Cor. 11:4; Gal. 1:6–9)?

Ethics: Love and Sin

There is a major difference also between the Elder and his opponents concerning ethics. Central to Johannine Christianity is the love commandment; it is the community's fundamental ethical principle. Jesus gave them this new command (John 13:34–35; 2 John 5–6). Yet, to the Elder, all of the actions of the schismatics show that they do not keep this command. They hate their brothers (1 John 2:9–11). They are like Cain, evil and murderous (1 John 3:11–15). They see their brothers in need and turn away (1 John 3:16–18). They claim to love God yet they hate their brothers (1 John 4:19–21). The most telling loveless action of the opponents was their secession itself; they broke the unity of the community. To the Elder that showed that "they did not really belong to us . . . none of them belonged to us" (1 John 2:19). It is evident that the opponents deny both of the central tenets of Johannine Christianity, faith in Jesus as God's Son and love among his disciples (1 John 3:23).

The opponents also claim not to sin. They may even believe that they are incapable of it, having moved beyond that possibility spiritually. They "have no sin" (1 John 1:8), and they "have not sinned" (1 John 1:10); so they claim. They are not the kind of "gnostics" whose personal assurance of salvation caused them to be libertines, as in Corinth.[18] The Elder never accuses them of any specific immorality. All of his "ethical" charges against them are general ("walk in the darkness," 1 John 1:6; "does not do what he commands," 2:4 [cf. 3:24; 5:3; 2 John 5–6]; does not "walk as Jesus did," 2:6; "sins," "breaks the law," "keeps on sinning," "does what is sinful," will "lead you astray," 3:4–10; "under the control of the evil one," 5:19; cf. 3:8, 10), or relate either to their "lying" about Jesus (the doctrinal issue; 1 John 1:6; 2:22; cf. 4:20, lying about their relationship with God), or to their failure to love their brothers and sisters (the schism and its results, see above). Instead, the false teachers are "super-spiritual" gnostics, claiming to be living life with God on a much higher plane than the Johannine Christians who remain loyal to the Elder.[19]

Spirituality

Just what were the schismatics' exalted spiritual claims? There were seven of them, although they overlap and are all different expressions of one common assertion of their spiritual superiority.

Specifically, they claim (1) "to have fellowship with" God, who "is light"[20] (1 John 1:5–6). The Elder contends that they are lying, since they "walk in the darkness" (1:6). But the opponents claim (2) "to be in the light" (2:9), an assertion the Elder denies, since they hate their brothers (2:9–11). Similarly, the secessionists claim (3) to "live (lit., "abide" or "remain"; Gk. *menō*) in him" (2:6), or to "be in him" (cf. 2:5). The Elder contends that this assertion of an intimate, mystical relationship with God is belied by their unchristlike lifestyle (2:6).[21]

As gnostics (Gk. *gnōsis),* they claim (4) "to know God," in the sense of close, personal communion and esoteric, saving knowledge (1 John 2:4; cf. 3:6; 4:7–8). First John 2:20 implies that these opponents may also have been claiming, more absolutely, to "know," i.e., to have broad spiritual knowledge, to be enlightened; hence, the Elder assures his readers, "You all know." He counters the false teachers further by pointing out that their claim to know God is invalidated by their disobedience to God's commands (2:4) or God's word (2:5), by their habitual sin (3:6), and by their lack of love (4:7–8).

The schismatics also claim (5) "to love God" (1 John 4:10, 20). They boasted about their devotion to God; perhaps they religiously practiced spiritual disciplines as evidence of their devotion. What counts, the Elder replies, is not our love for God, but God's love for us (4:10). And the true evidence of love for God is love for one's brothers and sisters in the community (4:20–21). As we have already seen, the opponents have failed to meet this test.

Much of the language of 1 John implies that both sides claimed (6) "to be God's children," or "to be born of God," or "from God." "We are the children of God," the writer assures his beleaguered readers (3:1–2, 10; 5:19; cf. 5:2), but *they* are the "children of the devil" (3:10) and are under the control of the devil (5:19; cf. 4:4). We have been "born of God" (3:9; 5:1, 4a, 18) and are "from God" (4:4, 6), but they are "not from God" (4:6) but are "from the world" (4:5).

Finally, the opponents claimed (7), as we have already seen, to have the Spirit and to prophesy by the Spirit (4:1–2), a claim which the Elder rejects by testing the spirits and finding that the schismatics cannot affirm that "Jesus Christ has come in the flesh." This proves they are not speaking by the Spirit of God (4:2).

These claims to an exalted spirituality caused a consider-able loss of confidence among the Johannine Christians who were loyal to the Elder. Repeatedly, throughout 1 John (e.g., 2:26–27; 3:19–22; 4:17–18; 5:13–20), the author seeks to answer their self-doubts and to assure them that it is they, and not the assertive and self-recommending secessionists, who are right with God.

Politics[22]

All of these differences, and perhaps other factors un-known to us today, led to a clash between the Elder and his opponents over power and authority. We have already seen that they claimed to have equal spiritual power, as prophets speaking by the Spirit. In a community that relied on the Holy Spirit as the Paraclete and Spirit of Truth (John 14:16–17) to teach them all things (14:26), to testify about Jesus (15:26), and to guide them into all truth (16:13), this controversy over who speaks by the Spirit caused considerable confusion among the members and was part of the secessionists' strategy to undermine the Elder. "Listen to us, the spiritual elite," they asserted. "We, and not the Elder, speak by the Spirit."

This struggle for influence and teaching authority over the Johannine churches led to a schism in the churches. The gnostic false teachers left the community (1 John 2:19; the Elder main-tains that they never really belonged to it, though why he thinks so remains unknown), but they continued to try to influence the remaining members to join them (2:26; 3:7). They were traveling the circuit of the Johannine house churches in an attempt to spread both their teaching and their influence (2 John 10). The Elder is also sending out his representatives (2 John 3, 5–8) and is himself contemplating visits to the churches (2 John 12; 3 John 14).

At least one church leader, Diotrephes, has seized this op-portunity to declare his house church completely independent of the Elder. He "loves to be first"; he has refused to recognize the Elder's authority and has attacked him maliciously; he will not admit to his church the Elder's representatives, and he has the power to "excommunicate" (Gk. *ekballō*, "throw out") those who want to welcome them (3 John 9–10).[23]

To counter the general threat to his leadership, the Elder expresses his authority in several ways in his letters. He begins by appealing to the tradition of which he is the living representative. In 1 John 1:1-3 he claims to be either an eyewitness to Jesus' ministry himself or, more likely, the heir[24] of "those who from the first were eyewitnesses and servants of the word," as Luke put it (Luke 1:2). "We have heard . . . seen . . . looked at . . . touched . . . the Word of life" (1 John 1:1). He occasionally uses "we" or "us" elsewhere in the epistles to tie himself to this authoritative apostolic tradition (1 John 1:4–5; 4:14; 3 John 9–10; cf. 5:20).[25] A particularly striking instance of this is in 3 John 12, where the Elder says "you know that our testimony is true." This echoes the words of the community about the Beloved Disciple in John 19:35 and 21:24. By implication, the author is claiming this heritage of authority. He reinforces this important tie by reminding the readers of the teaching they have had "from the beginning," the foundation with which he, and not his opponents, is connected (1 John 2:7, 24; 3:11; 2 John 5–6).

Another way in which the Elder subtly asserts his authority over the readers is his addressing them as his "children," "dear children" (1 John 2:1, 12, 13, 18, 28; 3:7, 18; 4:4; 5:21) or "my children" (3 John 4). Paul did the same, and thereby both men expressed their parental concern for those in their charge. Like Paul, the Elder may even have given them birth in the sense of being an agent in their conversion (cf. 1 Cor. 4:14–15; Gal. 4:19; 1 Thess. 2:7, 11).

The Elder's assumed authority over his readers is further demonstrated in his giving them commands: 2:7–8, the new/old command (cf. 2 John 5–6); 2:15, "Do not love the world"; 2:24, "See that what you have heard from the beginning remains in you"; 2:27–28, "remain in him," "continue in him"; 3:7, "do not let anyone lead you astray"; 3:13, "do not be surprised"; 3:18, "let us . . . love . . . with actions and in truth"; 4:1, "do not believe every spirit"; 4:7, "let us love one another"; 5:21, "keep yourselves from idols"; 2 John 8, "Watch out" (lit., "guard yourselves"); 2 John 10, "do not take him into your house or welcome him." He also tells them what they "should," "ought to," or "must" do: 2:6, "must walk as Jesus did"; 3:11, "should love one another"; 3:16, "ought to lay down our lives for our brothers"; 4:11, "ought to love one another"; 5:16, "should pray"; 3 John 8, "ought . . . to show hospitality"; cf. 3 John 6.

Though the Elder has a strong sense of his authority over and responsibility for the Johannine community to which he is writing, he often expresses his relationship to them in an egalitarian way, as one of them, on the same level as they are. Thus, there is a certain "democratic" tone to his style of communication. Though he can use the parental "children" (and its variants), he often uses "dear friend(s)" (1 John 2:7; 3:2, 21; 4:1, 7, 11; 3 John 1, 2, 5). The church members can simply be called "the friends here" and "the friends there" (3 John 14). Or he addresses them all as "brothers [and sisters]" (3:13), or he says, "we [all of us] are the children of God" (3:1–2, 10; 5:19). In 1 John 2:20, 27, the Elder instructs them about their common "anointing" and knowledge, and that they do not even need a teacher (meaning the secessionists, certainly, but perhaps also the Elder would include himself), since all have the Paraclete to teach and guide them (John 14:16–17, 26; 16:13). He prefers "to visit you and talk with you face to face" (2 John 12; cf. 3 John 14), on the same personal level. Instead of threatening the rebel Diotrephes, when the Elder comes, he "will call attention to what he is doing," as if the community itself is expected to come to the right conclusion and do what should be done (3 John 10; in contrast to 2 Cor. 13:1–2, 10).[26]

The Elder can speak harshly about the false teachers and does not hesitate to do so, given the gravity of what is at stake (the continuation of orthodox and "apostolic" Christianity). Yet, it is rather amazing, given the rejection of the Elder and his teaching by the secessionists and the rebellion of Diotrephes, that the author expresses his authority as mildly and "democratically" as he does.[27] The harshness of the Elder's language has been overstated and, in any case, runs against the grain of modern inclusivist, relativist thinking.

Occasion and Purpose

The letters of John were called forth, therefore, by this crisis of the secession of the false teachers. First John was written to address the heart of the conflict directly, refuting the heretical views of the schismatics and encouraging the remaining Johannine Christians to continue to be faithful both to the Elder personally and to his teaching. Second John warns a particular church against receiving the itinerant secessionist teachers and urges their exclusion from hospitality. Third John commends Gaius for showing hospitality to the Elder's traveling representatives and urges him to continue to do so, especially in view of Diotrephes' rejection of the Elder's authority.

Genre and Language

There is no doubt about the literary genre of 2 and 3 John, and there is no agreement about the genre of 1 John. Second and Third John are letters, the former to a church and the latter to an individual. They have most of the usual marks of personal letters in the Hellenistic era: the names of the sender and the recipient, a greeting formula (a blessing or a health wish) the body, and closing formulas, sometimes including greetings.[28] But, as to 1 John, there are many proposals, none entirely satisfactory. First John is clearly neither a letter nor a more formal epistle. It contains none of the letter elements, but it was written to a specific and geographically limited audience well known to the author, who never names himself or his readers, except to call them "children," "dear children," or "brothers [and sisters]." While there is a homiletic quality to 1 John, its lack of any clear organization makes it appear more like a collection of sermon fragments or notes than a connected discourse. While there are similarities to the Gospel of John, which it seems to presuppose, it is not a commentary in any ancient or modern sense.[29] A simpler solution is needed. Several times the author indicates that he is writing (1:4; 2:1, 7–8, 12–14, 21, 26; 5:13). Since 1 John is like no other NT document in form, perhaps it is best to follow the author's own suggestion for it and call it a "writing."[30]

As to the language of the letters of John, it is highly antithetical or dualistic.[31] The author prefers to express himself in contrasts in order to state or to clarify his teaching. These motifs of contrast are interrelated. They overlap one another and present the author's doctrinal and ethical concerns in a variety of ways. Repetition, with and without nuance, is a prominent stylistic characteristic. The author's language has a way of doubling back on itself, as in a spiral, before it moves ahead into a new expression of thought.[32]

Antitheses which occur at least twice are:

The Elder and his group versus . . .	the secessionists
God, Christ, Spirit versus . . .	various opponents
Secessionist claims versus . . .	the Elder's refutations
Love versus . . .	hate, not love, or fear
Truth versus . . .	error, lie, or deceit
To know versus . . .	to not know
Sin, unrighteous, evil, or disobedience versus . . .	not sin, righteous, good, or obedience

To abide or remain versus . . .	not to abide or to pass away.
To believe or confess versus . . .	not to believe or confess, or to deny
Confident, reassuring, or not condemning versus . . .	ashamed, or condemning
Greet, support, receive, or welcome versus . . .	not greet, not receive, or not welcome
Has God or the Son versus . . .	does not have God or the Son
Life versus . . .	death or not life
See, appear, or be manifest versus . . .	not see, not appear, or be blind
Light versus . . .	darkness
Write versus . . .	not write

Theological Themes

Having covered at length the views of the opponents of the Elder and indicated therein the broad outlines of his response to them, I have touched upon most of the topics of Johannine theology in the epistles. A brief overview is all that is needed here.[33]

The two principal themes of the Johannine epistles are summarized in 1 John 3:23: "And this is his [God's] command: to believe in the name of his Son, Jesus Christ, and to love one another as he commanded us." Christology and ethics dominate the Elder's theological agenda. The former issue is focused on the humanity of the Christ. The secessionists, with their gnostic world view, apparently accept his divinity but reject that he "came in the flesh" (1 John 4:2; 2 John 7; cf. 1 John 1:1-3). They cannot affirm that the human Jesus is the Christ or the Son of God (1 John 2:22–23; 4:3, 15; 5:1, 5, 20). As a corollary, they have no place for his death in their scheme of salvation. Consequently, our author emphasizes the importance of the blood or sacrificial death of Jesus for salvation, an emphasis not present in the Gospel of John (1 John 1:7, 9; 2:2; 4:10; 5:6–8; cf. 3:16).

The heart of the author's ethical teaching is the old, yet new, love command (1 John 2:7–11; 3:11–18, 23; 4:7–8, 11–12, 19–21; 2 John 4–6), in the form in which the community has had it "from the beginning" (1 John 2:7; 3:11; 2 John 5–6): "A new command I give you: Love one another. As I have loved you, so you must love one another" (John 13:34). Given the schism which has torn the Johannine community, the Elder's application of the love command is always within the community among his remaining loyal disciples. There is no reflection on love for neighbor in general or love for the opponents or one's enemies.[34] It is the chief moral failure of these secessionists that they fail to love their former brothers and sisters whom they have left (1 John 2:19).

The Elder is also concerned about the moral issue of sin, and this concern as well is driven by the opponents' claims that they do not sin (1 John 1:8, 10). While the Elder wants to maintain that true Christians also should not (1 John 2:1) or, in a habitual sense, do not sin (3:6, 9; 5:18), he teaches that we should confess our sins, live in fellowship with one another, realize that Christ is our advocate and atoning sacrifice for sin, and know that we have been cleansed from sin and forgiven (1:7–2:2; 4:10; cf. 2:12). True Christians, in contrast to the opponents, will obey God's commands and live a righteous, loving life, "walking as Jesus did" (1 John 2:3–6, 29; 3:3, 7, 10–18, 22–24; 4:7–8, 11–12, 19–21; 5:2–3; 2 John 4–6; 3 John 6–8, 11).[35]

While there are also in the epistles theological perspectives on God (e.g., as "light"—1 John 1:5; or as "love"—4:8, 16), the Spirit, the world, eschatology, and other themes that are distinctively Johannine and which are even different from their presentation in the Gospel,[36] none of them are as prominent as the concerns for Christology and ethics outlined above.

Outline or Structure

Despite the dozens of commentaries on 1 John and their authors' concerted attempts to set forth the structure of this writing satisfactorily, none have been widely accepted and all differ from one another.[37] It is best to treat 1 John as a series of interrelated pericopes, in which the Elder-composer brings back, as in a musical reprise, several themes or motifs. For example, the entire epistle could be organized, with very little "slippage," around four major topics to which the author repeatedly returns for emphasis and clarification, as he attempts to meet the continuing threat of the secessionists' teaching and their efforts to lead his community astray:

A. Faith/doctrine: 1:1–4; 2:18–27; 4:1–3; 5:4b–12, 21
B. Sin/obedience: 1:5–2:2; 2:15–17, 28–29; 3:3–10; 5:16–17
C. Assurance: 2:3–6, 12–14; 3:1–2, 19–24; 4:4–6, 13–18; 5:13–15, 18–20
D. Love: 2:7–11; 3:11–18; 4:7–12, 19–5:4a.[38]

Lacking any major division based on content,[39] our outline of 1 John recognizes fourteen separate units in the letter (see the Table of Contents). In deciding where to make a division between the end of one unit in 1 John and the beginning of another, it is important to recognize the author's use of "linking concepts," i.e., he often ends the previous section with an idea that also briefly introduces or "links" the new section. See the Additional Note on 1 John 5:4b.

The structures of 2 and 3 John are simple and direct, with opening greetings, main bodies (with two or three concerns), and closing words.

The Text

This commentary is based on the NIV translation of the New Testament, which first appeared in 1973 and was revised in 1978 and 1984. I have noted in the commentary the few minor changes which have occurred in the text of 1–3 John. Many of the comments and notes, however, use the Greek NT. I have worked with K. Aland, M. Black, et al., *The Greek New Testament*, 3d ed. (Stuttgart: United Bible Societies, 1983, corrected). Occasionally, text critical matters were referenced in Nestle-Aland, *Novum Testamentum Graece*, 26th ed., and in B. M. Metzger, *A Textual Commentary on the Greek New Testament* (London/New York: United Bible Societies, 1971). The best MSS for the Johannine epistles are the uncials Codex Vaticanus from the Alexandrian group and Codex Sinaiticus which, while also Alexandrian, contains other readings.[40]

Notes

---

1. The language, style, and issues discussed are so similar that there is no reason to postulate separate authors, though R. Bultmann thought so (*Epistles,* p. 1), citing 2 John's imitation of 1 John and 3 John's different historical situation. R. E. Brown, *Epistles,* has a chart delineating the similarities among the three writings (pp. 755–56). Cf. also I. H. Marshall, *Epistles,* p. 31: "The common authorship of all three Epistles remains the overwhelmingly probable hypothesis."

2. For those who see the differences between the Gospel and the letters as more decisive, see: Brown, *Epistles,* pp. 19–30; C. H. Dodd, *Epistles,* pp. xlvii–lvi; D. M. Smith, *First John,* pp. 12–13. Those who emphasize the similarities include: A. E. Brooke, *Epistles,* pp. i–xviii; D. Guthrie, *Introduction,* pp. 876–81; W. F. Howard, "The Common Authorship of the Johannine Gospel and Epistles," *JTS* 48 (1947), pp. 12ff.; W. G. Kümmel, *Introduction,* pp. 442–45; Marshall, *Epistles,* pp. 32–42; and J. R. W. Stott, *Letters,* pp. 20–28. The chart in Brown, *Epistles,* pp. 757–59, lists extensive similarities between the Gospel of John and 1 John.

3. Based on the internal evidence of the Fourth Gospel alone, Lazarus is a good candidate for the beloved disciple. If comparisons to and evidence from the Synoptic Gospels are introduced, then a good case can be made for the apostle John. The external evidence uniformly supports the latter, but it is from the late second century and is not well founded. Arguments concerning the external evidence and its worth may be found in Guthrie, *Introduction,* pp. 241–71, 864–69 (pro), and in Kümmel, *Introduction,* pp. 234–46, 442–45 (con). On the identity of the beloved disciple, see R. E. Brown, *Gospel, I–XII,* pp. xcii–xcvii, and idem, "The Role of the Beloved Disciple," in *The Community of the Beloved Disciple* (New York: Paulist, 1979), pp. 31–34.

4. See R. A. Culpepper, *The Johannine School,* SBLDS 26 (Missoula, Mont.: Scholars, 1975).

5. For a discussion on the implications of the prologue to 1 John for the authorship question, see Brown, *Epistles,* pp. 158–61; M. de Jonge, "Who are 'We'?" in *Jesus: Inspiring and Disturbing Presence* (Nashville: Abingdon, 1974), pp. 148–66; and R. Schnackenburg, *The Johannine Epistles. A Commentary,* trans. R. H. and I. Fuller (New York: Crossroad, 1992), pp. 48–56. Marshall believes that the prologue can mean only that the author of 1 John was an actual eyewitness; otherwise his readers would take him for an imposter (*Epistles,* p. 107).

6. See M. Hengel, *The Johannine Question* (Philadelphia: Trinity International, 1991), passim.

7. See the discussion in Kümmel, *Introduction,* pp. 241–44 and Marshall, *Epistles,* pp. 42–46.

8. That the author of the letters was a disciple of the Fourth Evangelist is held by Dodd, *Epistles,* p. lvi; R. Kysar, *I, II, III John,* p. 14; Schnackenburg, *Johannine Epistles,* p. 273, "perhaps an apostolic disciple"; S. Smalley, *1, 2, 3 John,* p. xxii, and is allowed by F. F. Bruce, *Epistles,* p. 30 (though he prefers common authorship, p. 31) and by Marshall, *Epistles,* pp. 46–47.

9. O. Cullmann, *The Johannine Circle* (Philadelphia: Westminster, 1976).

10. See Brown, *Gospel, I–XII,* pp. xxiv–xxxix, for a contemporary view of how the Fourth Gospel was composed. A contrary, more traditional view is found in D. A. Carson, *Gospel,* pp. 68–87.

11. On Ephesus, see G. L. Borchert, "Ephesus," *ISBE*, vol. 2, pp. 115–17.

12. A helpful but somewhat speculative reconstruction of the history of the Johannine community is the subject of Brown's *Community*. See also Brown, *Epistles*, pp. 69–115.

13. Most scholars hold that the letters were written after the Gospel. The letters appear to assume the teaching of the Gospel, or at least its tradition, and it makes more sense if the theology of the Gospel had become a source of debate and conflict within the Johannine community, as the letters appear to suppose. See Brown, *Epistles*, pp. 30–35. For a contrary view, see K. Grayston, *Epistles*, pp. 12–14.

14. The following analysis shows the passages in the epistles which form the basis for our discussion of the issues over which the Elder and the opponents were in conflict.

Doctrine (Christology)

Jesus came in the flesh, but they deny it	1 John 1:1–3; 4:2; 2 John 7
His blood or death as a sacrifice	1 John 1:7; 2:2; 4:10; 5:6–8
They deny the human "Jesus," or "the Christ," or "the Son"	1 John 2:18, 20, 22–23; 4:15; 5:1, 5, 12–13, 20; 2 John 7, 9
They reject God's testimony about the Son	1 John 5:10
We have the "truth"	1 John 1:6, 8; 2:4, 21; 3:19; 4:6; 5:6; 2 John 1–4; 3 John 1, 3–4, 8, 12; cf. 2:27; 5:20
They deceive, lie, lead astray, or are in error	1 John 2:21–22, 26; 4:6, 20; cf. 1:6; 8; 2:27; 4:1; 5:10
They have a false god	1 John 5:21

Doctrine (pneumatology)

You have received the true anointing, and it remains in you	1 John 2:20, 27
We have the Spirit, or the true Spirit	1 John 3:24; 4:2, 4, 6, 13
They have a false, antichrist, not-from-God spirit	1 John 4:1, 3–4, 6; cf. 2:18; 2 John 7
The Spirit testifies to Jesus' humanity	1 John 5:6–8

Ethics (love)

They hate their brothers and are like the murderer Cain	1 John 2:9–11; 3:11–15; 4:20
They do not love	1 John 4:8; 20–21; cf. 3:23; 4:11–12; 2 John 5–6; 3 John 6

They have worldly goods but will not help their brothers and sisters in need	1 John 3:17–18
They love the world and its possessions	1 John 2:15–17

Ethics (sin)

They lie and do not live by the truth	1 John 1:6, 8; 2:4
They make God out to be a liar	1 John 1:10; 5:10
They claim to be without sin or not to have sinned	1 John 1:8, 10
They do not do what God commands or live as Jesus did	1 John 2:4, 6; cf. 3:24; 5:3; 2 John 5–6
They sin, break the law, and do wrong	1 John 3:4, 6, 8–10; 5:18; cf. 2:29; 3:3
They are under the control of the evil one	1 John 5:19; cf. 3:8, 10
They seek to lead others astray morally	1 John 3:7
They commit the sin which leads to death	1 John 5:16
They accept support from non-Christians	3 John 7

Spirituality

They claim to have fellowship with God	1 John 1:6
They claim to know God or just "to know"	1 John 2:4; 3:6; 4:7–8; cf. 2:20
They claim to abide or to be in God	1 John 2:5–6
They claim to be in the light	1 John 2:9
They claim to love God	1 John 4:10, 20
They claim to have the Spirit and to speak by the Spirit	1 John 4:1, 3
They claim to be born of God or to be the children of God	1 John 3:1–2, 9–10; 4:4, 6; 5:1–2, 4, 18–19

Politics

The conflict with opponents is mentioned directly	1 John 2:19; 2:26; 3:7; 4:1, 3; 2 John 7, 9–10; 3 John 9–10
The writer is strongly connected to the community's tradition	1 John 1:1–5; 2:7, 24; 3:11; 4:14; 2 John 5–6; 3 John 9–10, 12; cf. 5:20.
He calls the readers "dear children" or "my children"	1 John 2:1, 12–13, 18, 28; 3:7, 18; 4:4; 5:21; 3 John 4

He expresses himself "democratically":

"dear friends"	1 John 2:7; 3:2, 21; 4:1, 7, 11; 3 John 1–2, 5, 14
"brothers"	1 John 3:13
all are God's children	1 John 3:1–2, 10; 5:19
we have a common anointing and all know	1 John 2:20
no one needs a teacher	2:27
his desire to talk face to face	2 John 12; 3 John 14
his solution to the Diotrephes crisis, "to call attention to what he is doing"	3 John 10
The Elder gives commands, advises, or uses the language of obligation	1 John 2:1, 7–8, 15, 24, 27–28; 3:7, 11, 13, 16–18; 4:1, 7, 11–12; 5:16, 21; 2 John 4–6, 8, 10–11; 3 John 4, 6, 8, 11
indirectly	1 John 1:7, 9; 2:3–6, 17, 29; 3:3, 6, 9, 14, 21–24; 4:21; 5:2–3, 18

See also Brown, *Epistles,* pp. 762–63.

15. On Cerinthus, see Brown, *Epistles,* pp. 766–71.

16. Another view of the controversy over the Spirit in 1 John is found in Brown, *Community,* pp. 138–44.

17. "Spirit of truth" and "spirit of error" also appear in the Dead Sea Scrolls, with which the Johannine writings show some familiarity. See esp. 1QS 3:13–4:26, and M.-E. Boismard, "The First Epistle of John and the Writings of Qumran," in J. Charlesworth, ed., *John and Qumran* (London: Chapman, 1972), pp. 156–65.

18. On "gnosticism" and its manifestation in Corinth, see W. Schmithals, *Gnosticism in Corinth* (Nashville: Abingdon, 1971). For a more helpful characterization of Paul's opponents in Corinth, see Carson, *Introduction,* pp. 279–82.

19. For a contemporary critique of this attempted spiritual imperialism, see F. Schaeffer, *The New Super Spirituality* (Downers Grove, Ill.: InterVarsity, 1972).

20. That "God is light" (1 John 1:5) was affirmed by the Zoroastrians of Persia (modern Iran), among whom the Jews lived during the exile. The Psalmist saw God as clothed in light (Ps. 104:2) or as "my light" (Ps. 27:1). The Qumran community understood themselves to be God's children and, therefore, "sons of light" (cf. 1QS 1:9f.). Jesus claimed to be "the light of the world" (John 8:12; 9:5). On "light," see H.-C. Hahn and C. Brown, "Light," *NIDNTT,* vol. 2, pp. 490–96; H. Conzelmann, *"phōs," TDNT,* vol. 9, pp. 310–58; C. H. Dodd, *The Interpretation of the Fourth Gospel* (Cambridge: Cambridge University, 1953), pp. 201–12.

21. See E. Malatesta, *Interiority and Covenant: a Study of* einai en *and* menein en *in the First Letter of Saint John,* AnBib 69 (Rome: Biblical Institute, 1978).

22. While, as a college president, I have considerable allegiance to Otto von Bismarck's definition of "politics" as "the art of the possible," it is used here in its general sense as "competition between groups or individuals for power and leadership" (*The New Merriam-Webster Dictionary*, p. 562).

23. Diotrephes is not likely to be one of the false teachers. The Elder, who criticizes him on several grounds, has no doctrinal objections. Diotrephes apparently rejects the views of the secessionists, as well as the authority of the Elder. He seeks to be independent. See the commentary on 3 John 9–10.

24. See the discussion of authorship above.

25. See the discussion of "we" above. A "we" which may represent the Johannine community also occurs in the Gospel of John (1:14, 16; 3:11; 21:24; cf. also 4:22, 42; 6:68–69; 9:4, 31; 16:30; 19:35; 20:25). See the discussion of the possible meanings of "we" in 1 John 1:1–3 in Brown, *Epistles*, pp. 158–61.

26. E. Schweizer has elaborated on this "democratic" tendency in the Johannine churches in *Church Order in the New Testament*, SBT 32 (London: SCM, 1961), pp. 117–30.

27. Of course this is not "amazing" to those who believe that the Elder had so little authority that he had no choice but to be "democratic"; cf. J. L. Houlden, *Epistles*, pp. 1–20. Brown is severely critical of the Elder in *Community*, pp. 131–35. On criticism on the Elder, see R. A. Whitacre, *Johannine Polemic*, SBLDS 67 (Chico, Calif.: Scholars, 1982). pp. 176–86; M. M. Thompson, *1–3 John*, pp. 155–56, 163.

28. G. A. Lee, "Letters," *ISBE*, vol. 3, pp. 107–8.

29. Brown, *Epistles*, pp. 90–92.

30. Cf. Smalley, *1, 2, 3 John*, who calls 1 John a "paper," p. xxxiii.

31. For a complete discussion of this topic, with comparisons to the Fourth Gospel, Revelation, Galatians, James, and 1QS in the Dead Sea Scrolls, see T. Johnson, *The Antitheses of the Elder: A Study of the Dualistic Language of the Johannine Epistles* (Ph.D. diss., Duke University; Ann Arbor: University Microfilms, 1979). The final chapter contains an interpretation of this language from a social science perspective.

32. Cf. A. Plummer, *Epistles*, p. lix–lx: "The movement of the Epistle largely consists of progress from one opposite to another. And it will nearly always be found that the antithesis is not exact, but an advance beyond the original statement or else an expansion of it."

33. On the theology of the epistles, see Brown, *Community*, pp. 109–44; Grayston, *Epistles*, pp. 22–27; Kysar, *I, II, III John*, pp. 20–23; G. E. Ladd, *A Theology of the New Testament* (Grand Rapids: Eerdmans, 1974), pp. 609–16; J. Lieu, *The Theology of the Johannine Epistles* (Cambridge: Cambridge University, 1991); Marshall, *Epistles*, pp. 49–55; Stott, *Letters*, pp. 56–60; Thompson, *1–3 John*, pp. 21–25.

34. In fact, the readers are told not to love the "world" (1 John 2:15). However, the Elder defines what he means by "world" in the following verse. Nevertheless, the contrast with John 3:16 is striking.

35. Sin is also a concern in the matter of the "sin unto death" in 1 John 5:16–17. The sin in mind here, and perhaps also in 1 John 3:6 and 9, is rejection of Jesus. For Johannine Christians unbelief in Jesus is the only unforgivable sin (cf. John 16:9; cf. 6:28–29).

36. The standard treatments of the theology of the Johannine epistles usually discuss the similarities and differences between the Gospel and the letters. See above n. 33.

37. See the chart of proposed divisions of 1 John in Brown, *Epistles*, p. 764.

38. Note the purely chiastic order ABCDC′B′A′ through 2:27. No such pattern is discernible in the rest of the letter.

39. Perhaps the letter's midpoint is after 3:10, since in 3:11 the author writes again, as he did in 1:5, "this is the message you ['we have' in 1:5] heard," the only uses of *angelia* ("message") in 1 John. But this is no division based upon a real shift in content. The most that can be said is that there is *"more* frontal attack on the secessionist adversaries" in 1:1—3:10 and *"more* loving address to the author's adherents" in 3:11—5:21 (Brown, *Epistles*, pp. 125–26).

40. See W. L. Richards, *The Classification of the Greek Manuscripts of the Johannine Epistles*, SBLDS 35 (Missoula, Mont.: Scholars, 1977).

1 John

Just as the Gospel of John begins with a prologue (John 1:1–18), so do the letters. In both, the Word (*logos*) is the central theme. Here too the Elder introduces some of his principal concerns: the reality of the incarnation, eternal life, and fellowship with the community of believers.

The tone of the prologue is authoritative: the author speaks with the first generation of Christians ("we"), emphasizing his solidarity with apostolic "orthodoxy," and he repeatedly uses verbs of personal experience (v. 1: "heard," "seen," "looked at," "touched"; v. 2: "seen," "testify"; v. 3: "seen," "heard") to underscore his direct connection with the incarnation of the Word. Thus, it is evident from the beginning of the epistles that such an emphasis is necessary because of the crisis situation of the readers: false teachers who do not have the author's authority are dividing the community and are threatening its central truth: Jesus the Christ, God's Son, come in the flesh (1 John 2:18–19, 22–23; 4:1–2; 2 John 7; cf. John 1:14).

1:1 / The exact subject of the prologue is not clear. The author speaks about it in several ways. He uses the neuter pronoun *ho* (which the NIV translates as **that which** and **which** in v. 1, and as **what** in v. 3), and he describes it primarily in terms of its appearance (*ephanerōthē*, twice in v. 2). He says it is **concerning the Word** (a masculine noun) **of life**. Then, in v. 2, he calls it **the life**, a feminine noun, and **the eternal life**.

The original readers of the letter, who not only knew the prologue to the Gospel of John but were familiar with the author's vocabulary and style, would have had no difficulty in identifying the subject as God's **Son, Jesus Christ** (v. 3), **the Word** who "became flesh and made his dwelling among us" (John 1:14), who is also **the life** (John 14:6). All of these ways of speaking of Jesus highlight the inseparability of the person, his message, and the experience of the Christ event.

From the beginning, while containing an allusion to "in the beginning" (John 1:1; Gen. 1:1), refers here to the **beginning** of the Christian movement, the teaching and experience of Jesus, which led to the formation of his disciples (John 15:27; 16:4) and ultimately to the founding of communities of Christians throughout the Mediterranean world. The author uses the expression elsewhere in the letters: **from the beginning** the Johannine community has had a command to follow (2:7; 2 John 5–6), a message ("what you have heard," 2:24) to heed and to allow to abide in them (1 John 3:11), and the "fathers" have known him who is **from the beginning** (2:13–14).

Four verbs in the perfect and aorist tenses and two nouns referring to parts of the body emphasize as concretely as possible the physicality of **the Word of life: heard, . . . seen with our eyes, . . . looked at, . . . our hands have touched**. The polemical context of these assertions is the denial of the incarnation made by the Elder's opponents (4:3; 2 John 7).

The NIV, in order to make the rough Greek sentence more clear to the modern reader, introduces the main verb from v. 3 (**we proclaim**) into v. 1. The **Word of life**, who was thus apprehended by our physical senses—**this we proclaim**.

1:2 / The emphasis in v. 2 is on the communication to the recipients of this Word of **eternal life**. Note the progression in time of the verbs. **The eternal life** was **with the Father** (*pros ton patera*; cf. 1 John 2:1: "we have an advocate," *pros ton patera* and John 1:1: "and the Word was," *pros ton theon*). Next he **appeared** (or was manifested) **to us**. Therefore, **we have seen** him, and now are able to **testify**, and **proclaim to you** what we have thus experienced. This same kind of progression in revelation and communication is also found at the opening of the book of Revelation (Rev. 1:1), where we have a sequence of God—Jesus Christ—angel—John—his servants.

1:3 / Verse 3 summarizes what has been said in vv. 1–2 and then moves on to a new affirmation. The author (and the apostolic community he represents, hence the **we**) **proclaims** this message about the **Word of life**, in order that those who hear it might join "the circle of salvation," i.e., those who **have fellowship with** God (which, according to John 17:3, is eternal life). It is essential to be in **fellowship with** the author, because the author is in **fellowship with the Father and with his Son, Jesus Christ**. The Elder's opponents, the secessionists—those who have left the community (2:19) and are antichrists (2:18), false prophets (4:1), deceivers (2 John 7), and liars (2:22)—are not in fellowship with the author, and they no longer have either the Father or the Son (2 John 9; cf. 2:22–24). They are outside the "circle of salvation." It is evident here that **fellowship** (*koinōnia*) is not simply a matter of love and hospitality (though for the Elder it is also that), but is primarily a matter of eternal life and death.

1:4 / There is a textual problem in v. 4. Does the author write **to make our joy complete**, or to make *your* joy complete? Some MSS, the ones on which the KJV was based, not the best or earliest ones, have the more understandable "your joy," and in John 16:24 Jesus tells his disciples to "Ask . . . and your joy will be complete." Copyists, knowing this verse, and favoring what is easier to understand, would have more likely altered the original "our" to "your" than vice versa. (The difference between "your" and "our" appears even less in Greek than in English.) Thus, most translators believe that the harder-to-understand reading, **our joy**, is more likely to be what the author actually wrote.

What, then, does the author mean? Writing is another form of proclaiming the message which he has been describing in vv. 1–3. What he and the founding generation **testify** and **proclaim** to all who would hear (so that they might have mutual **fellowship** with God), the author now **writes** about to his own community, that group of Christians for which he has special responsibility. To do so gives him **joy**; it is fulfilling (NIV: **complete**), because it extends the circle of fellowship to others and keeps in the circle those who may be tempted to leave it (and follow the secessionists). To **write**, then, about this Word of life meets not only the original readers' needs but the author's as well.

Additional Notes §1

1:4 / On the textual problem, see Metzger, *Commentary*, p. 709.

§2 *Walking in the Light and the Problem of Sin (1 John 1:5—2:2)*

The next two sections of 1 John are on the theme of walking in the light. The first section, 1 John 1:5—2:2, addresses the theme in relation to the issue of sin, while the second section, 1 John 2:3–11, focuses on walking in the light in relation to obedience, especially to the love command. The terms **walk**, **light**, and **darkness** occur throughout the section (1:5–7; 2:6, 8–11) and unify it. The Elder's opponents are always present in the background. They have made certain claims (e.g., **If we claim** in 1:6, 8, 10; "The man who says" in 2:4; "Whoever claims" in 2:6; and "Anyone who claims" in 2:9) which the Elder must raise and refute. In 1 John 1:5—2:2 the theological and ethical principles of light and darkness are stated and then worked out in relation to the problem of sin. The Elder and his opponents view this subject quite differently. Perhaps the author begins his teaching with this subject because it was the one which was most troublesome spiritually to his community. It also allows him to introduce the incarnate Jesus in his role as redeemer from sin.

1:5 / **God is light**. This is both a theological and a moral statement, i.e., it describes the essential nature of God, as well as God's character in relation to humanity. Later (4:8, 16) the Elder will affirm that God is love. Here, though, the emphasis is first upon the character of God as good, pure, and holy. **Light** implies integrity, truthfulness, and authenticity. It is also the nature of light to shine, to manifest itself, to reveal, and this God has done in him who is the light of the world (John 3:19; 8:12; 9:5).

The author claims that this understanding of God is what Jesus taught; it is **the message** (*angelia*) which the first generation **heard from him** and now **declare**s (*anangellō*; the same verb is translated as **proclaim** in vv. 2–3) to those who follow. It is also what they learned from observation of his life (John 14:9: "Anyone who has seen me has seen the Father").

The last part of the verse strongly affirms, as if in bold contrast to an unspoken claim to the contrary, that there is absolutely **no darkness** in **God**. **Light** and **darkness** are favorite antithetical concepts in the Johannine writings (John 1:4–5; 3:19–21; 8:12; 12:35–36, 46; 1 John 2:8–11; cf. Rev. 21:24 and 22:5). **Darkness** stands for evil, sin, and impurity. It implies deceit, falseness, and inauthenticity. **Light** and **darkness** are ultimately incompatible, and, while in all human character and behavior there is gray, in **God** there is nothing unworthy, undependable, or morally ambiguous. **God is light**.

1:6 / **If we claim**. The opening of v. 6 begins a series of three pairs of contrasting **If**-clauses (1:6a and 7a, 1:8a and 9a, 1:10a and 2:1b). The **we** is now not the special and limited "we" of the first generation of witnesses to the Word, so prominent in 1:1–5, but includes every Christian. (In each instance a **claim** from the false teachers is answered with the true Johannine teaching from the Elder. The secessionists, who have divided the community (1 John 2:19), have left a strong impression on the remaining Johannine Christians. In fact, they continue to visit the house churches of those loyal to the Elder to win them over (2 John 10–11). The Elder must counter their teaching lest he lose his flock.

The first **claim** of the schismatics is **to have fellowship with** God; yet at the same time they **walk in the darkness**. After the opening verb **claim**, which is in the aorist tense and marks a definite assertion, the tenses of the verbs are all continuous present: "we are having **fellowship**" . . . "we are **walk**ing" . . . "we are lying" . . . "we are not doing." The author points out the falseness of a lifestyle, an ongoing pattern of behavior, characterized by such a contradiction.

To have fellowship with means "to live in communion with," "to be in a right relationship with," to be part of one body, unified, at peace, and sharing the same life. This is its sense in v. 3. It is the saving fellowship of union with God, akin to the Pauline "in Christ." Such a close relationship cannot be maintained while a person (or group—the Elder has the heretics in mind) **walk**s **in the darkness**. This phrase deliberately contrasts and recalls **God is light** from the previous verse. It implies moral, spiritual, and, for the Elder, doctrinal error. It is thinking and action that are inconsistent with the nature of God and that are incompatible with the claim to be in **fellowship** with God. **Darkness** and **light** are moral and spiritual realms. They are mutually exclusive. For the author, one is either in the light or in the darkness (cf. 2:9–11), just as one is either a child of God or a child of the devil (3:10; 5:19), either from God or from the world (4:5–6).

Lying and **truth** is another frequent contrast in the letters of John, and its first appearance is in v. 6. Those in the sphere of darkness **lie and do not live by the truth**. From the author's viewpoint, their lie consists in the false claim to be in an ongoing, right relationship with God (**to have fellowship with him**) while they **walk in the darkness**. Since light, God's nature (v. 5) and locus (v. 7), and darkness, the opponents' situation outside the community of truth, are mutually exclusive, the secessionists are lying.

It is not just their words which are false; their lives are: "and we are not doing the truth" (lit.), or as the NIV insightfully translates it, we **do not live by the truth**. For the author(s) of the Gospel and letters of John, **truth** is not so much a set of propositions to be believed and confessed, as it is a way of life to be lived and put into practice (cf. 3:22). The standard for this life of truth is God's revelation in Jesus Christ (John 14:6: "I am . . . the truth").

1:7 / If the behavior and attitude of the secessionists, described in v. 6, are unacceptable, what is the positive alternative? The Elder says, **walk in the light**: be continuously thinking and living in God's sphere of being. Brother Lawrence might have said, "Practice the presence of the God who is Light."

This is the only conduct consistent with the nature of God (**as he is in the light**). Rather than claim **fellowship** with God while walking in the darkness (v. 6), live in ongoing **fellowship** with God **in the light**. That is the only authentic alternative. Just as in the Sermon on the Mount God's character is the pattern and model (Matt. 5:48: "Be perfect, therefore, as your heavenly Father is perfect"), and just as Paul told the Philippians, "Let your manner of life be worthy of the gospel" (Phil. 1:27, RSV), so the Elder holds up a divine standard for human conduct.

Two consequences follow for those who **walk in the light**. They **have fellowship with** other true Johannine Christians, and they are **purified from all sin**. We would have expected the author to say that **walk**ing **in the light** issues in **fellowship** with God, in order to parallel v. 6. But he assumes that truth and moves on to a new one: it is only those who **walk in the light** who are truly members of the author's community, and, by extension, of the Christian community at large. We saw above in v. 3 that part of the author's purpose was to complete and to strengthen the circle of salvation. Those who broke with the Elder and with the truth and who have left the fellowship are in serious spiritual danger. They are now outside the community of life (vv. 1–3). Therefore, **walk**ing **in the light** keeps one in the community, in **fellowship** with other faithful believers.

The second result of continuous contact with the **light** is that **the blood of Jesus, his Son, purifies us from all sin**. The closer one's **fellowship** with God and with those who **walk** with God, the more aware one will be of **sin** in one's life. The secessionists fled **the light** (cf. John 3:19–21), claiming continuous **fellowship** with God, while their pride, dishonesty, and lack of love belied them. They could not "own up" to their **sin**s. But, the Elder teaches, if we persist **in the light** (**confess**ing **our sins**, v. 9), we will discover that God loves us and has sent **his Son** to be "an atoning sacrifice for our sins" (1 John 4:10).

The blood of Jesus refers to his sacrificial death on the cross. It is the Christian's agent of purification and cleansing, and it draws its meaning from the Jewish sacrificial system. The Elder emphasizes, contrary to the opponents' rejection of Jesus' physicality, that it is **the blood of Jesus** which is the effective antidote for **sin** in the believer's life, not denial of the existence of **sin**. In fact, this antidote keeps on working: the present tense of the verb *katharizō* stresses continuous purification.

The term **sin** or sins (*hamartia*) occurs seventeen times in the Gospel of John (the verb *hamartanō* occurs three times) and seventeen times in the much smaller book of the letters (all in 1 John; the verb *hamartanō* occurs a surprising ten times). Clearly the problem of **sin** vexed the Elder's community. Most of the references to **sin** are in the singular, calling attention to the principle or fact of sin in human life (e.g., 1:8), rather than to individual acts of **sin**. Certainly, though, **from all sin** includes both. For the Elder, **sin** means lawlessness (*anomia*, 3:4) and unrighteousness (*adikia*, 5:17) or wrongdoing (NIV), any departure from God's norm or standard of **light** as revealed in **Jesus** Christ.

1:8 / The second claim of the secessionists is **to be with-out sin** (lit., "we do not have sin"). They claim that they do not need to be purified from **sin** by the blood of Jesus (v. 7), since they are sinless. They do not sin at all (v. 10). They do not see them-selves as sinners in disposition or in practice. Some interpreters understand the claim in v. 8 as an assertion not to have a sinful nature or a principle of sin operating in one's life (Brooke, *Epistles*, p. 17; Stott, *Letters*, pp. 81–82).

Why do the opponents believe that they are "without sin"? Perhaps it is because they believe that their exalted spirituality has put them in a state beyond sin such that they are free from it, or that it is irrelevant to them. In any case, they **deceive** (*planaō*, "lead astray" or "go astray") themselves. Denying their sinfulness, they believe something about themselves that is con-trary to the universal experience of human nature and patently not true in their particular case.

To be self-deceived means that **the truth is not in us**, i.e., in our hearts or inmost being. If it were, we would recognize and admit our condition, stay in the light, and be forgiven. "Our self-understanding is false" (Kysar, *I, II, III John*, p. 39).

1:9 / If the opponents' attitude and belief are wrong (vv. 6 and 8), the right approach to sin is to keep on walking in the light (v. 7) and to be honest about one's **sins** (v. 9). **If we confess our sins** is the true alternative to claiming **to be without sin**. The word **confess** (*homologeō*) means, literally, to say the same thing, thus, to agree or to admit. When **we confess our sins**, we agree with God and the community that they are **sins** (which the secessionists would not do). Then our self-understanding is true, and we have the basis for an effective solution to the sin problem. Confession was likely not only in private to God but publicly to the community (cf. Matt. 3:6; Acts 19:18; Jas. 5:16; and Didache 4:14 and 14:1, an early Christian document written about the same time as the letters of John).

There are (as in v. 7) two consequences of openly acknowl-edging our **sins**. God, who **is faithful and just**, will (a) **forgive us our sins** and (b) **purify us from all unrighteousness**. Literally, the verse says, **If we confess our sins, he is faithful** (*pistos*) **and just** (*dikaios*), with the result that he **will forgive** (*hina aphē; hina* with the subjunctive mood is here a result or consecutive clause) **us** the **sins** and cleanse (*katharizō*, **purify**; cf. v. 7) **us from all unrighteousness** (*adikias*).

He is God, as in vv. 6–7. His character is **faithful and just**. That is, he is true to his people and to his promises (especially to **forgive** on the basis of the blood of Jesus, v. 7), and he puts things right which are wrong (especially people, in a right relationship with himself). **Faithful and just** are terms which reflect God's covenantal connection with his people (Brown, *Epistles*, pp. 209–10).

These qualities in God are seen as he acts redemptively toward those who humbly acknowledge their need (v. 9a). God **forgive**s and cleanses his people from all their **unrighteousness**. These two verbs show that the problem of sin in one's life cannot be solved by human action (v. 6, claiming to be right with God when one is not, or v. 8, denying that one is a sinner). Even confession only opens the door to an answer; it is not self-efficacious. God must act, and God does. As in all of Scripture, salvation is from God. The form of salvation here is forgiveness and cleansing from sin. The verbs are parallel and functionally synonymous. **From all unrighteousness** (*adikias*) recalls God's character as just (*dikaios*, v. 9b).

1:10 / This is the third claim of the false teachers in chapter 1, all presented with the identical words **If we claim** (*ean eipōmen*). The assertion in this verse goes beyond that of v. 8. Not only do the opponents claim not to "have sin" as a principle or disposition within them, they claim not to have committed specific sins. Hence they do not need redemption by the "blood of Jesus" (1:7). Gnostically inclined, the death/blood of Jesus offended them, as did any "enfleshment" of the divine Christ (4:2; 2 John 7). Their own "perfectionism" and high, yet self-deceived, spirituality could do without the cross, as modern psychologies of self-actualization and "success" often do.

Such a claim (**we have not sinned**) has serious consequences. First, while the writer might have been expected to argue that such an assertion makes the claimant **a liar**, he goes beyond this to a more profound, and more spiritually dangerous, theological conclusion: to deny that one has sinned is to **make him**, God (as in v. 9), **out to be a liar**. (The same accusation and warning occurs in 5:10, this time with respect to believing God's testimony about Jesus, his Son.) One does not only lie about one's own condition, but, more seriously, one blasphemes God by, in effect, calling God **a liar**. This is so because God has said that we have sinned, and honest confession of one's sins is prerequisite to benefiting from "the message" of salvation from sin and eternal life through Jesus' death (1:5–7).

The second consequence of denying that we have sinned is that we "cut ourselves off from what he has to say to us" (J. B. Phillips, *The New Testament in Modern English*, p. 500). Literally, the text says, "and his word (*logos*) is not in us." The **word** or *logos* of which the writer speaks is the same as in v. 1: it is the message or "word of life" which finds its embodiment in the person, words, and deeds of Jesus Christ (vv. 1–3), the Word made flesh (John 1:14). The Elder says that making this false assertion, as the secessionists do, means that they have separated themselves, not just from the community (1 John 2:19), but from the gospel: God's life-giving word **has no place** in their lives. They are not, from the Elder's standpoint, Christian believers, even if they originally claimed to be or still do. The right response to the reality of sin will be seen in 2:1b.

2:1 / The first part of v. 1 is parenthetical, intended to remind the readers that what the Elder has written so far, about forgiveness and the purifying death of Jesus (1:7, 9), is not a license to sin. Just because sin is an inevitable reality and forgiveness is available does not mean that the believer should take a lenient attitude toward it. (Paul faced the same concern in Romans 6:1: "Shall we go on sinning that grace may increase?") In fact, the author says that it is one of his purposes in writing (cf. 1:3–4) that the community **will not sin**, that they will completely reject **sin** as a way of living. The Christian ideal remains **not** to **sin** (John 5:24; 8:11; 1 John 3:6).

He calls his readers **my dear children** (lit., "my little children"). The Greek *teknia* is a diminutive expressing affection (Marshall, *Epistles*, p. 115). It also implies parental authority and is complemented by the possessive pronoun "my." The Elder is very concerned about his community, not only because of the schism and false teaching, but also for their positive spiritual understanding and maturity. He also uses for the first time the first person singular, "I," after using "we" throughout chapter 1.

The second half of v. 1 is the answer to 1:10 (just as v. 7 answers the claim in v. 6, and v. 9 responds to v. 8). Rather than assert that one has not sinned, the faithful must acknowledge (**if**

anybody does sin; cf. 1:9) and recognize **Jesus Christ** as their solution. The rest of vv. 1 and 2 explain (in addition to 1:7) how this is so.

Jesus is described in a formal way with his title, **Jesus Christ**. This is in part because another descriptive title follows, **the Righteous One**, and because v. 2 is like a creedal statement. He is **the Righteous One** (also 2:29; 3:7; cf. Acts 3:14; 7:52; and 1 Pet. 3:18; as God is **righteous** in 1:9), not only in view of his sinless character (John 8:46) but because he saves and advocates for sinners.

He is our *paraklētos,* translated in the NIV as **one who speaks . . . in our defense**. The Spirit is the *paraklētos* in John 15:26 and "another *paraklētos*" in 14:16–17, in which it is implied that Jesus himself is the original. Before God, or in the presence of **the Father** (*pros ton patera;* cf. 1:2), **Jesus** intercedes for sinners and **speaks** on their behalf. The same function is attributed to him in Rom. 8:34 and Heb. 7:25.

2:2 / The second part of the Elder's christological answer to the problem of **sins** is that Jesus is **the atoning sacrifice**. He who is our advocate (*paraklētos*) is also our **atoning sacrifice** (*hilasmos*). Much debate has occurred over this word. Outside the Bible and in some OT passages it means to appease an angry or offended party (usually a divine being) with a **sacrifice**. Inside the Bible, including other OT texts, it means to expiate, cover, or remove the offense of sin. The context in 1 John clearly favors the latter. In 1 John 4:10 it is God who, out of love for the world, sends the Son as its *hilasmos,* and in 1:9 God is "faithful and just" and forgives and cleanses those who confess their **sins**. The NIV translation, **atoning sacrifice,** is a good one; it retains the idea of blood **sacrifice** (1:7) from the OT sacrificial system, while pointing to the purpose of Jesus' death: reconciliation (at-one-ment) with God. Jesus is such an effective *paraklētos* "in our defense," because he is "the Righteous One" and because his own death for **our sins** is the ground of his advocacy. He pleads with his own blood.

The Elder strongly emphasizes that Jesus' **atoning** death is potentially effective **not only for** the **sins** of the community but **for the sins of the . . . world**. He even adds the word **whole** (*holou*) to underscore this further. Perhaps the gnostically inclined opponents understood the salvation which Christ brought as redemption or enlightenment for an elect few. It is certain that they would have found the author's insistence on the importance of Jesus' blood **sacrifice** in death a complete offense.

Additional Notes   §2

1:6 / The structure of 1:6—2:1 has been most clearly set forth in Brown, *Epistles*, p. 191.

In sociological terms, a schism is a form of disruptive or divisive social conflict, a kind of factionalism within a specific community or group. On the phenomenon of schism, see J. Wilson, "The Sociology of Schism," *A Sociological Yearbook of Religion in Britain-4*, ed. M. Hill (London: SCM, 1971), pp. 4–5, and J. P. Gustafson, "Schismatic Groups," *Human Relations* 31 (1978), pp. 139–54. On schism as it relates to the Johannine community, see Johnson, *Antitheses*, pp. 231–60.

Strictly speaking, the terms "heresy" and "heretical" belong to a later time when there was a more clearly established church-wide "orthodoxy." But it is also appropriate within the Johannine frame of reference, since the Elder and his followers have well defined doctrinal views, based on the tradition of the Beloved Disciple and the Fourth Gospel. To deviate from this teaching is "heretical." See W. Bauer, *Orthodoxy and Heresy in Earliest Christianity* (Philadelphia: Fortress, 1971); H. D. Betz, "Orthodoxy and Heresy in Primitive Christianity," *Int* 19 (1965), pp. 299–311; J. Bogart, *Orthodox and Heretical Perfectionism in the Johannine Community*, SBDLS 33 (Missoula, Mont.: Scholars, 1977); and J. D. G. Dunn, *Unity and Diversity in the New Testament* (London: SCM, 1977).

While the false teachers may **walk in the darkness**, it would be a mistake to think of them as immoral or licentious. They are not like the Corinthian "gnostics," for whom bodily life was spiritually irrelevant. In fact, as 1:8, 10 make clear, they claim a high standard of holiness. There is no list of sins which the Elder can cite against them. The only accusations of immorality or unethical conduct which the Elder ever directly makes against the opponents are lying and breaking the love command, both of which the opponents themselves would deny. The dispute which has divided the community is primarily doctrinal and personal, not ethical: the schismatics do not accept the community's Christology, and they reject the authority of the Elder. The latter calls their claims "lies" and their secession from the group a rejection of the obligations of love among disciples.

The positioning of believers and unbelievers in opposing spiritual realms (**darkness**/light) is typical of the world view of the first-century Jewish group known as the Essenes. It may be found in a form closest to the Gospel and letters of John in the Manual of Discipline (or Community Rule, 1QS) and the War Scroll (or War Rule, 1QM) of the Dead Sea Scrolls.

See G. Vermes, *The Dead Sea Scrolls in English* (Baltimore: Penguin Books, 1975), pp. 71–94, 122–48. Given the close similarities between the language and conceptuality of the Scrolls and that of the Johannine literature, some scholars think the Dead Sea writings or the movement which produced them influenced the Johannine community. See Charlesworth, *John and Qumran* and R. E. Brown, "The Qumran Scrolls and the Johannine Gospel and Epistles," *New Testament Essays* (Garden City, N.Y.: Doubleday, 1968), pp. 138–73.

The other occurrences of the contrast between **truth** and its opposites are in 1:8, 10; 2:4, 21–22, 26–27; 4:6; 2 John 1–4, 7. A thorough study of this language of contrast may be found in Johnson, *Antitheses*.

The concept of *doing* the truth is also common in the Dead Sea Scrolls and other Jewish intertestamental literature. See I. de la Potterie, *La vérité dans Saint Jean* (2 vols.; AnBib 73–74; Rome: Biblical Institute, 1977, and A. Thiselton, "Truth," *NIDNTT*, vol. 3, pp. 889–94.

1:7 / The false teachers would not have welcomed this reference to Jesus' full corporeal humanity, given their denial of his incarnation (4:2; 2 John 7).

In the Gospel of John, references to **the blood of Jesus** occur in John 6:53–56, a passage which recalls the elements of the Lord's Supper, and in John 19:34, where the beloved disciple sees blood and water flow from the wounded side of the crucified Jesus. In the letters of John, the term appears three times in 1 John 5:6–7, a passage in which the author strongly affirms that Jesus "did not come by water only, but by water and blood." The blood is an important witness to his identity. Finally, if the book of Revelation also comes from the Johannine community, which it almost certainly does, then there is further evidence of the importance of the blood of Jesus for Johannine Christology. In Rev. 1:5, Jesus "has freed us from our sins by his blood." In 5:9, as the slain Lamb he has purchased with his blood people from every tribe and nation. In 7:14 the tribulation martyrs have "washed their robes and made them white in the blood of the Lamb." Finally, in 12:11 the saints have overcome Satan by the blood of the Lamb. While the Word of God appears in a robe dipped in blood in 19:13, it is likely not his own blood but the blood of his enemies. See also F. Laubach, "Blood," *NIDNTT*, vol. 1, pp. 220–24.

Referring to Christ as **Jesus, his Son** includes the author's preferred name for his human nature, Jesus, and a title that points in the Johannine literature to his deity, Son of God.

The 1984 edition of the NIV changed the phrase "every sin" to **all sin**.

1:8 / In the Gospel of John "to have sin" means to be in a state of guilt. Thus, the opening **If**-clause may be translated, "If we boast, 'We are free from the guilt of sin' " (Brown, *Epistles*, pp. 205–6).

The schismatics not only are self-deceived about their spirituality, but they deceive others and lead them astray. In 1 John 2:26 the Elder has written "about those who are trying to lead you astray." In 3:7 he warns, "Do not let anyone lead you astray." In 4:5–6 he contrasts "the Spirit of truth" in those who "are from God" with "the spirit of falsehood" (*planēs*, error, deceit) in those who "are from the world." 2 John 7 calls these people *planoi*, "deceivers."

1:9 / **Confess** occurs four times in the Gospel of John and six times in the letters. First John 1:9 is the only instance in which *homologeō* means to confess or admit sins. All of the other uses are in the positive sense of making a confession of faith, esp. in Christ. See John 1:20; 9:22; 12:42; 1 John 2:23; 4:2–3, 15; 2 John 7.

On **confess**, see O. Michel, *"homologeō," TDNT*, vol. 5, pp. 199–220.

2:1 / The Elder uses three different terms for his parentally caring yet authoritative relationship to the readers in his community: *teknion*, little child (2:1, 12, 28; 3:7, 18; 4:4; 5:21; cf. John 13:33), *teknon*, child (3:1, 2, 10; 5:2; 2 John 1, 4, 13; 3 John 4; cf. John 1:12; 11:52) and *paidion*, child (2:14, 18; John 21:5). They are virtually interchangeable, though the Elder prefers *teknion* for his relationship to the readers and *teknon* for their relationship to God. See Brown, *Epistles*, pp. 213–15.

There is a shift in emphasis from the Spirit as the Paraclete to Jesus as the Paraclete probably because the opponents of the Elder also claimed to be prophetically inspired by the Spirit (4:1–2; R. A. Culpepper, *1 John, 2 John, 3 John*, Knox Preaching Guides (Atlanta: John Knox, 1985), pp. 20–21.

Jesus' role as *paraklētos* is in contrast to Satan's: "Believers now have someone who defends them before God instead of accusing them" (Brown, *Epistles*, p. 217; cf. Matt. 10:32). The name "Satan" means "accuser" (cf. Job 1:6–12).

2:2 / See the history of the debate over the meaning of *hilasmos* in Brown, *Epistles*, pp. 217–22. First John 2:2 and 4:10 are the only two uses of *hilasmos* in the NT, although linguistically related terms occur in Luke 18:13; Rom. 3:25; Heb. 2:17 and 9:5.

This is the first use of *kosmos*, **world**, in the Johannine letters and, unlike most uses of the term in the Gospel and epistles of John, it is positive, or at least neutral (like John 3:16–17; 4:42; 8:12; and 1 John 4:14). The world is usually seen as the sphere of Satan's activity (1 John 5:19) and, therefore, as opposed to God and God's people (1 John 2:15–17; 3:13; 4:4–5; John 15:18–19). In his study of *kosmos*, Brown suggests that "the overall effect of such contradictory statements within the same works is to create a theological sequence wherein the divine intent is initially salvific toward the world, but people prefer darkness to light (John 3:19); and so 'the world' becomes the name of those who refuse Jesus and choose Satan as their father, 'the Prince of this world' (cf. 1 John 3:1, 10)" (*Epistles*, p. 224).

§3 *Walking in the Light Tested by Obedience (1 John 2:3–11)*

The next section of 1 John continues the theme of walking in the light begun in 1:5. In 1:6, 8, 10 the Elder dealt with the three false claims of the opponents with respect to sin. Now he deals with another trio of false claims, all of which relate to being in a right relationship with God/Christ: knowing God/Christ, v. 4; abiding in God/Christ, v. 6; being in the light, v. 9. In each instance, just as in the previous section, he answers them with a test of the claim's authenticity: obeying Christ's commands, vv. 4–5; walking as Jesus did, v. 6; loving other Christians, v. 10. All of the answers have this in common: they emphasize obedience or the Christian walk as the test of claims to a profound spirituality.

2:3 / The NIV does not translate the opening Greek particle, *kai*. But, like the *kai* which begins 1:5 (which the NIV also does not translate), it marks the beginning of a new section. The rest of the verse literally says, "By this **we know** (present tense) **that we have come to know** (perfect tense) **him, if we** keep **his commands**." The **If**-clause explains the expression "by this": "this" is obeying God's/Christ's commandments. The Greek text's "By this" (*en toutō*) does not occur in the NIV.

The issue in vv. 3–5 is knowing God/Christ. The word **know** is used four times in these three verses. First, the Elder states the general principle by which Christians are assured that they truly know God/Christ (v. 3); then he takes up the opponents' false claim (v. 4) and refutes it (v. 5; Barker, "1 John," p. 315). "Knowledge" was an important concern to the gnosticlike secessionists. The very name "gnostic" means "one who knows" (from *gnōsis*). This knowledge was special; it conveyed salvation. To know God is eternal life (John 17:3). It meant fellowship with God (1:6) and walking in the light (1:7; 2:9). But, how can one be sure that one really knows God/Christ? This was a question on the minds of the loyal Johannine Christians as they listened to the seceding teachers' assertions. The Elder's answer is as profound today as it was relevant then: **we know that we have come to know him if we obey his commands**.

The word **obey** in the NIV is *tēreō*. Its literal meaning is "keep." It is a favorite Johannine term, occurring eighteen times in the Gospel and seven times in 1 John. It connotes both preserving or protecting, especially when its object is a person, and obeying or observing when its object is God's or Jesus' word(s) or commands (cf. John 14:15, 21–25). "Keeping his commands is the sure test that we have come to know God" (Culpepper, *1 John*, p. 25). One's claim must be validated by one's conduct. The evidence is obedience.

What **commands** does the author have in mind? In the context of 1 John it can only be faith in Jesus and love for other Christians (1 John 3:23). There is no substantial evidence anywhere in the letters of John for any other moral or ethical concern. The opponents are never accused of other sins or immorality. They have violated the most fundamental standards of all, even if their lives appear morally upright: they deny that the human Jesus is the divine Christ, and they do not love their Christian brothers and sisters in the community.

2:4 / Verses 4, 6, and 9 begin in the same way, a stylistic feature which is not clear in the NIV. All three verses quote or paraphrase a claim of the secessionists and introduce it with the formula "the one who says" (*ho legōn*). In this verse the claim is: "I have come to know him" (perfect tense). It is a claim to intimate, personal, saving knowledge of God. It is experiential, not merely intellectual. The perfect tense connotes a reality that began at some time in the past and continues on into the present.

Anyone who makes this claim and at the same time is not keeping God's/Christ's **commands** (especially to love others and to believe in Jesus, 3:23) is a liar. This is the same contradiction between confession and conduct which we saw in 1:6–10 (Kysar, *I, II, III John*, p. 45). In typically antithetical style, the author immediately contrasts the word **liar** with its opposite, **truth**, as in 1:6 (cf. 1:8; 2:21; 4:6). Such people (*en toutō*; lit., "in such a person") lack integrity; they claim one thing in words, but its reality is not demonstrated by their actions.

2:5 / Verse 5 is the positive contrast and answer to v. 4. It is not the disobedient person who truly knows God, but the one who **obeys his word**. The emphasis is on the continual present tense of the verb, "keeps on obeying." **His word** (*autou ton logon*) is synonymous with "his commands" (*tas entolas autou*; NIV, **what he commands**) in v. 4. The antithetical style of the author is also seen in the contrast of **truly** in v. 5 with **liar** in v. 4.

The Elder's opponents claimed to know God (v. 4), but their disobedience to God's commands proved them false. In v. 5, the Elder affirms that the obedient Christian grows in the *agapē* (**love**) of God until that **love** is mature, perfect, or **complete**. Here, knowing God and growing in **God's love** complete the parallelism between the verses. To know God is to experience *agapē* love, and such knowledge or **love** (also claimed by the opponents; cf. 4:10) is demonstrated by doing what God has commanded. "The proof of love is loyalty" (Stott, *Letters*, p. 96), and in the letters of John that means believing in Jesus and loving one's brother or sister in the community of faith (1 John 3:23; cf. John 6:28–29).

Divine **love is truly made complete** in the person who **obeys his word**. **Made complete** translates *teteleiōtai*, another favorite Johannine term. It signifies a process of spiritual maturity which begins with faith in Jesus and ends at his appearing in becoming like him (1 John 3:2). Growing in love for God is an important part of spiritual growth, as is love for others, a point the author will make forcefully later (cf. 2:9–11; 4:20–21).

The last part of v. 5 looks forward, as the NIV punctuates it, to v. 6. **This is how we know we are in him**. The "how" is defined in the verse which follows. But we should take note that once again the subject is assurance (a confidence in short supply in the Johannine community because of the threat and boasts of the secessionists). How can we know that we are truly in a right relationship with God? This is what the phrase "to be **in him**" connotes. It means "fellowship . . . with the Father and with his Son, Jesus Christ" (1:3), to "walk in the light, as he is in the light" (1:7), and to "know him" (2:3). But how can we **know** we are **in him**?

2:6 / The Elder's answer is a practical one: **walk as Jesus did.** This verse contains the fifth stated claim of the Elder's opponents, the secessionists, who had denied the full humanity of Jesus (1 John 4:2; 2 John 7) and separated themselves from the community (1 John 2:19). They claim **to live in him**. Actually, the Greek original is stronger: they claim to abide or to dwell (*menō*) in him. *Menō* means to live in an ongoing, close, personal relationship with God/Christ. It parallels to live in "fellowship with him" (1:6), to "walk in the light" (1:7), "to know him" (2:3–5), and "we are in him" (2:5). The Elder's opponents claimed to have this profound relationship with God/Christ unbroken by sin (1:8, 10), whereas the believer confesses sin (1:9) and counts on Christ as advocate (NIV, "one who speaks . . . in our defense" [2:1]) and "atoning sacrifice" (2:2).

The Elder insists that the opponents' claim be tested by a life in imitation of Jesus. You **must walk as Jesus did.** This test, he is convinced, they cannot pass, because they do not keep God's commands (2:3–4), as Jesus did. Above all, they do not love as Jesus loved (John 13:34). "The test of our religious experience is whether it produces a reflection of the life of Jesus in our daily life; if it fails this elementary test, it is false" (Marshall, *Epistles*, p. 128).

2:7 / Walking as Jesus did (v. 6) leads the author to think of Jesus' example and his "new command" of love (John 13:34–35). He addresses his readers as "beloved" (*agapētoi*; the NIV's **Dear friends** misses the connection with the love command implicit in the address), loved not only by the Elder, but loved also by God (4:9–10) and by Jesus (John 13:34). With a play on the idea of the **new command** in John 13:34, he says that he is really writing to them not about a **new command** but about an old command, one which they have had *ap' archēs*, **since** or from **the beginning**. **Since the beginning** refers to the founding tradition of the Johannine community in the teaching of Jesus, as remembered and passed on to them by the disciple whom Jesus loved, their founder. It means "since the beginning of the Christian movement, as we have known it" (cf. 1:1; 2:13–14, 24; 3:11; 2 John 5–6; also John 15:27, in which Jesus says to his disciples "from the beginning [*ap' archēs*] you are with me"). This foundational teaching gave them a **new command**, to love one another "as I have loved you." By now it is to them an **old one.**

He calls this command (*entolē*) **the message** (*logos*, or "word"; 1:1, 10; 2:5) which they heard (aorist tense, at a definite time in the past). The writer can use the words *logos*, *entolē*, and *angelia* (1:5; 3:11) for written and oral communication synonymously. The content of the message is, in this case, not the gospel (*euangel-*

ion), a word which never appears in the Gospel or letters of John, but the ethical imperative to love one another.

2:8 / But, in a sense, it is also **a new command**, both because it was called the "new command" by Jesus (John 13:34), and also because of the new age which has dawned with his coming. It is a command which belongs, not to the old era of the law of Moses, but to the new day of grace and truth in Jesus Christ (John 1:17). Stott points out that the **new command** was and remains new in emphasis (the whole Torah hangs on it; Matt. 22:40), in quality, as measured by Christ's love for them (John 13:34), in extent, including enemies (Matt. 5:44), and by our continued, fresh, daily application of it to new circumstances (Stott, *Letters*, p. 98).

It is the latter sense which the Elder has in mind here, especially within the life of this community torn by schism and attacked by false teachers. Following the example of Jesus ("as I have loved you"), believers are to let the **truth** of love shine forth from their lives. Jesus and his disciples (of the first generation and today) are the streaks of dawn from the rising of a new era in human history, the kingdom of God inaugurated by Jesus Christ and bringing into time the age to come, ever longed for by the people of God (cf. Col. 1:12–13). When Christians love, there is evidence that **the darkness is passing and the true light is already shining** (cf. Eph. 5:8–9; 1 Thess. 5:4–8).

2:9 / Verse 9 contains the sixth and final claim of the opponents of the Elder. It closely integrates the themes of light/darkness and love/hate in a profound moral and spiritual antithesis. These schismatic false teachers claim **to be in the light.** This is also implied in 1:5–7, where walking in the light in fellowship with God is at issue.

To be in the light is the equivalent of having fellowship with God (1:6), knowing God (2:3–4), being in him (2:5), and abiding in him (2:6), all claims which both the opponents and the author's community are making of themselves. But the opponents' claims are belied by their behavior. They "walk in the darkness" (1:6); they "lie and do not live by the truth" (1:6); they "deceive [themselves]" (1:8); they "make him [God] out to be a liar" (1:10); they do "not do what he [God/Christ] commands" (2:4); and they do not "walk as Jesus did" (2:6). In v. 9 the indictment against them is that they **hate** their **brother**s and sisters. Just as **love** is characteristic of those who truly walk in the **light**, so **hate** describes those who walk in the **darkness**.

What is this hatred to which the Elder refers? It was seen most profoundly in the deliberate schism or splitting of the community which the false teachers caused when they left the fellowship (1 John 2:19), but roots of it may have been put down earlier, since the author claims that "they did not really belong to us." In fact "their departure showed that none of them belonged to us" (1 John 2:19). Hatred for their former brothers and sisters may also be evidenced by their claims to spiritual superiority (1:6, 8, 10; 2:4, 6, 9), by their lack of help for Christians in need (3:17–18), by their denial of the fundamental christological belief of the community, Jesus Christ come in the flesh (4:2; 2 John 7), and perhaps by their refusal to accept the Elder's authority in matters of faith and practice (e.g., 3 John 9–10).

The Elder adds the little phrase *heōs arti*, translated by the NIV as "still" (NASB, "until now"). Those who live in hatred for their brother and sister Christians have yet to experience the light of the new age which has dawned in Christ; they are not yet in the Kingdom but are **still in the darkness.** They are living in an era that has passed, instead of in God's new future which has come in Jesus.

The moral and spiritual differences between the Elder's community of true, faithful, persevering believers and the secessionist false teachers could not be more profound.

2:10 / Verse 10 states the positive alternative to the opponents' claim to be in the light while "hating" their brothers. It is only the person who **loves his brother** or sister who also remains or abides (*menō*) **in the light**. One cannot be or stay **in the light** while cultivating negative, critical, and compassionless attitudes and actions toward other believers. The two spiritual states are incompatible. God is light; to **live in the light** is to walk in continuous fellowship with God (see also the comment on 1:5 and 2:9). But it is also to live in loving fellowship and community with one's brothers and sisters in the faith. An otherworldly, self-isolated spirituality is not authentic life before God. Love among Christians is the touchstone of true discipleship (John 13:35).

The second half of v. 10 is difficult to understand. Literally, it reads: "and there is no cause for stumbling (*skandalon*) in him [or, in it]." The NIV translation is ambiguous. It seems to mean that such loving believers have nothing in their lives which will make them fall. There are two other options. It could mean that the Christian who loves others has or does nothing to cause others to stumble (Kysar, *I, II, III John*, p. 50), i.e., love excludes giving unnecessary offense. Or, thirdly, if the pronoun is translated as "it" instead of **him** (see NIV footnote), the meaning then would be that there is no cause for stumbling in it, i.e., in the light. Loving others is living in the light, a condition in which there is no cause for offense as long as one stays there. You can see where you are going morally and spiritually and, as a result, don't fall yourself or cause others to do so (Smalley, *1, 2, 3 John*, pp. 61–62).

2:11 / Verse 11 directly contrasts to v. 10 and returns to the negative side of the theme first expressed in v. 9: people who do not love **brother** and sister Christians are lost and **blinded in the darkness**, despite their claim (v. 9) to be in the light. Note the continuing use of pairs of contrasting words in this passage: light/darkness and love/hate. This kind of moral and spiritual antithetical language is used throughout the letters of John. The Elder sees the world and his community's part in it in black-and-white, dualistic terms. He prefers to state situations in language which leaves no middle ground, no ambiguity, and no question. This way of speaking is characteristic of groups in crisis and conflict, as the Johannine Christians were due to both their earlier schism with Judaism and the recent secession of the gnosticlike false teachers (1 John 2:19).

How dark the situation is for those, like the secessionists, who **hate** their **brother** or sister, is emphasized in a threefold way. They are **in the darkness**, they **walk around in the darkness**, and **the darkness has blinded** them. But "God is light" (1:5) and "is in the light" (1:7); therefore the opponents described here are not where God is. In 1:6 **walking in the darkness** was contrasted with walking in the light, or being in fellowship with God. Thus, the false teachers are not in communion with God. They do not know where they are going, despite their claims to possess knowledge (2:4). Like the Pharisees in John 9:39–41, the schismatics claim to see but actually are blind (cf. also the summary indictment of Jesus' opponents in John 12:35–40.) Blinded by the darkness, these false teachers are likely not only to stumble themselves but to cause others to stumble. Thus, there is an implied contrast also with v. 10b.

Additional Notes   §3

2:3ff.   /   In this passage and elsewhere in 1 John it is not possible to know whether the author intends God or Christ when he uses the pronouns "he," "him," or "his." A good case can be made for either person. The Elder may be referring to both. God/Christ will be used throughout this section.

2:5   /   **Word** (*logos*) and "commands" (*entolai*) are also used interchangeably in John 14:21 and 14:23. *Logos* can, of course, have a broader meaning, as we have already seen in 1:1 (where it refers to Christ, the Word of life), and in 1:10 where it is a synonym for the gospel, God's message (*angelia*, cf. 1:5).

The Greek phrase *hē agapē tou theou*, "the **love** of God," could be translated in three ways: as a subjective genitive (God's love for the obedient Christian), as an objective genitive (the obedient Christian's love for God), or as a qualitative genitive (God's kind of love, divine love—the likely meaning in 2:5; Stott, *Letters*, p. 96). Given the fluidity of the language of the author, such fine distinctions as NT scholars make may be overly precise interpretation.

This is the first use of "love" (*agapē*) in the letters of John, where it occurs thirty-one times as a verb and twenty-one times as a noun. The term of fond address, *agapētos*, also occurs ten times. It is a high frequency word in these letters (one-fifth of the entire NT usage). For a detailed study of the use of *agapē* in the letters of John, see Brown, *Epistles*, pp. 254–57 and in the Gospel of John (Brown, *Gospel, I–XII*, pp. 497–99). Love is the free decision of one person to give himself or herself up for the highest good and well-being of another person without regard to reward. It is best seen in God's love for humankind in the sending of the Son to be the Savior of the world (1 John 4:7–12).

The Gospel and letters of John contain nine of the NT's twenty-three uses of the term *teleioō*, to "make **complete**, fulfill." 1 John always uses it in relation to "love" (2:5; 4:12, 17–18).

We are in him. "To be in" (*einai en*) is one of the writer's favorite expressions. It occurs eighteen times in these letters. See, e.g., 1:5 ("in him there is no darkness"), 1:7 ("as he is in the light"), 1:8 ("there is no truth in us"), 1:10 ("his word is not in us"), 2:4 ("there is no truth in such a person"), 2:5 ("we know that we are in him"). Kysar says that it describes "the relationship which determines one's being," or "the primary factor which shapes the behavior and character of a person" (*I, II, III John*, p. 46).

2:6   /   The secessionists' earlier claims are in 1:6, 8, 10; 2:4, and the sixth claim occurs in 2:9, which ends the series of direct quotations of or references to the spiritual self-descriptions of the schismatic false teachers.

Menō, **to live in**, is a favorite Johannine term. It occurs forty times in the Gospel of John and twenty-seven in the letters of John. "Remain," "abide," and "dwell" are its primary meanings. The NIV translates it variously as "live" (1 John 2:6, 10, 14, 17; 3:6, 24; 4:12, 13, 15, 16; 2 John 2), "remain" (1 John 2:19, 24, 27; 3:9, 14), "continue" (1 John 2:28; 2 John 9), "be" (1 John 3:17), and leaves *menō* untranslated in 1 John 3:15. See the concise study of *menō* in Brown, *Epistles*, pp. 259–61.

The name **Jesus** is not in the Greek text; instead the special Johannine use of the term *ekeinos* appears. *Ekeinos* means "this one," "that one," or simply "he." In 1 John it always refers to Jesus (3:3, 5, 7, 16; 4:17; cf. also John 1:18; 3:30; 7:11) and "was common as a designation in the circle of the author" (Bultmann, *Epistles*, p. 26).

2:7–8 / These verses contain typical Johannine antitheses: **new/ old** and **light/darkness**. New/old occurs only here and in 2 John 5, and never in the Fourth Gospel. Light/darkness is more frequent, occurring in the epistles here and at 1:5–7, and in the Gospel in seven passages (1:5; 3:19–21; 8:12; 9:4–5 [day/night]; 11:9–10 [day/night]; 12:35–36; and 12:46). John 1:5 refers, as in 1 John 2:8, to the dawning of a new age of light which the darkness cannot overcome. In 3:19 light has come into the world and divides humankind into two camps of moral contrast. Jesus declares himself to be that light in 8:12 (so also 9:5), while in 9:4–5 his time on earth is called "day" after which comes the "night." Day/night occurs also in 11:9–10. The meaning is more difficult to discern but appears to be christological: "walk" by the day/light which is Christ. This is precisely the connotation of 12:35–36. Jesus has come into the world as light, so that those who believe in him may escape the darkness (12:46). On the antithetical language of the Gospel and letters of John, see Johnson, *Antitheses*, pp. 31–161.

2:9–10 / **Light / darkness** and **love / hate** are also intertwined in the Manual of Discipline of the Dead Sea Scrolls (1QS), the language of which is closely related to the Johannine writings (see Charlesworth, *John and Qumran*). Cf. 1QS 1:9–10; 3:24–26; 4:5–13; Johnson, *Antitheses*, pp. 169–71.

When the Elder writes of **love / hate** for the **brother**s and sisters, he is referring exclusively to members of the Johannine community. He is wrestling with a local issue, albeit one which has relevant application today. There is no reflection on "love of neighbor" or "love of enemies" in the Johannine Gospel or epistles. The focus is on the importance of love among the threatened yet believing community, among disciples (cf. John 13:34–35; cf. D. Rensberger, *Johannine Faith and Liberating Community* [Philadelphia: Westminster, 1988], pp. 124–31).

2:11 / This social conflict-based cause of the antithetical language of the letters of John is explored in depth in Johnson, *Antitheses*, pp. 224–60. See the Introduction for discussion of the historical setting of 1–3 John.

There is a close parallel to 2:11 in John 12:35. Jesus warned those who had not yet put their trust in him (12:36) that "the man who walks in the dark does not know where he is going." The Elder's opponents had denied that the divine Christ was actually Jesus (1 John 2:22); they had not put their trust in him, and so, like those described in John 12:35 and 1 John 2:11, they walk in the darkness and have lost their way.

§4 The Victorious Community and the World (1 John 2:12–17)

This section of 1 John is composed of two distinct parts. Verses 12–14 describe the victorious Christian community, addressing three groups of family members: children, young men, and fathers. Verses 15–17 exhort this faithful community not to love the world but to continue to do God's will in it. The author's purposes in this passage are to strengthen the Johannine Christians' confidence, so that it will not be further eroded by the secessionist false teachers, and to warn them against the kind of worldly compromise which characterized the opponents' lifestyle.

Verses 12–14 have a special structure as the indented printing of the NIV clearly shows. There are several parallel structures in these three verses. Though one cannot tell this from the NIV translation, the first three sentences (vv. 12–13) begin with "I write" (*graphō*), while the last three sentences begin with "I wrote" (*egrapsa*). Further, three groups of persons are addressed, all viewed as parts of one family or community of believers, well known to the author: "children" (12a, *teknia*; 14a, *paidia*), "young men" (13b, 14c), and "fathers" (13a, 14b).

These groups may stand for different levels of Christian maturity or experience in the community, although the Elder can also call the whole community "children" (*teknia* in 2:1, 28; 3:7; 4:4; 5:21; and *paidia* in 2:18). What is said of each group also does not appear to be age- or experience-related but is true of the whole community. So referring to these groups is best thought of as a stylistic device that sets forth several truths about the spiritual victory of the whole Johannine fellowship.

The variation of the verbs for "write" is to be understood in exactly the same way. There is no significant difference in meaning between the author's use of *graphō* and *egrapsa*. One of the characteristics of the aorist is definiteness: at most, then, v. 14 is saying "I am definitely writing to you because . . ." In fact, all the author's uses of "write" in 1 John until 2:14 (1:4; 2:1, 7, 8, 13) are present tense (*graphō*), while all of his uses of "write" after 2:14 (2:21, 26; 5:13) are aorist (*egrapsa*), without any apparent change of significance (Brown, *Epistles*, p. 297). Stylistic variation is one of the chief literary characteristics of the Johannine writings as a whole (e.g., in John 21:15–17 of sheep/lambs and the verbs for "love" and "feed").

It should also be noted that there is disagreement among biblical scholars as to the best interpretation of the word which the NIV translates "because" (*hoti*) in each of these verses. The same Greek word can also mean "that." The connections between the halves of the sentences in all these cases would then be declarative rather than causal: "I write to you that . . . " rather than "I write to you because . . ." But, as Marshall puts it, "It does not make a lot of difference to our understanding of the passage whether we use 'because' or 'that' to introduce John's statements" (*Epistles*, p. 136).

2:12 / The decisive fact which the Elder here wants to underscore for his readers is that their **sins have been forgiven.** The past has been taken care of; they have been cleansed. **Forgiven** is in the perfect tense, implying an act begun at a specific point in the past (conversion) and whose effects continue on into the present (they stand forgiven). This forgiveness is renewed on a daily basis by confession (1:9).

Forgiveness is based on **his name.** It is **on account of his name** that the community enjoys its victory over sin. In 1:7 and 2:1–2 the writer states the christological foundation of forgiveness: "the blood of Jesus . . . purifies us from all sin" and "Jesus Christ, the Righteous One, . . . is the atoning sacrifice for our sins." The **name** of Jesus is also the object of the believer's faith in 3:23 and 5:13. It is by faith in **his name** (who he is and what he has done) that we are **forgiven** and have eternal life.

2:13 / The second decisive victory of the Johannine Christians who have remained loyal to the Elder is knowledge of God/Christ. The **fathers** (possibly a reference to the community's more experienced leaders, but certainly representative of all Christians) have come to know **him who is from the beginning.** Their spiritual experience is not bogus but authentic. As the author writes in 2:3 and 2:5: "We know that we have come to know him" and "we know we are in him." He grounds these true claims on the obedient, Christlike lifestyle of the readers, a verification the author's opponents lacked. Thus, the community can be assured of its position before God; they do not need to be thrown into doubt and uncertainty by the false teachers.

Him who is from the beginning recalls 1 John 1:1, the Word of life, "which was from the beginning," and John 1:1, "In the beginning was the Word." This points to Jesus as the one to whom the writer is referring. In 13c (NIV; Gk. 14a) the children are said to know the Father, while in 14a (NIV; Gk. 14b) the fathers know him who is from the beginning, a pointless repetition unless the two phrases refer to different persons.

The third victory of the Johannine community is conquest of **the evil one**. This is attributed to the **young men**. Brown translates *neaniskoi* as "young people," a good reminder that all that is said here applies also to the women of the fellowship, though predominantly male terminology is used (Brown, *Epistles*, ad loc). Although **young men** may refer to a younger and less mature subgroup within the whole (Smalley, *1, 2, 3 John*, p. 70), representatively their victory is one in which all Christians share.

Overcome is in the perfect tense, again, as in all these verses, implying a past reality with continuing consequences. It is Christ's past victory, by his death and resurrection, over the powers of evil and darkness which gives believers the victory today. They have conquered **the evil one** because Christ has done so, and they are in him. In 1 John 4:4 the "dear children" have "overcome" the false prophets who deny Jesus, and in 5:4–5 those truly "born of God" have "overcome the world" by their faith in Jesus as God's Son.

The evil one in the Johannine literature refers to the devil, rather than to an abstract power of evil, though the two are clearly related. In John 17:15 Jesus prays that his disciples be kept from the evil one, while in 1 John 5:18 he fulfills his own request by keeping God's children safe so that the evil one cannot harm them. "The whole world is under the control of the evil one" (1 John 5:19), who in John 12:31 is called "the prince of this world." The murderer Cain belonged to him (1 John 3:12). It is this personified power, God's ancient enemy, Satan (Rev. 12:9), whom the Johannine community has already overcome. Their victory is realized in the present because of what Christ has done in the past.

With v. 13c the cycle of addressees begins again. This time the **dear children** (*paidia*) are said to be victorious because they **have known the Father**, a favorite Johannine term for God. As in 13a, the issue is assurance of real spiritual knowledge in the face of the assertive gnostic false teachers who claimed a special and superior knowledge of God. The children, here clearly the whole community, need not worry or be confused. They know **the Father**; indeed they **have known** him from the beginning of their Christian experience until now (the thrust of the perfect tense). This true knowledge of God is authenticated by their obedience to God's commands (2:3–4), proof the opponents cannot match.

2:14 / The first half of v. 14 is nearly an exact repetition of v. 13a. Only the tense of the verb has changed. This change of tense is stylistic, as we discussed in the introduction to this section. At most it adds a note of intensity and definiteness to the assertion that the **fathers have known him who is from the beginning**, that is, Jesus, God's Son, the Word (1 John 1:1; John 1:1). Although many theories have been offered concerning the Elder's reason for repeating this assertion about the **fathers** in nearly identical terms, none of them are convincing, and the reason remains unknown.

The second half of v. 14 contains the final admonition to the community, addressed to the **young men**. The "because clause" contains three elements this time, only one of which is identical to v. 13b, the previous address to this subgroup: **you have overcome the evil one**. To this the writer adds two new descriptions of their victorious condition as God's faithful community: (a) they are **strong** and (b) **the word of God lives** in them. The word **strong** refers to their spiritual strength, likely (in view of the mention of Satan) their ability to resist temptation (possibly the temptations to be mentioned in v. 16). But the source of their strength is **the word of God** which abides or dwells (NIV, **lives**; *menei*) in them. Here God's word is, as in 1:10, the truth about Jesus, who is himself "the Word of life" (1:1). This saving message dwells in the **young men** and gives them strength to **overcome the evil one**. What is true of the **young men** is true of every member of the community, the Elder's and the Christian community today.

2:15 / Verses 12–14 have described the victorious, faithful community. The Elder has assured them of their wealth of spiritual resources: they are forgiven (12), they know Jesus (13a, 14a), they have overcome the evil one (13b, 14b), they know the Father (13c), they are strong, and the word of God dwells in them (14b). Now he warns them against losing what they have gained by compromising with **the world**. The Elder's opponents are still in the background. In his view, they **love the world**, and the world loves them (4:5). They have given in to its desires and do not share their material possessions with their needy brothers and sisters (3:17). The faithful Johannine Christians are not to be like them.

Do not love the world. This is an odd command coming from the community which wrote, "For God so loved the world" (John 3:16). The resolution lies in different senses of **world** in the Gospel and letters of John. In this verse **world** is like "mammon" in Jesus' saying about the impossibility of serving two masters (Matt. 6:24). Loving God and loving **the world**, in this sense, are mutually exclusive, like the Old Testament prophets' insistence that Israel could not serve both Yahweh and Ba'al. The nation had to choose (Josh. 24:14–24; 1 Kgs. 18:21). James agrees in 4:4: "Friendship (*philia*, love) with the world is hatred toward God." Here the **world** is Satan's domain, in the control of the evil one (1 John 5:19). It does not mean "the created universe, nor the human race as such . . . but the life of human society as organized under the power of evil" (Dodd, *Epistles*, p. 39). The command is a present tense imperative connoting a way of life characterized by not loving the **world**, nor the things **in the world** (NIV, **anything in the world**).

Before the Elder clarifies in v. 16 what he means by **anything in the world**, he finishes v. 15 by stating the fundamental incompatibility of both loving God and loving the Satan-controlled world. One cannot do both. To love the world is to be devoid of love for the Father; the writer leaves no middle ground. Authentic love for God and "worldliness" cannot coexist in the same person at the same time. By this strong antithesis the Elder challenges his readers to purity of life (1:6, 9; 2:1; 3:3), especially so that there might be a difference between them and the "worldly" lifestyle of the false teachers.

2:16 / The **for** at the opening of v. 16 indicates that v. 16 is giving a reason for the assertion in v. 15b that love for God and for the world are an impossible contradiction. Why? Because

everything in the world (cf. in v. 15 "anything in the world") has its origin not in the Father but in the world itself. God and the world are an absolute antithesis as sources of value. They stand over against each other like light and darkness, truth and error. The controversy which has pitted the Elder and his remaining loyal band of followers over against the popular false teachers has caused him to see the choices facing Christians in clear black-and-white terms. Just as one must choose which side of the schism one is on, so one must choose whether to serve and love God or the world (cf. Matt. 6:24).

What is **everything in the world** of which the author is thinking? He defines it in three phrases: the desire (*epithymia*) of the flesh, the desire (*epithymia*) of the eyes, and **the boasting of what he has and does** (lit., "the boasting in the life," *hē alazoneia tou biou*). This is the essence of the "worldly" person; it is a way of feeling, looking, and expressing oneself. This approach to life is self-centered: the thoughts, decisions, and activities of every-day life are dominated by **the cravings** of one's own "flesh" (*sarx*; NIV, **the sinful man**), the longings (NIV, **lust**) of one's own eyes (TEV, "what people see and want"), and the personal **boasting** in material possessions (*tou biou*; cf. 3:17, where the phrase *ton bion tou kosmou*, lit., "the life of the world," means the material posses-sions of this world, the physical resources which one could use to help people in need).

2:17 / A further reason for not loving the world (v. 16 was the first reason) is that it is temporary, passing away, and impermanent, while the true Christian **lives forever** (cf. 2 Cor. 4:18). The focal point of the antithesis is now the believer (rather than God) and the world.

The world and its desires (lit., "desire"; cf. the two refer-ences to desire in v. 16) **pass away** (*paragetai*), in the sense that this age is ending and God's reign is coming, just as "the darkness is passing (*paragetai*) and the true light is already shining" (2:8); indeed, it "is the last hour" (2:18), when the end-times "anti-christ" who was supposed to come has already appeared (2:18; 4:3) in the form of the false teachers with their denial that the Christ is the fully human Jesus (2 John 7; cf. 4:2–3).

By contrast with the ephemeral world, the one **who does the will of God** abides forever. This description of the faithful member of the Johannine community derives from the Gospel of

John. Jesus' food is to do God's will (John 4:34), he seeks not his own will but the will of the one who sent him (5:30), and he has come down from heaven to do not his own will but the will of him who sent him (6:38). The man born blind tells the Pharisees that God listens only to "the godly man who does his will" (in this context, Jesus; 9:31). Jesus' true followers also do God's will by looking to the Son and believing in him (6:40), and if they do God's will, they will discover whether Jesus' teaching is from God (7:17).

Such obedient, believing members of the Elder's community will **live** (lit., "abide," *menō*) **forever**. They are not like the world which **passes away**. The antithesis here is really between life and death. Johannine Christians have already passed from death to life (3:14–15; John 5:24). They have life through their faith in the Son, which those who reject Jesus do not have (5:12). This is part of the Johannine "realized eschatology," in which formerly anticipated blessings of the age to come are now realized in the earthly experience of those who believe in Jesus. They do not wait to receive eternal life until the resurrection but have it as a present possession by faith in Jesus (John 3:16, 36; 5:24; 6:47, 54; 11:26; 20:31).

Additional Notes   §4

2:13 / Realized eschatology is one of the principal theological themes of the Gospel and letters of John. Spiritual realities expected to happen only in the future reign of God have become a part of the present experience of believers in Jesus. Victory in the judgment, the defeat of Satan, the reception of eternal life, the indwelling of the Spirit, and other "events" were all viewed in Judaism as future hope, but the Christian community, especially the Johannine community, though also Paul, claims these blessings as available in the present to those who believe in Jesus. See G. E. Ladd, "Eschatology," *ISBE*, vol. 2, pp. 136–37.

In editions of the Greek New Testament, such as the UBS text and Nestle's, and in most modern translations, v. 14 begins at v. 13c. The NIV and NASB are exceptions.

2:14 / On the repetitive language of 2:12–14, see Smalley, *1, 2, 3 John*, pp. 66–79.

2:16 / "The desire of the flesh" (NIV, **the cravings of sinful man**) is a phrase common to Paul's writings but does not occur elsewhere in John's. In the letters of John, "flesh" (*sarx*) occurs only here, in 4:2, and in 2 John 7, where the reference is to the full humanity of Jesus, the incarnation (cf. John 1:14, "The Word became flesh" [*sarx*]), a teaching which the opponents denied. "Flesh" may mean "all that satisfies the needs and wants of human beings taken as such" (Brown, *Epistles*, p. 310).

Boasting (*alazoneia*) means pretentiousness, ostentation, or over-confidence. Here in 1 John this attitude is based on the security one feels in material possessions. It is exemplified by the rich man in Jesus' story who said to himself, "You have plenty of good things laid up for many years. Take life easy; eat, drink, and be merry." But of him God said, "You fool! This very night your life will be demanded of you" (Luke 12:19–20). The Elder believes that this "worldly" attitude is also characteristic of the secessionists.

§5 *The Truth and the Lie: A Warning against Antichrists (1 John 2:18–27)*

This section of 1 John is unified by its concern for maintaining the truth which has been given to the Johannine community over against the lie of the antichrists. The antichrists are those who have seceded from the community (2:19) and who deny that the fully human Jesus is the Christ, the divine Son of God (2:22). The Elder's aim is to reassure the remaining loyal Christians that they have the truth and to urge them to remain in it (2:24, 27).

2:18 / The two key notes of this verse are the announcement of **the last hour** and the introduction of **the antichrists**. Both are concepts drawn from Jewish eschatology. The author sees his situation as eschatological; he and his community are living at the end of an era of darkness and at the beginning of a new age of light. **The last hour** is the turning point, the remaining hour of darkness before the dawn (2:8, 17a). In this transition there will be tribulation and conflict. Jewish and early Christian eschatology expected demonic opposition to God's work in bringing about "the age of the Messiah" (the Christ), and it is clear that the community was familiar with this teaching: **you have heard that the antichrist is coming**. But now this opposition, **many antichrists**, has already appeared in multiple form. **Antichrist** has become a collective whole, the believing community's opponents, those who deny the Christ. (In what sense the Elder's enemies deny Christ will be made clear in v. 22.) By the appearance of these forces of evil, **we**, the community, **know it is the last hour.** As many have done since, the author reads the signs of his own day as signs of the end of history and identifies actual living persons with symbolic end-time figures.

2:19 / This verse is the most important verse in the letters of John for understanding the historical setting of these epistles. It also helps to explain the intensity of the author's opposition to his opponents. At one time they had all been part of the same community, but one group left (**they went out from us**) and became secessionists. They are the false teachers whom the author now calls the "antichrists." A schism had occurred within the Johannine community, splitting it in two. Similarly, in an earlier time the community itself as a whole had been painfully separated from Judaism by expulsion from the synagogue.

The Elder is adamant, however, that the seceding group never really belonged to the community (lit., "they were not from us"). They had belonged to the group in the sense of being part of the same organization (from which **they went out**), but they did not belong to the group in the sense of sharing its core beliefs. How they could have been or become part of the group in any sense is never explained. The best historical guess is that they were Gentile converts who had been influenced by the emerging gnostic ideas of the Hellenistic world, and who had never really given up their Greek philosophical world view. It had led them to deny that the divine savior, the Christ, was ever embodied in the fully human person, Jesus. For them, the divine Logos (the Word) could not have become flesh and dwelt among us (John 1:14).

The Elder wants his readers to realize that the secessionists' schism of the community is the proof that they are not really true Christians. If they were, they would have stayed (note the antithesis between **they went out** and **they would have remained**). But it was necessary that the schism occur, so that the true stripes of the opposition could be manifested. Paul argues similarly in 1 Cor. 11:19. **None of them belonged to us**, not one. All of those who have left were not authentic Christians; the schism has served to make this clear. Paul foresaw the possibility of such a division among those claiming to be Christians in Acts 20:30.

2:20 / In contrast (**But you**) with the secessionists, the Elder's readers **have an anointing from the Holy One** which causes them all to **know** (NIV adds **the truth**, words not in the Greek text). They do not need to be shaken by the false teachers' claims or spiritual pretensions. The Elder's purpose in vv. 20–23 is to reassure the community that *they* have the truth and not the lying secessionists.

The term **anointing** (*chrisma*) refers to their reception of the Holy Spirit, probably at baptism or in a service of anointing with oil which was practiced in some quarters of early Christianity. This **anointing** is referred to again in v. 27, where its qualities of abiding in believers and of teaching them are underlined. All of these indicators point to its identification with receiving the promised Holy Spirit spoken of in John 14:17, 26. The **Holy One** who gives the Spirit could be either God the Father or Jesus. In the Fourth Gospel, both are said to grant the Spirit (the Father, John 14:16, 26; Jesus, 15:26; 16:7). The context of the parallel passage in vv. 27–28 favors Jesus as the **Holy One**.

This Christ-given presence of the Holy Spirit within the Johannine Christians empowers them to **know** (cf. v. 27 where the anointing teaches them). The second half of v. 20 is the result of the first half. Over against the secessionists' claim to a special and superior knowledge of God, seen already in 2:4 and reflected in the author's previous reassurances in 2:3, 5b, 13ac, 14a, the Elder asserts the readers' true knowledge of God. They are the true "knowers," not the self-proclaimed "gnostics." The original text's assertion here is broader than that implied by the NIV's addition of the direct object, **the truth**, which the translators borrowed by analogy from the next verse. Furthermore, **all of you** know, not just some of the members. Because all have received the Spirit, all are knowing; there is no exclusive, elite group with "inside" spiritual knowledge of divine mysteries, such as the false teachers are likely to have claimed.

2:21 / Because the Spirit-anointed, faithful Johannine Christians **know the truth**, the author was writing not to inform them as if they were ignorant, but simply to remind them that they do **know the truth** and, therefore, they have nothing to fear from the schismatics. He was worried not about their knowledge but about their assurance in the face of the aggressive claims of the seceding false teachers. "Do not be intimidated by them," he implies. In fact, the loyalists know something that the others don't: **no lie comes from the truth** (lit., "every lie is not from the truth"). The Elder wants to remind his "dear children" (v. 18) that the new teachings of the secessionists were not derived from the truth which the community holds to be central and sacred. Their error (**lie**) and deception have arisen from sources outside the fellowship. The false teachers cannot claim that their teaching is consistent with the historic teaching of the Johannine community, based as it was on the teaching of Jesus as preserved and interpreted by the beloved disciple in the Gospel of John (but undoubtedly this is exactly what the former Johannine "Christians" were claiming!).

2:22 / **Who is the liar?** That is, what is the essence of "the lie" (v. 21) which has deviated so destructively from the historic "truth" of the Johannine Christians? What is the false teaching which threatens to lead the community astray (v. 26)? **The liar** is the one **who denies that Jesus is the Christ.** At stake in the conflict with the secessionists is whether **the Christ** can be identified with **Jesus**, the one (1 John 1:1) who came in the flesh (John 1:14; 1 John 4:2; 2 John 7), who came by water and blood (5:6–7), and who shed his blood for our sins (1 John 1:7; 2:2; 4:10). Both sides in the controversy believed in the Christ, the divine Son of God; the secessionists denied that this divine being who appeared on earth was in every respect the same as the human being Jesus. When the writer of these letters uses the name "Jesus," he is usually implying the historical, enfleshed, fully human Christ. *That* Christ the secessionists, with their Greek assumptions about the body and human nature, could not accept. Thus, they are to the Elder **the antichrist.** The prefix "anti" in Greek may mean "in the place of," as a substitute, either neutrally or with negative connotations, such as a false Christ, or antagonistically, "against Christ," or "opposed to Christ" (BAGD, pp. 73–74). That the negative connotations are clearly in the writer's mind is seen in his association of the term with **liar** and denier (cf. 2 John 7).

Further, to deny **Jesus** is to deny not only **the Son** but **the Father** as well. The two are inseparable, as v. 23 makes clear.

2:23 / One cannot have **the Father** without **the Son.** If one denies **the Son**, and if **the Father** and **the Son** are an indivisible unity ("I and the Father are one," John 10:30; "No one comes to the Father except through me. If you really knew me, you would know my Father as well," John 14:6b–7a; "Anyone who has seen me has seen the Father," John 14:9b), then to deny Jesus is to deny God. In this way, the Elder extends the horrifying implications of the secessionists' christological error.

Antithetically, the second half of v. 23 affirms the positive truth, which is the experience of the remaining, loyal-to-the-Elder Christians (in contrast to the secessionists): by confessing (NIV, **acknowledges**) **the Son**, one **has the Father.** Verse 23 makes it clear that Christology is everything. Denying or confessing

Jesus is the key to a right relationship with God (**has the Father**) and to fellowship with the true community of believers, who acknowledge that the human Jesus is the Christ, God's Son.

2:24 / The Elder's purposes in this section of 1 John are to clarify for the remaining Johannine Christians what the present situation actually is with regard to the opponents and their secession (18–19, 22–23), to reassure them of their own spiritual standing vis-à-vis the false teachers (20–21, 26–27), and in vv. 24–25 to exhort them to remain loyal to what they have already received, the community's tradition. This is the teaching which they **have heard from the beginning** (cf. 2:7; 3:11; 2 John 5–6). He urges them to let it **remain** in them, to abide and to last, so that they stay faithful to the gospel. **What you have heard** implies oral preaching. What the writer heard he proclaims to his readers (1:1, 3, 5), the message (*logos*) which they have heard **from the beginning** (2:7; 3:11), just as Paul passed on to his churches as sacred the tradition which he had received (1 Cor. 11:2; 15:1–3; Gal. 1:11–12). If the readers allow this teaching to remain in them, then, as a consequence, they themselves **will remain in the Son and in the Father**. There is a direct tie between faithfulness to the gospel and remaining in fellowship with God and God's Son.

2:25 / There is a **promise** which belongs to the Christian who perseveres to the end, "remaining in the Father and the Son" (v. 24): **eternal life**. To be and to remain in the Son (and the Father) is life. This gift from God of **eternal life** is in the Son, just as it is also in the Father (cf. John 5:26, 40; 1 John 5:11). To be in the Son (to have the Son, 5:12) is to have or to abide in **eternal life**. In John 17:3 **eternal life** is to know God and Jesus Christ, another expression that is the virtual equivalent of believing, abiding, and being in. As always in the Gospel and letters of John, this **eternal life** is a present possession, a formerly eschatological blessing now realized in those who believe in Jesus and love their brothers (John 5:24; 1 John 3:14).

2:26 / The Elder sums up this section of warning against the antichrists with a verse of reminder and a verse of reassurance. Verse 26 briefly summarizes what he has been writing about at least since 2:18. **These things** may even refer back to the beginning of the epistle.

The opponents are here described as **those who are trying to lead you astray** (lit., "the ones deceiving you"). The verb "to deceive" (*planaō*) and its two cognates *planos* and *planē* are found six times in the letters of John. We may deceive ourselves about our sin (as the false teachers are doing; 1:8), and, as in 2:26, 1 John 3:7 warns against those who would deceive the readers. In 4:6 God's Spirit of Truth is contrasted with the demonic Spirit of Error (*planē*), while 2 John 7 refers directly to the secessionists as deceivers (*planoi*) and as antichrists. It is evident not only that the break-away party is **trying to** deceive (or **lead astray**) the remaining Johannine Christians, but that it has succeeded in doing so, at least to the point of seriously shaking the confidence of the community with its erroneous claims.

2:27 / Therefore, to assure the community, the Elder returns once again to the subject of the **anointing**, which he first mentioned in v. 20. This *chrisma* is the Holy Spirit, in the Gospel of John called the Paraclete (John 14:16, 26; 15:26; 16:7). The author makes four assertions about this **anointing**:

(1) It was received from God/Christ. This is one of those verses in which it is impossible to identify with certainty the person to whom the pronoun **him** refers, just as in 2:25 the **he** who is the source of the promise of eternal life is unclear. The origin of their **anointing** is divine.

(2) The **anointing remains** in them. It is not an experience which comes and goes, but an endowment, an abiding reality that resides in their lives to empower them for occasions such as this one, i.e., to resist temptation and assertive false teaching.

(3) The **anointing teaches you about all things**. The readers do not need to be intimidated by authoritative-sounding leaders who bring new doctrines or who deny old ones. They can trust the Spirit to teach them and to lead them into all truth, just as Jesus promised (John 14:26; 16:13). If they would listen to their Spirit-teacher, they would not need any human teacher in spiritual matters. Even the Elder's letter would be unnecessary!

(4) The **anointing** is **real, not counterfeit** (lit., "is true [*alēthes*] and it is not false" [*pseudos*]). The secessionists were claiming that only their **anointing** was valid or truly effective, while those who remained with the Elder had a false or weak **anointing.** It was either spurious or inoperative. "Not so," the Elder claims. "Your anointing is true (authentic, genuine). It really happened and

remains within you. So, do not let anyone cast doubt upon your spiritual experience. You are the only living expert on your relationship with the Spirit of Jesus. No one else knows your heart."

In the light of all this, the author urges his readers to **remain in him**, just as Jesus commanded his disciples in John 15:1–10. This is, above all, what the Holy Spirit, **the anointing, has taught**: do not be led astray but remain loyal to Jesus, the true Christ (v. 22), and to the community of those who, like the Elder, have resisted the secession of the antichrists (vv. 18–19).

Additional Notes   §5

2:18 / See the excellent summary of the Jewish eschatological background in Brown, *Epistles*, pp. 332–36.

The expression, **the last hour**, which occurs only here in the NT, corresponds to "the last days" (Acts 2:17; 2 Tim. 3:1; Heb. 1:2; Jas. 5:3; 2 Pet. 3:3), a time introduced by the first coming of Christ which will include persecution and suffering for God's people, and which will be brought to conclusion by the return of Christ. All Christians, from Jesus' time to today, are living in "the last days." The Gospel of John prepares the reader of 1 John for understanding the concept of a final hour of suffering which leads to glory. Throughout the Gospel there is both an eschatological hour, a time which is coming (John 4:21, 23; 5:25, 28; 16:2, 4, 25) and Jesus' own "hour" (John 2:4; 7:30; 8:20; 12:23, 27; 13:1; 16:32). These are brought together in John 17:1 in which Jesus' own hour, the time of suffering and death, is also the eschatological hour that leads to glory and life.

The entire book of Revelation, also a part of the Johannine literature, is devoted to this cosmic, end-times conflict between the forces of good and evil, light and darkness, God and Satan.

The Johannine community, or the Elder who writes these letters as their leader, the successor to the beloved disciple, the community's founder, may have coined the term **antichrist**, for this is its first appearance in all literature. It occurs also in 1 John 2:22; 4:3; and 2 John 7 and nowhere else in the NT or earlier writings (cf. "false Christs," *pseudochristoi* in Matt. 24:24).

2:19 / Signs of this schism from the synagogue may be seen in John 9:22, 34; 12:42; and 16:2. See J. L. Martyn, *History and Theology in the Fourth Gospel*, rev. ed. (Nashville: Abingdon, 1979). The history of the Johannine community is one of conflict and controversy, and these social conflicts played a major role in determining the community's outlook and the language in which it is expressed. See W. A. Meeks, "The Man from Heaven in Johannine Sectarianism," *JBL* 91 (1972), pp. 44–72, and Johnson, *Antitheses*, pp. 224–60.

2:20 / Elsewhere in the NT Jesus is called **the Holy One** in Mark 1:24; Luke 4:34; John 6:69; Acts 3:14; and Rev. 3:7. It also occurs in the apostolic fathers, 1 Clem. 23:5 and Diogn. 9:2.

The best MSS support the reading **all of you know**; another group changes the *pantes* (nominative) to *panta* (accusative), and translates the verse "and you know everything." The harder to explain reading is more likely to be original than the one which supplies an object for the verb *oidate*, a verb normally never without an object.

2:21 / Note the continuing highly antithetical language and the dualistic conceptuality behind it. Here **truth/lie** give it expression, as they do in 1:6: "we lie and do not live by the truth"; 1:8: "we deceive ourselves and the truth is not in us"; 1:10: "we make him [God] out to be a liar and his word is not in us"; 2:4: "[he] is a liar and the truth is not in him"; 2:27: "the anointing . . . is real and not counterfeit"; 4:6: "the Spirit of truth and the spirit of falsehood"; 2 John 1–4, 7: "I love in the truth, . . . all who know the truth, . . . because of the truth, . . . in truth and love, . . . walking in the truth, . . . many deceivers, . . . such [a] person is the deceiver. . . ." For our author, on account of the conflict, the schism, and the struggle for authentic Christianity in which he was involved, the boundaries between truth and error have become sharp and clear; there are no ambiguities. He is not unlike many Christians today for whom controversial but complex moral and theological issues are just as transparent.

2:22 / The term **liar** is associated with Satan in John 8:44 and 2 Thess. 2:9. He is also "the deceiver" (see 2 John 7 where antichrist and deceiver are associated), who deceives the whole world (Rev. 12:9; 20:3, 8, 10). The Elder is implying that the false teachers are under demonic influence when he uses terms like **antichrist**, **liar**, and deceivers (2 John 7) to describe them.

"Denying" Jesus has important theological nuances in the NT. Peter denied Jesus (John 18:17, 25, 27), and those who deny him risk being themselves denied when he returns (Matt. 10:33). John the Baptist "confessed" and did not "fail to confess" (note the typical Johannine antithetical style) that he was not the Christ (John 1:20). The "Men of Israel" denied Jesus, "the Holy and Righteous One" before Pilate (Acts 3:12, 14). Second Peter 2:1 speaks of false prophets and false teachers who "deny the sovereign Lord who bought them," just as Jude 4 mentions "godless men" who "deny Jesus Christ our only Sovereign and Lord." The faithful churches of Pergamum and Philadelphia (Rev. 2:13; 3:8) have not denied their faith in Jesus' name. Thus, to deny Jesus is the most serious of theological errors.

See the "Introduction" for a more complete description of the Elder's opponents, their probable historical and cultural background, and their beliefs.

There is no evidence, apart from their denial of Jesus as the Christ, that the opponents held what the Elder would consider as heretical views of the Father. They are not accused of separating the Father from the Creator, as Marcion and other "gnostically" influenced teachers did in the second century.

2:23 / The expression "to have the Father," or "to have God," is unique in the NT to the letters of John (2:23; 5:12; 2 John 9). It does not even occur in the Fourth Gospel (cf. John 8:41, where Jesus' interlocutors claim God as their Father). It may be that the Elder is using the language of his opponents, just as Paul does in 1 Corinthians and in Colossians.

2:24 / Both 1 John 5:20 and John 17:21 speak to "being in" (*einai en*) the Father and the Son. This is the only passage which speaks of "abiding in" (*menein en*) both persons. The two senses are equivalent. See the comment on 1 John 2:6, 10 for discussion of the Johannine concept of "abiding," and Malatesta, *Interiority*, passim.

2:25 / Some scholars understand the **he** in this verse as Jesus (Smalley, Brown), or both Jesus and the Father (Houlden, *Epistles*; Kysar, *I, II, III John*). Normally in the NT God is the giver of **eternal life** or life through the agency of the Son.

§6 The Children of God and the Children of the Devil (1 John 2:28—3:10)

This section of 1 John is unified by the idea of the children of God: who they are and how one can identify them by their lives. It is a passage dominated by ethics, particularly an ethical concern for righteousness and sin. It compares two "families": the children of God and the children of the devil. In the background, as always, are the Elder's opponents, the secessionists, whom he strongly contrasts to his own "dear children."

The unit is built on a structure of four antitheses, four pairs of opposing statements:

A.	1. Everyone who does what is right	(2:29b)
	2. Everyone who sins	(3:4a)
B.	1. No one who lives in him	(3:6a)
	2. No one who continues to sin	(3:6b)
C.	1. He who does what is right	(3:7b)
	2. He who does what is sinful	(3:8a)
D.	1. No one who is born of God	(3:9a)
	2. Anyone who does not do what is right	(3:10b)

All of these contrasting pairs have the same grammatical structure: they begin with a definite article (often with *pas*) followed by a present tense participle (the participle in 3:9a is the perfect tense with the force of the present). Seeing this, it becomes clear that the subsection 3:1–3 is a parenthetical celebration of the reality of being God's children, inside a larger unit concerned about what the lives of those who claim to belong to God should be like.

2:28 / Just as the last unit began with an eschatological note ("this is the last hour," 2:18), so does this one. Two common NT words for the return of Christ occur in this verse: *phanerōthē* and *parousia*. The former may be translated **when he appears**, an action of Christ himself, or "when he is manifested," leaving the initiation of Christ's return to the Father. The second term, *parousia*, **coming**, was used in the Hellenistic world for the visit of a king to a foreign province.

The link between this and the preceding verse is clear: the command **continue in him** is identical in both, though one would not know this from the NIV which uses "remain" in v. 27 and **continue** in v. 28. Perhaps the NIV translators chose to vary the reading because they sensed correctly that the author's emphasis in v. 28 is different. He is thinking about his community remaining faithful to Christ, persevering until his return and not going the way of the secessionists. When Christ comes, because they have **continue**d in fellowship with him, they will be **confident** (lit., "have confidence"; *parrēsian* may also mean "boldness") and **unashamed**. (Note the implied antithesis between **confidence** and **shame**; cf. also 3:19–21 and 4:17–18). The little phrase **before him** suggests a scene in which believers personally appear before Christ, as people coming into the presence of a king, and react to him as ones who either already know him or have reason to fear for their lives.

2:29 / Keeping the readers' minds on Christ, the Elder now raises the subject of Christ's nature or character. This will be his dominant theme throughout this section. **He is righteous**, or just (*dikaios*, cf. 1:9, where "God is faithful and just"; 2:1–2, where Jesus Christ is "the Righteous One"; and 3:7 which also refers to Christ as "righteous"). **Righteous**ness is not just holiness or freedom from sin, but includes the OT idea of putting things right or making them just. Here the readers are reminded that the person whose character is like Christ's (**everyone who does what is right**, lit., "everyone who is doing [practicing] righteousness") **has been born** of God. The family likeness will be present. Those born of God will resemble Christ, because they will share a common characteristic: doing justice or practicing righteousness.

To be **born of him**, that is, born of God, is a profound idea. In the Fourth Gospel, those who believe in the Word "become children of God" and are "born of God" (John 1:12–13). Repeatedly, Jesus tells Nicodemus that he must be "born from above" (3:3, 7), or be born of water and the Spirit (3:5, 8). In the letters of John, being born of God occurs in 2:29; 3:9 (twice); 4:7; 5:1, 4, 18 (twice). In two of these verses Jesus is the one who has been born of God (5:1, 18; cf. John 1:14, 18); the other times it is the Christian. To be born of God, one must believe that *Jesus* is the Christ and live a life of righteousness and love (2:29; 3:9; 4:7; 5:18; cf. Eph. 5:1, 2).

It is likely that the Elder's opponents were also using the phrase "born of God" and were claiming to be God's special children. Indeed, this may be another instance of the author using the opponents' own language to refute them. He was confident that if one looked at the character of the secessionists, one would not see lives that reflected the righteousness of Jesus, and on that basis, their claim to be children of God would clearly be false.

3:1 / The idea of being born of God is so inspiring to the Elder that he exclaims (lit.), "Behold! What great love the Father has given to us that we should be called children of God!" He explores this theme for three verses before returning to the contrast between sin and righteousness begun in 2:29.

It is **love** which has motivated God to claim us as his children. While the two previous references to **love** (*agapē*; 2:5, 15) were to human love, this is the first reference to God's love. (God's love will be the author's main focus in 4:7–10, 12, 16–18.) God's **love** has been **lavished on us**. The perfect tense connotes **love** which has been and continues to be given to us, with the continuing consequence that we are **called children of God**. People are born into God's family (2:29; John 1:13) and are given the right to become **children of God** because they have "received" the Word and have "believed in his name" (John 1:12–13). These are the people for whom Jesus died, including believers from "the Jewish nation," as well as "the scattered children of God" (future Gentile believers), that he might make them one (John 11:52; 17:20–23; cf. John 10:16). Such people "do what is right" (1 John 2:29) and thereby show that they are in reality what God called them to be (**and that is what we are!**).

The Elder reinforces the divine origin of the believing community because its status as God's children is unknown to **the world**; the surrounding culture does not see it and confirm it. The Johannine Christians must hold on to their true identity "against the stream." But, in being unknown to the world and in having a secret identity, the community can take special pride, for prior to them Jesus (NIV, **him**) was also "unknown" to his contemporaries (John 1:10–11; 8:19; 14:7, 9; 15:18–21; 16:3; cf. 3:32; 4:10; 7:27–28; 14:17; 17:25).

3:2 / The emphasis in v. 2 falls on the temporal dimension, i.e., on **now** and **not yet**. The author has just forcefully affirmed that he and his readers are **children of God** (3:1); that is what they are **now**, in reality, at the present moment. What their future identity **will be** (lit., "what we shall be") **has not yet been made known**. Paul says that "the creation waits in eager expectation for the sons of God to be revealed" (Rom. 8:19), and that "no eye has seen, no ear has heard, no mind has conceived what God has prepared for those who love him" (1 Cor. 2:9). While there is much about our existence in God's future of which we are and will remain ignorant until the right time comes, we can know *something* about it, namely, that we will continue on our present trajectory of becoming like Christ (cf. Rom. 8:29; 1 Cor. 15:49; Phil. 3:21): **we shall be like him**. Still **children of God**, we shall become more like "the One and Only" (John 1:14, 18) Son of God. The image of God lost in creation will be restored in Christ as we become like him, the New Man and New Adam (cf. Col. 3:10; 1 Cor. 15:45; Rom. 5:14).

This will happen **when he appears** (*phanerōthē*). *Phaneroō* is used in the letters of John to describe both the first (1:2; 3:5, 8; cf. John 1:31;) and second coming of Jesus (2:28; 3:2). The letters of John, written later in the first century than the Gospel (see the Introduction) and after the schism which has brought the "antichrist" to light (in the group of the secessionists; 2:18, 22; 4:3; 2 John 7), reflect a more vivid awareness of the return of Jesus; they have, compared to the Fourth Gospel, a heightened eschatology (2:18, 28; 3:2–3; 4:17). The Gospel of John, though unique in its strong emphasis on "realized eschatology," has a place for a genuinely futuristic eschatology as well (cf. 5:28–29; 14:3).

The writer and his community expectantly look forward to the coming of Jesus (2:28). They believe that when he appears, they will be transformed to become like Christ (cf. 1 Cor. 15:51–52) and that this change will occur, at least in part, because **we shall see him as he is**. To see, to gaze upon, and to meditate upon what one sees is to move in the direction of becoming like that which preoccupies one's attention. There will be a transforming vision at the return of Jesus in which believers will be purified of all that still separates them from complete likeness to Christ (cf. 2 Cor. 3:18).

3:3 / In v. 3 the author begins to return to his theme of a righteous life as the sign of authentic membership in the family of God. The eschatological **hope** (the only occurrence of the term in the Gospel and letters of John), grounded **in him**, i.e., in Christ/ God, which he has just outlined, does not only offer his readers comfort and assurance about their future (needed because of the threat of the schismatic false teachers); it also has a present, practical application. Anyone who looks forward to a vision of Christ/ God, the result of which will be to become like him, does not delay the process of transformation but **purifies himself** or herself now. Becoming like Christ/God begins now (note the ongoing present action of the verb). The change in view is holistic: moral, spiritual, attitudinal, and behavioral. The standard or model is Christ (**as he is pure**; cf. 3:5), or perhaps more accurately, in the light of the Christology of the Johannine writings, the model is God as revealed in the person, teaching, and life of Christ, God's Son.

3:4 / After a three-verse celebration of being God's children (3:1–3), the writer returns to the subject begun in 2:29. The first half of v. 4 contrasts the idea stated in 2:29b:

2:29b: everyone who does what is right
3:4a: **everyone who sins.**

Throughout this section (vv. 4–10) the Elder wants to show his readers how different are the lives of those who claim to be God's children (the secessionists, the false teachers who left the community; 2:19) and those who really are (3:1–2).

Everyone who sins is more literally translated "everyone who practices sin." The author's emphasis is on the continuous, habitual commission of sin as a way of life, not occasional or unintentional sin. In 1:7—2:2 he already acknowledged that believers commit sins and that the way to deal with them is to be confessing them and to be receiving God's forgiveness. But continuous, deliberate sinning **breaks the law** (lit., "practices lawlessness"; *anomia*). Ongoing, unconfessed sin **is lawlessness**, rebellion, an attitude, evidenced in action, that does not respect God's standards. Such rebellion was expected in "the last hour" when the antichrist would arise and lead people astray (2:18). Just as Jesus also accuses his opponents in the Gospel of John of not practicing the law (7:19), so the Elder sees his opponents (the false teachers and "antichrists" who left the Johannine churches; 2:18–19) as lawless.

3:5 / **But** such a rebellious attitude-in-action is directly contrary to God's self-revelation in Christ. Verse 5 contains two affirmations about Jesus' (**he**; *ekeinos*) relation to sin, both of which make it impossible for someone to claim to be in fellowship with God/Jesus while continuing to sin (cf. 2:6).

The first christological statement is that **he appeared so that he might take away our sins**. **He appeared** (*ephanerōthē*) is one of the writer's favorite expressions for the first and second coming of Jesus (1:2; 2:28; 3:2, 8; 4:9; John 1:31; it is also used of Jesus' post-resurrection appearances in John 21:1, 14). The purpose of Jesus' incarnation was to **take away our sins** (lit., "take away sins"; cf. 1:7; 2:2, 12; 3:8b; 4:10; John 1:29: "the Lamb of God who takes away the sin of the world"; 3:16–17; Rev. 1:5), not that we might be able to continue in them!

The second christological truth is that **in him is no sin**. This declaration of Jesus' sinlessness goes back to John 8:46 ("Can any of you prove me guilty of sin?") and to the portrayal of Jesus as the innocent, sacrificial lamb of Isaiah 53:7, 9. Other NT writers shared this conviction. Paul wrote in 2 Corinthians 5:21: "God made him who had no sin to be sin for us." The author of Hebrews said that Jesus "has been tempted in every way, just as we are—yet was without sin" (4:15), and that as our high priest he was "holy, blameless, pure" (7:26; cf. 1 Pet. 2:22, 24).

3:6 / Verse 6 draws the conclusion toward which v. 5 directly points and applies the moral point of these christological affirmations. If what is stated about Jesus in v. 5 is correct, then it is impossible to claim (as the schismatics were doing) that they **live in him**, have **seen him**, or have **known him**, when they prove by their continued false teaching and rejection of love that they **keep on sinning** and **continue to sin**.

Verse 6 also contains the second pair of the four pairs of antithetical statements which form the structure of this unit (2:28—3:10) of 1 John:

3:6a: No one who lives in him . . .
3:6b: No one who continues to sin . . .

(The other pairs of counterposed statements occur in 2:29b/3:4a; 3:7b/3:8a; and 3:9a/3:10b.)

Living, or more literally, abiding in him (*ho en autō menōn*) is an important and characteristically Johannine spiritual reality. It is the central theme of John 15:1–10, abiding in Christ the Vine, and it is promised to "whoever eats my flesh and drinks my blood" in John 6:56, a clear reference to the elements of the Lord's Supper. In the letters of John, the opponents claim to "live (*menō*) in him" (2:6), but this is contradicted by their conduct. The Elder's loyal followers are urged to "continue (*menō*) in him" (2:28–29), and he promises that if "what they have heard from the beginning" abides in them, then they will abide in the Son and in the Father (2:24). See the discussion of these verses above (cf. also 3:24; 4:13, 16).

The author continues to use present tense forms of the verb (**keeps on sinning**: *hamartanei*; **continues to sin**: *ho hamartanōn*) to underline that he is talking about the habitual, unrepented of, practice of sin. "His objection is to a continued life-style and outlook on sin that is incompatible with being a Johannine Christian" (Brown, *Epistles*, p. 403).

Far from abiding in Christ, those who practice sin as a way of life have neither **seen him** nor **known him**. It is possible that no one in the Johannine community of the author's day had physically seen or known Jesus during his life on earth, neither the Elder and his followers nor his opponents. Like 3:6, 3 John 11 claims that "no one who practices evil has seen God." In what sense, then, did Johannine Christians claim to have seen God/ Christ, a claim which they deny to their adversaries?

To see Jesus is to discern his real identity and to believe in him (Smalley, *1, 2, 3 John*, p. 164). This is a common theme in the Gospel of John (1:34; 6:36; 9:40–41; 12:37–46; 14:7, 9: "If you really knew me, you would know my Father as well. From now on you do know him and have seen him. . . . Anyone who has seen me has seen the Father"; 19:35; 20:29: in which the reference is to not seeing physically and yet believing, a different emphasis from the one in 1 John 3:6 and its parallels). To see him, then, is to recognize his true identity as the Christ, the Son of God (John 20:31), the one who came in the flesh (1 John 4:2; 2 John 7).

To see him accurately in this way is to "know him." We have observed the repeated use of *ginōskō* in the Gospel and epistles of John to indicate spiritual perception, especially in the claim to have a true understanding and a close relationship with God/Christ (see, for example, 1 John 2:3–5, 13–14: 3:1; 4:6–8; cf. John 1:10; 6:69; 10:14, 38; 14:7, 9, 17; 16:3; 17:3: "this is eternal life: that they may know you, the only true God, and Jesus Christ, whom you have sent"). The Elder denies that his opponents, who reject the true identity of Jesus (2:22–23; 4:2–3; 5:10; 2 John 7, 9), have any authentic knowledge of God/Christ at all.

3:7 / That the secessionist false teachers have been in the writer's mind throughout this section is clear from the opening of v. 7: **do not let anyone lead you astray**. The Elder has already described the opponents as those who deceive themselves (1:8) and has warned the remaining Johannine Christians "about those who are trying to lead you astray" (lit., "those who are deceiving you"; 2:26).

The point of this admonition is similar to 2:29, and there is a nearly identical comparison to God/Christ. In 2:29 it was not entirely certain whether the Elder was referring to the Father or the Son with the pronouns "he" and "him." In this verse the context strongly suggests that the antecedent is Christ (3:5, 8b). The author wants his readers to observe the conduct of those who are attempting to deceive them, not what they say but what they do. For it is the person who actually **does what is right** (lit., "practices righteousness" or "justice," *dikaiosynē*) who truly **is righteous** (*dikaios*; "just"), not the person with the most exalted or spiritual-sounding claims. Who really lives a just life, a life that looks like the way Jesus lived (**just as he is righteous**; cf. 2:6, 29; 3:3, 5b)? Follow that person. The Elder is certain that the daily lives of his opponents will fall far short of the standard of Christlikeness.

3:8 / The second half of the third pair of contrasting phrases which help form the framework of this section (2:28—3:10) is in v. 8; its partner was in v. 7:

> 3:7b: He who does what is right
> 3:8a: **He who does what is sinful**

This set of antithetical statements helps the writer make the bold contrast between the children of God (3:1–2) and the children of the devil (3:8, 10) that is the principal theme of this section of 1 John. These two groups, which are in fact the two sides of the schism (2:19), are his own loyal followers and the secessionist false teachers and their adherents. **He who does what is sinful** (lit., "the one who practices sin") describes the Elder's opponents, just as v. 7b described the ideal Johannine Christian as one who practices righteousness.

These two opposing sides are also different in origin. First John 2:29 made the point that the person who practices righteousness has been born of God. In 3:1–2 it was emphasized that the readers are indeed God's children. Their character will be like Christ, a central teaching of 3:2–3, 5–7. But the antichrists (2:18, 22), who are trying to lead the readers astray (2:26) and who continually practice sin (3:4, 6), have a different origin; they are **of the devil**.

The reason for this assertion is given in v. 8b: **because the devil has been sinning from the beginning**. If a life of continual rebellion (*anomia*, 3:4) and sin (3:6) characterizes the Elder's opponents, it is clear that they became this way because of their association with the devil, for he has been a continual sinner from the first. The Elder probably has in mind Satan's lies in the Eve/Satan story in Genesis 3:1–7 and Cain's murder of Abel in Genesis 4:1–8 (cf. 1 John 3:12). Both are referenced in John 8:44, where Jesus says that the devil "was a murderer from the beginning. . . . he is a liar and the father of lies." The secessionists' character reveals their parentage, their family of origin, their spiritual roots.

Recall that in v. 7 the standard of righteousness is Christ, the one who "appeared so that he might take away our sins" (3:5). He also **appeared** (*ephanerōthē*, "was manifested") for another reason: **to destroy the devil's work** (cf. John 12:31; 16:11; Heb. 2:14). These two reasons for the first coming of Christ are parallel, since sin is and has been the devil's work **from the beginning**. By conquering sin, Jesus destroys the evil effects of the devil's work and overcomes his efforts to thwart the coming of God's kingdom (or, in more Johannine terms, to prevent people from receiving and experiencing eternal life).

This is the first use of the full title, **the Son of God**, in the letters of John (4:15; 5:5, 10, 12–13, 20). "His Son" occurs in 1:3, 7; 3:23; 4:9–10, 14; 5:9–11, 20, while "the Son" appears in 2:22–24; 5:12; 2 John 9. Second John 3 has the more formal expression "the

Father's Son." "Son of God" is a favorite Johannine title for Jesus; it is common in the Gospel of John as well. "The Son," "the Son of God," and "his Son," as references to Jesus, occur 29 times in the Fourth Gospel, more than in all of Paul's letters. They express the unique and intimate relationship between Jesus and God.

3:9 / In v. 8 the writer described the origin of his opponents as "of the devil." In v. 9 he contrasts this with the origin of his followers as **born of God**. He had made this point earlier in 2:29. Those who have remained loyal to the Elder and have not followed the false teaching of the schismatics are "the children of God" (3:1–2). But the emphasis in vv. 9–10 is on the quality of moral life of these two opposing sides. God's true children, those **born of God**, will not **continue to sin** (lit., "does not practice sin"). Verse 6a affirmed the same truth with regard to those who live or abide in him: they do not keep on sinning.

The reason they do not, given earlier, was that it is inconsistent with knowing the righteous, pure, sinless, and sin-destroying God/Christ (2:29; 3:3, 5–8). In this passage a different explanation is offered. Such a person does not keep on sinning **because God's seed remains in him** (lit., "his seed abides in him"). In fact, it is not possible to **go on sinning**, because **he has been born of God**. What does the author mean by **God's seed** (lit., "his seed," *sperma autou*)? Because of the parallel structure of 9a and 9b, **God's seed** must be closely related to **born of God**.

> 9a: does not practice sin
> **because** his **seed remains** (*menō*) **in him**
> 9b: is not able **to go on sinning**
> **because he has been born of God**

It is possible that **God's seed** are Christians who abide in him (i.e., God). But the idea of Christians being **God's seed** is highly unusual; the Elder prefers "God's children." **God's seed** is more likely a force or principle within the Christian (**in him**) which **remains in him** and causes him/her to be **born of God**. If one attempts to identify this indwelling, life-generating power more precisely, the Holy Spirit, the Paraclete, fits the picture appropriately (cf. 1 John 2:27; 3:24; 4:13; John 3:5, 8; 6:63a; 14:16–17; 16:7–8; 20:22). The meaning, then, is that the Holy Spirit, abiding in the Christian, keeps the Christian from the continual practice of sin. Because of the presence and power of the indwelling Spirit of God, the Christian **cannot go on sinning**, for the Spirit of God has caused him/her to be born from above (John 3:3, 5–7) or **born of God**.

3:10 / Throughout this section of 1 John, the author has been distinguishing between two groups, **the children of God** (2:29; 3:1–2, 9), who are his own faithful followers, and **the children of the devil** (3:8), the secessionist false teachers and their disciples. He has repeatedly contrasted their ways of life, especially their attitudes and actions with respect to sin and righteousness (2:29; 3:3–4, 6–9). In v. 10 he offers a final test, a clear means by which to tell who is a **child of God** and who is not.

Literally translated, v. 10 reads: "By this the children of God and the children of the devil are evident (or manifest; NASB, 'obvious'): everyone who does not practice righteousness (NIV, **do what is right**) is not from God (*ek tou theou*; NIV, **not a child of God**), also the one who is not loving his brother."

The criterion of practicing or not practicing righteousness was mentioned previously in 2:29 and 3:7 (cf. 3:4, 8–9). It functions in v. 10, then, as a summary of the negative ethical aspect in the entire section. The new element is the return of the criterion of **love** for one's **brother**. It has not been stated since 2:9–10. There it was a means by which to test "anyone who claims to be in the light" (2:9). Here it distinguishes the true **children of God**. The author may also understand **love** as a concrete expression of practicing **what is right**.

The Elder knows that the false teachers, who have split the community with their secession (1 John 2:19) and by their denial that the Christ is the truly human Jesus (2:22; 4:2–3; 2 John 7), do not meet the test of **love**. They have abandoned their brothers and sisters, split the community, caused economic hardship (3:16–18), rejected the Elder's authority, and are actively trying to win over to their "heretical party" the remaining Johannine Christians.

In the Gospel and letters of John, the focus of **love** is within the community of believers. There is no command concerning love of neighbor or love of enemies, as in the Synoptic Gospels and Paul's writings. What is at issue is love among Jesus' disciples (John 13:34–35; 15:12, 17) and love among those who claim to be brothers and sisters in the same fellowship (1 John 2:9–10; 3:10–11, 14–18, 23b; 4:7–8, 11–12, 20–21; 5:1–2; 2 John 5–6; 3 John 6).

Only God is said to love the world (John 3:16); Johannine Christians are not instructed to (1 John 2:15–17).

The last half of v. 10 also is a transition to a new section of the epistle which will deal with the subject of authentic love among Christians.

Additional Notes   §6

This section and the two previous sections begin with an address to the community as the author's children. The first section (2:12–17) describes the Elder's community, the second (2:18–27) describes the secessionists, while the third (2:28—3:10) contrasts the two groups.

The structure of this unit has been illuminated by Brown, *Epistles*, pp. 417–20.

3:1 / This is the only use of *kaleō* in these epistles; John 1:42 and 2:2 are the only instances in the Gospel. The word does not have for the Elder the theological significance it carries for Paul (cf. Rom. 8:30).

See the discussion of **children of God** in Brown, *Epistles*, pp. 388–91 and in R. A. Culpepper, "The Pivot of John's Prologue," *NTS* 27 (1980–81), pp. 1–31.

In this verse **the world** stands in antithetical relationship to the fellowship of obedient Johannine Christians, just as in 2:15–17 the Father and the world were opposing objects of **the children**'s love.

3:2 / **Now/not yet**, another Johannine antithesis, makes its only appearance here in the letters; it is more common in the Gospel (2:4; 4:35; 6:17; 7:6, 8; 11:30; 12:16; 13:7, 36; 16:12–13, 25).

Phaneroō is also used in the Gospel of John of Jesus' showing himself to his disciples after the resurrection (cf. 21:1, 14).

On the increased eschatological awareness of the epistles, see Brown, *Community*, pp. 135–38; Smalley, *1, 2, 3 John*, pp. 93–101. On the eschatology of the Fourth Gospel, see Brown, *Gospel, I–XII*, pp. cxv–cxxi; W. F. Howard, *Christianity according to St. John* (London: Duckworth, 1943), pp. 109–15; Ladd, *Theology*, pp. 298–308.

Brown believes that the last three pronouns in this verse, **him, him,** and **he**, refer to God, not Christ, and that the relationship between the last two clauses cannot be decided with certainty. All we can know, he says, is that we shall see God as he is and be like God (*Epistles*, pp. 394–96). The Elder's ambiguous (to us) use of pronouns in reference to God/Jesus throughout 1 John means that there may be no clear separation here between Christ and God in the writer's mind (Smalley, *1, 2, 3 John*, pp. 145–47).

3:3 / Brown argues that the **him** in v. 3 is a reference to God (*Epistles*, p. 397). Bruce, *Epistles*, p. 88, and Stott, *Letters*, pp. 124–25, defend "Christ" as the intended referent; and Smalley, *1, 2, 3 John*, p. 149, sees "God in Christ" as the best solution.

3:4 / This is the only occurrence of *anomia* in the Gospel and letters of John. The Johannine literature does not usually measure the rightness or wrongness of one's actions against the standard of God's "law" (*nomos*) in the OT, as was done in other Jewish and Jewish Christian communities. In fact, several verses in the Gospel of John appear to relegate the law of Moses to Jesus' Jewish opponents as "your law" (8:17; 10:34; 18:31; "their law," 15:25), and Jesus' adversaries are portrayed as claiming the law as their special possession (7:19a, 49, 51; 12:34; 19:7).

3:6 / As was discussed in the Introduction and in the comment on 1:1–4, what the author and his community are claiming is continuity with those who had heard, seen, and touched Jesus, not that they had actually done so themselves.

3:8 / Jesus accused his opponents of being **of the devil** in his debate with "the Jews who had believed in him" (John 8:31) and who claimed to be children of Abraham (8:33, 37, 39) and children of God (8:41). On the contrary, Jesus replied, "You belong to your father, the devil" (8:44).

This way of speaking of the purpose of the coming of the Son of God is more characteristic of the Synoptic Gospels than of the Gospel of John. In the latter, overcoming the works of the devil (8:41) or Satan plays a minor role, whereas in the Synoptics one of the chief manifestations of the kingdom of God is Jesus' breaking the power of Satan (Matt. 12:28). Exorcisms, for example, are non-existent in the Fourth Gospel, but they are common in the Synoptics.

On the different yet compatible expressions of the core of NT theology in the Synoptics, John, and Paul, see G. E. Ladd, *The Pattern of New Testament Truth* (Grand Rapids: Eerdmans, 1968).

On the title **Son of God**, generally, see O. Michel, "Son of God," *NIDNTT*, vol. 3, pp. 634–48; M. Hengel, *Son of God* (Philadelphia: Fortress, 1976); O. Cullmann, *The Christology of the New Testament* (Philadelphia: Westminster, 1963), pp. 270–305; J. D. G. Dunn, *Christology in the Making* (Philadelphia: Westminster, 1980), pp. 12–64. On its use in the Gospel of John, see R. Schnackenburg, *The Gospel according to St. John*, 3 vols. (vol. 1: Montreal: Herder/Palm, 1968; vols. 2–3: New York: Seabury/Crossroad, 1980, 1982), vol. 2, pp. 172–86; L. Morris, *Jesus is the Christ: Studies in the Theology of John* (Grand Rapids: Eerdmans, 1989), pp. 89–106.

3:9 / This is the only occurrence of **seed** (*sperma*) in the letters of John. The three occurrences of it in the Fourth Gospel are "seed of David" (7:42) and "seed of Abraham" (8:33, 37). In Rev. 12:17 the dragon, Satan, makes war with the "seed" of the woman.

On the relationship between **sin** and the Holy Spirit in the Gospel and letters of John, the Spirit convicts of sin (John 16:8) and moves the

Christian to confess sin (1 John 1:9), and to claim continually the advocacy of Jesus, who takes away the sins of the world (2:2, 12; 3:5). The Johannine ideal is not to sin (2:1; 3:6) but to practice righteousness (2:29; 3:7), though the Elder recognizes that Christians do sin, and he speaks forcefully against those who claim that they do not (1:8, 10). Christians are to "walk in the light" (1:7) by the power of the indwelling Spirit (3:9) and to claim the blood of Jesus which keeps on cleansing us from all sin (1:7).

3:10 / The proselyting activity of the secessionists is especially evident in 2 John 7–10.

On the meaning of love in the Fourth Gospel and the epistles of John, see F. F. Segovia, *Love Relationships in the Johannine Tradition*, SBLDS 58 (Chico, Calif.: Scholars, 1982); Brown, *Community*, pp. 131–35.

§7 *Loving One Another (1 John 3:11–18)*

Verses 11–18 are unified by the theme of loving one another. Love among the members of the community was first raised in 1 John 2:10 (as love for one's "brother" or sister) and was the link into this section of the letter in 3:10b. The background to this emphasis on love is the schism which has divided the community (1 John 2:19) and has set former community members against one another. The schismatics have shown a flagrant, Cain-like disregard for their fellow believers. The Elder is greatly concerned that there be sacrificial, practical love among the remaining Johannine Christians.

3:11 / The word **message** (*angelia*) occurs only twice in the NT: here and in 1:5. It may signal a major division within 1 John after which love and faith are primary issues and before which light and truth were the principal concerns. Both sections have in mind the false teachers who have broken away from the fellowship and whose teaching actively threatens the Elder's loyalists.

In 1:1 "the Word of life" was "from the beginning, which we have heard." In 1:5 "God is light" was "the message we have heard." In 2:7 the new yet old command (love; cf. John 13:34–35) was "the message (*logos*) you have heard," "since the beginning"; 2:24 also referred to "what you have heard from the beginning," the tradition of Jesus as the Christ (2:22). Here **the message you heard from the beginning** is the command that **we should love one another**; it is closest in thought to 2:7 and especially to 2 John 5–6, where the nearly identical expression occurs. All of these passages are, in the Elder's mind, parts of the sacred tradition of the community, passed down to the present Johannine Christians from Jesus through the disciple whom Jesus loved (John 21:24). They have had this teaching **from the beginning** of their existence as a Christian fellowship.

All of the references to positive human **love** in the Gospel and letters of John are to love for God or Jesus (John 14:15, 21, 23–24; 1 John 4:10, 20–21; 5:2–3), or among disciples (13:34–35; 15:12, 17), or for members of the community (1 John 2:10; 3:10–11, 14, 18, 23; 4:7, 11–12, 19–20; 5:1–2; 2 John 5). There is no command to love one's neighbor outside the community, or to love one's enemies. Given the conflicts which plagued Johannine Christians from the start, externally with Judaism (reflected in the Gospel of John) and internally with the secessionists (Johannine epistles), ethical reflection was cast inward, and the overriding concern was ever community survival. If the "world hates you" (John 15:18–19; 1 John 3:13), persecutes you (15:20), puts you out of the synagogue, and kills you (16:2; cf. John 9:34), it is all the more important that the believers form a close bond of love and support among themselves.

3:12 / The Elder next presents **Cain** as the opposite of what he has just stated. The NIV translation, **Do not be like Cain, who belonged . . . and murdered**, makes the best of an awkward Greek construction (lit., "Not like Cain was from . . . and killed"). There is no direct command (but an implied one, by negative comparison), and the relative pronoun, **who**, does not appear.

Cain, cited directly in the Bible only in Genesis 4, Hebrews 11:4, and Jude 11 (but cf. John 8:44), had become a figure of speculation in other contemporary Jewish circles. Philo wrote four treatises on Cain, and Josephus referred to him in *Antiquities*. A later Jewish legend says that Cain was the son of the devil by Eve (Brown, *Epistles*, p. 443). It is likely that the Elder was aware of some of this extrabiblical speculation.

The writer makes two assertions about **Cain**. He was "from the evil one" (lit., NIV, **belonged to the evil one**), just as Jesus' opponents in the Fourth Gospel "belong to your father, the devil" who "was a murderer from the beginning" (John 8:44), and just as the Elder's opponents are "the children of the devil" (1 John 3:10). **Cain** had his origins in **the evil one** and was on his side. Secondly, he **murdered his brother**. He engaged in a violent act which caused his brother's death. All of the other uses of this verb for **murder** (*sphazō*) in the NT are in the book of Revelation, and all refer to brutal killing (of Jesus the Lamb, 5:6, 9, 12; 13:8; of the beast, 13:3; of the martyrs, 6:9, 18:24; and of people murdering each other, 6:4). The two brothers, representing evil and good, also represent the two sides in the community, the Cain-like secessionists and the faithful followers of the author. **Do not be like Cain** also means "Do not be like the false teachers. They are from **the evil one**; and they hate us and are trying to destroy us" (cf. 3:15).

The Elder next gives a reason (*charin tinos*, "on account of what?") for Cain's brutality: **because his own actions were evil and his brother's were righteous**. The reader of Genesis 4 has few clues to the evil of Cain's actions or to the righteousness of his brother's prior to Abel's murder. Cain "worked the soil" (4:2) and "brought some fruits of the soil as an offering to the Lord" (4:3). Abel "kept flocks" . . . and "brought fat portions from some of the firstborn of his flock" (4:2, 4). "The Lord looked with favor on Abel and his offering, but on Cain and his offering he did not look with favor" (4:4–5), for which judgment the text gives no reason. "Cain was . . . angry" and "downcast" (4:5). God implies in his speech to Cain that Cain had not done right and had sinned (4:7), after which Cain invited Abel to the field and murdered him (4:8). The author may have been relying here on the total symbol of Cain as an evil and violent man in Genesis and on extrabiblical speculation. It is part of his overall antithesis between righteousness and evil, the true Christians and the secessionists. Cain's actions were evil because he was evil, in origin and in character, in contrast to "the children of God" (3:10).

3:13 / The thought continues directly into the next verse, as the NIV has it. No new paragraph is called for, as in some versions. In the light of the example of the brothers, Cain and Abel, the readers, whom the author cites as **my brothers**, should **not be surprised**. (Perhaps they had been **surprised**, not expecting aggressive opposition from those who had seceded.) The same kind of animosity that Cain displayed toward his brother **the world** shows toward the Johannine Christians. **The world hates you**. Jesus had already warned the community about this (in identical words) in his discourse to his disciples in John 15:18. Just as those who practice evil "hate the light" (John 3:20), or as the world hates Jesus (7:7; 15:18, 23–25) and his Father (15:23–24), so **the world**, which includes not only the Elder's opponents, the false teachers, but also their supporters and others who persecute the community (John 15:20; 16:2) and aid the secessionists (cf. 1 John 4:5), hate, oppose, and seek to destroy the readers and their faith. We had already heard about this hatred of brother for brother in 1 John 2:9 and 11, where it was proof that the opponents' claim to be "in the light" was invalid.

3:14 / All the **we**'s in this verse stand in direct antithesis to "the world" spoken of in v. 13. **We know**, but "the world does not know" (3:1). The world hates, but **we love our brothers**. The world **remains in death**, but **we**, in contrast, **have passed from death to life**. The community's identity is strengthened by negative comparison with the status of the world.

We have passed from death to life is a precise quote from John 5:24, assuming as most NT scholars do, that the letters of John were written after the Gospel. We noted above that "if the world hates you" is also nearly a direct quote (slightly different word order) from John 15:18. The Elder is reminding his readers that the tradition they have received speaks to their current situation. It warns them and encourages them.

Johannine theology understands the passage **from death to life** as an accomplished fact, something that has already occurred, for those who believe in Jesus and **love our brothers**. Eternal **life** is a present possession; no fear of judgment or condemnation need exist (John 3:36; 5:24; 1 John 4:17–18; 5:11–12). "Passing from death to life is another way of phrasing what John 3:5 refers to as 'entering the kingdom of God' " (Brown, *Epistles*, p. 445). This is the first occurrence of the **death/life** antithesis in these letters (cf. 3:15; 5:12, 16). It occurs much more frequently in the Gospel (e.g., 3:16, 36; 5:24–29; 10:17–18, 28; 11:21–25; 21:22–23). Verses 14a and b are set in sharp, dualistic contrast: on the one side are the terms **anyone, not love**, and **death**; on the other, **we, love**, and **life**.

Love for one another within the Christian community is seen by the Elder as a reason for knowing that we have already received eternal **life** and have overcome **death**. It is a sign that we belong to God's eternal kingdom and that we have been literally "born from above" (John 3:3, 7) or "born of the Spirit" (John 3:5). The opposite is also true: **Anyone who does not love remains in death**. Active **love** for one another is the key to **life**. Without it, one's claim to be a Christian is in jeopardy; it does not ring true. Without practical caring for other **brothers** and sisters within the community (cf. 3:17–18), one's existence is still under the dominion of **death**; one has not been liberated into **life**. **Love** shows who is really alive.

3:15 / The themes of **life** and death, love and **hate** continue into v. 15. **Hate** for one's **brother**, mentioned previously in 2:9–11, caused Cain's jealous murder of his brother (3:12), and it shows that one belongs to the evil one (3:12), is like the world (3:13), and is still under the dominion of death (3:14). The only other NT use of the word **murderer** (*anthrōpoktonos*) is in John 8:44, where Jesus calls the devil "a murderer from the beginning." Behind those who **hate** their **brother**s and sisters in the Christian community and who are still trying to lead them astray with lies and deception (1:6, 8, 10; 2:4, 21–22, 26; 3:7) is the devil, whose children the secessionist false teachers are (3:10). Jesus taught that beneath the action of murder lies the feeling of hatred (Matt. 5:21–22; cf. Deut. 19:11).

Just as love for one's brothers and sisters leads to life (3:14), so **hate** leads to death, and not only the death of others through murder, but one's own death as well, since **you know that no murderer has eternal life** abiding **in him**. This final statement makes a strong parallel with the previous verse:

14b:	Anyone who does not love	abides (*menei*) in death.
15:	**Anyone who hates** (=murderer)	
	and no murderer	**has eternal life abiding** (*menousan*) in him.

This is the only verse in the Johannine writings which directly speaks of eternal life remaining or abiding (*menousan*; the word is untranslated in the NIV) in the believer (cf. John 6:27). More commonly, the Christian "has eternal life" (John 3:15–16, 36; 5:24; 6:40, 47, 54; 1 John 5:12–13; cf. 10:10; 20:31,) but as 1 John 3:14 shows, this is not just an eschatological hope; it is a present possession which abides in those who believe in Jesus and love their brothers and sisters. The secessionists, rejecting both faith in Jesus (2:22–23; 4:2–3) and love for one's brothers and sisters (2:9–11; 3:11–15) remain in death (3:14) and do not have **eternal life** in them. They are not Christians, and, in the author's view, they never were (2:19).

3:16 / Continuing the theme of **love**, the Elder offers an experiential and operational definition (lit., "By this we have come to know love"): **Jesus Christ** (the Greek text only has "he," *ekeinos*) **laid down his life for us**. This is one of the most common elements in early Christian creeds (1 Cor. 15:3; Gal. 1:4; 2:20). Two aspects of the Greek text of this verse reinforce the idea of **love**. The Greek word order itself emphasizes **for us**; it is put first, just as Christ put us first in the gift of **his life**. The verb **laid down** (*ethēken*) stresses that Jesus gave up his own life willingly, thus showing the motivation of love. So in the Gospel of John, Jesus, "the good shepherd," voluntarily "lays down his life for the sheep" (10:11, 15, 17–18). The death of Jesus is also the decisive evidence of God's love (John 3:16; Rom. 5:8; 1 John 4:9–10).

Here, as in many other places in the NT, the conduct of **Jesus** is taken as the example or model for Christians to follow. (In 1 John 4:11, it is God's love which provides the pattern.) This is true in general, but also with specific reference to his suffering and death (cf. 1 Pet. 2:21–23; Heb. 12:3–4; 13:12–13). In John 15:12, Jesus tells his disciples, "Love as I have loved you" (cf. 13:34), and in the next verse he says, "Greater love has no one than this, that he lay down his life for his friends." Jesus' actions demonstrate the sacrificial element in authentic *agapē* love. Love is a personal commitment to give oneself to foster the highest good and well-being of others. Sometimes giving oneself for others means more than giving one's time or money or energy; it may mean giving one's very life.

3:17 / As a concrete instance of this love and the lack of it among the secessionists, the Elder turns to **material possessions** and how they are handled. He envisions a situation in which someone **has material possessions** (lit., "the life of the world," *ton bion tou kosmou*), **sees** (*theōrē*, "stares," "gazes") **his brother** lacking them, and yet refuses to help him. This may have been the very condition of the writer's community, especially if those who withdrew were numerous and the community had been a network of interdependent house churches (as 2 and 3 John seem to suppose). In 2:16 the writer knows of people, likely the schismatics, who boast of "the world's goods" (*tou biou*). They boast of what they have, and they do not share it with others (even their former brothers and sisters) who are **in need** (lit., "having need"). What is missing is the element of **pity** (lit., "closes his innards [heart] from him"). Not only do they not help the needy brother or sister, but they deliberately "shut off a feeling of compassion that the needy would instinctively arouse" (Brown, *Epistles*, p. 450).

The three previous clauses in v. 17 all lead to the question: **how can the love of God be in him?** Does the author mean love for God, love from God, or God's kind of love? It is not easy to decide. First John 4:20 expresses the first alternative, but here the writer means God's kind of love, divine love. Just as eternal life does not abide (*menousan*, untranslated in the NIV) in one who hates his brother (3:15), so it is unthinkable that God's love abides (*menei*, untranslated in the NIV) in such a merciless person. The question implies a negative answer.

3:18 / Verse 18 is a fitting conclusion to the teaching on **love** for one another in vv. 11–18. Influenced by the negative example in v. 17, the present tense command in this verse is also negative: "let us not be loving." The command is followed by four nouns in two pairs: **with words** (the Greek is singular, "word," *logō*) **or tongue** (*tē glōssē*), **but with actions** (again the Greek is singular, "action," or "deed," *ergos*) **and in truth** (*alētheia*). Genuine love must be practical, visible, and active. Just as God's/Jesus' love is made manifest in the giving of his life for us (3:16), and just as the secessionists' lack of love is seen concretely in their failure to help their brothers and sisters in need (3:17), so authentic love is a matter not of **words** ("I/we love you") but of practical **actions**.

The most difficult aspect of interpreting v. 18 concerns the relation of the second word in each pair to its partner. At first glance, they do not appear to be parallel. While **word** and **tongue** are roughly similar, **actions** and **truth** are not. **In truth** can mean "in reality," as opposed to mere intention or even deceptive lies. But in the letters of John, **in truth** usually means "within the sphere of God's truth," i.e., God's revelation of the way things really are in Christ, who is the truth (John 14:6); much as in Paul's writings "in Christ" can represent "in the sphere of Christ," where he is the all-determining reality. The writer means, then, something like "deeds of truth," or "actions which come from the truth." The **words** and **tongue** phrase could also be parallel, since **words** come from the **tongue**. The Elder means that his readers should love, not with mere spoken words, but with the kind of actions which knowing Christ (3:16) and having God's love within them (3:17) produce.

Additional Notes   §7

3:11   /   It is because of this teaching on love and other characteristics, reflected in the Gospel and letters of John, that the Johannine
community has been termed, sociologically, a sect. See Johnson, *Antitheses*,
pp. 260–302, and Rensberger, *Johannine Faith*, pp. 27–28, 124–26, 135–44.

3:14   /   On the antithesis of **death/life** in the Gospel and epistles
of John, see Johnson, *Antitheses*, pp. 36, 74–76, 85, 108–11.

3:15   /   The pseudepigraphal document Testament of Gad 4:6f. is
a close parallel to this verse. It includes the elements of **life** and death,
love and **hate**, and God and Satan.

You know implies that this is what the readers had been taught as
a part of common early Christian ethical tradition (cf. Matt. 15:19; Gal.
5:19–21; Rev. 21:8, 27).

3:16   /   The perfect tense of the Greek verb *egnōkamen* (NIV, **we
know**) implies knowledge based on experience.

On Jesus as a pattern for Christian conduct, see, e.g., Matt. 11:29
("learn from me"); Mark 10:42–45 (service); John 13:14–17 (foot-washing),
34 (love); Phil. 2:5 ("attitude"); 1 John 2:6 ("walk as Jesus did"); Dodd,
Epistles, pp. 84–85; W. Michaelis, "*mimeomai*," *TDNT*, vol. 4, pp. 659–74.

In contrast to Jesus' action, Peter promised to lay down his life for
Jesus (John 13:37), but Peter's deeds did not match his words (John 13:38;
1 John 3:18).

On v. 16 the exegesis of Smalley, *1, 2, 3 John*, pp. 192–95 is particularly helpful.

3:17   /   BAGD defines *bios* (NIV, **material possessions**) as "means
of subsistence" (p. 142a).

With **truth** as the link-word between this section and the previous one (the same stylistic technique may be observed in 2:17–18; 2:27–28; 3:10–11; 3:24—4:1; 4:6–7), the pastoral concern for assurance is foremost in vv. 19–24. The Johannine community has been split (1 John 2:19) by a group of secessionists with high-sounding spiritual claims (e.g., 1:6, 8, 10; 2:4, 6, 9; see the Introduction for discussion of them). They continue to press the remaining followers of the Elder to join them (2:26; 3:7; 2 John 10–11), and their version of the truth has caused confusion and insecurity among the Elder's readers (2:21; 4:6; 2 John 1–4; 3 John 1–4, 8). Thus the need for assurance. It was the author's use of the word "truth" in 3:18 which reminded him to strengthen the "hearts" (3:19–21) of his readers in the truth.

3:19–20 / Verse 19 begins with the common expression "by this," or "by this means" (*en toutō;* NIV, **this . . . is how**). It occurs twelve times in the letters of John at 2:3, 5c; 3:10, 16, 19, 24; 4:2, 9–10, 13, 17; 5:2. Sometimes the phrase refers to what follows, and sometimes it refers to what has just preceded it. Each instance can be decided only by careful study of the context of each passage. Here the reference is clearly back to vv. 16–18, in which the author has argued that authentic love is sacrificial and practical, as seen in the life of Jesus and in the lives of those who claim to follow him. This kind of love is **how we know that we belong to the truth**. His contention all along has been that the false teachers do not love their brothers and sisters (2:9–11; 3:11–18). But, the fact that his own followers do show love should further **set our hearts at rest**.

The grammar of vv. 19–20 is very difficult. Literally, they read, (19) "And by this we shall know that we are of the truth, and before him we shall assure [persuade?] our heart, (20) that [for?] if [when?] our heart condemns us, that [for?] God is greater than our heart and knows everything." The NIV solves these ambiguities well in v. 19 by giving the expression "by this" a double result: by this (i.e., by the fact that we truly love one another), (1) **we know that we belong to the truth**, and (2) **we set our hearts at rest**. The two phrases are virtually identical in meaning, though the first emphasizes that we are on God's side in the controversy (**the truth** as God has revealed it in Jesus; cf. 4:6), while the second focuses on the inner assurance this knowledge gives us.

"Heart" is singular (not plural as in the NIV), because it is the assurance of the whole community which is at stake, as if it had one heart (cf. 1 Cor. 1:10; Eph. 6:5; Col. 3:22). The phrase **in his presence** (lit., "before him") refers to God, as v. 20 makes clear. The issue is: how can we, before God who knows and judges all things truly, have the confidence that we are on the right road? Assurance is not a matter of convincing ourselves or of thinking positively; it is knowing the truth *before God*, or with God as a witness!

In v. 20 the NIV resolves the grammatical problems by leaving the first *hoti* ("that/for") untranslated, or by considering that the phrase *hoti ean* is better understood as *ho ti ean*, translated as **whenever**, though *ean* alone can mean this (BAGD, p. 211). The sentence means: **whenever our hearts condemn** (or convict) **us** (perhaps that we are unworthy to **belong to the truth** and that the opponents might be right after all—since they claim not to sin [1:8, 10]!), we can rest assured that we are God's by remembering the evidence of the love we have shown for one another (vv. 16–18).

The NIV then begins a new sentence, though in Greek vv. 19–20 are all one unclear sentence. The second half of v. 20 is meant as a comfort, not as a threat, to the spiritual assurance of the readers. One can take comfort from the fact that, whatever our hearts say, accusing or perhaps excusing us (cf. Rom. 2:15), God knows us truly; **he knows everything**. And **God is greater than our hearts**; therefore, the Elder implies, listen to what God says about you (you are forgiven, 1:9; you know God, 2:4–6; you know and belong to the truth, 2:20–21; 3:19; you are the children of God, 3:1–2, 10; you are loved, 4:10–11), not to your accusing heart.

Thus, the author gives his readers two grounds for assurance in vv. 19–20: (1) they love one another "with actions" not "with words," and (2) God's true and complete knowledge of them.

3:21 / This verse follows directly from the thought in vv. 19–20; no paragraph is needed as in the NIV. The circumstance the Elder now has in mind is one in which the assurance question, raised in vv. 19–20 ("how we set our hearts at rest . . . whenever our hearts condemn us") is settled. Now **our hearts** (lit., "our heart"— again it is the community's collective assurance that is in view more than the spiritual anxieties of private individuals) **do not condemn us**. And this is the way it should be, the way the Elder wants his community (his **Dear friends**; lit., "beloved ones," *agapētoi*) to think and feel. He wants them to **have confidence** (*parrēsia*, "boldness"; cf. 2:28; 4:17; 5:14) **before God** (*pros ton theon*; cf. the parallel construction with the same meaning in v. 19, *emprosthen autou*, "before him," or "in his presence"). They do "belong to the truth" (v. 19) and need not be spiritually threatened by the intimidating false teachers.

3:22 / There is a second consequence to having an un-condemning heart (v. 21): we not only have "confidence before God," but we get our prayers answered. A literal translation of v. 22a reads: "and whatever we ask we receive from him." Answered prayer may also be seen as a result of "confidence before God," because the latter enables the community to pray with faith. (Confident prayer is a concern of the Elder's again in 5:14–15.) Having full assurance of our right standing with God, we can **ask** so as to **receive**. Asking and receiving are common prayer language in the Gospel of John (11:22; 14:13–14, 16; 15:7, 16; 16:23–24, 26; 17:9, 15, 20) and in the NT (cf. Matt. 7:7–11; 18:19–20; 21:22; Eph. 3:20; Jas. 1:5–8; 4:2–3).

The Elder also connects receiving from God what we ask for in prayer with **obeying** (*tēroumen*, "we are keeping") **his commands**. We receive what we ask for because (a) we pray with uncondemning, confident hearts (vv. 21–22a), and (b) we are keeping **his commands and** are doing **what pleases him** (lit., "the pleasing things before him we are doing"; cf. John 8:29: Jesus always does what pleases God, and Eph. 5:10: "find out what pleases the Lord"). A similar thought is expressed in 2:3, where keeping God's commands is the way to assured knowledge of God. (For other results of obedience, cf. John 8:51; 9:31; 14:21; 15:10.) Here it is the way to effective prayer. It is only as the community realizes its true identity before God as his children (vv. 19–21) and faithfully does what God wants (v. 22b) that its prayers bear fruit. Keeping God's commands and doing what pleases him are synonymous. Precisely what **commands** the Elder has in mind is made very clear in v. 23.

3:23 / While it may appear to be an overstatement, in the Gospel and letters of John, there are really only two commandments: **believe in . . . Jesus Christ** and **love one another**. In John 6:28–29, when the multitude asks Jesus, "What must we do to do the works God requires?" Jesus answers, "The work of God is this: to believe in the one he has sent." In the Johannine letters, whenever God's commands are mentioned, it is soon made clear that love is what the author has in mind (2:3–11; 5:1–3; 2 John 5–6). Love among disciples is the distinctive "new command" which Jesus gave to his followers (John 13:34–35). Similarly, Jesus reduced the demands of the Torah to love for God and others (Matt. 22:37–40). "Faith active in love is a Pauline expression which our author would readily have accepted" (Dodd, *Epistles*, p. 94). This verse summarizes the two principal concerns of the three Johannine letters.

His command in v. 23 is God's command, since all of the pronouns in vv. 19–22 refer to God. Note the change from the plural "commands" in v. 22 to the singular in v. 23. For the Elder and the Johannine community as a whole, all Christian duty can be summed up in the twofold command: have faith in Jesus and love for one's brothers and sisters.

This is the first use of the verb **believe** (*pisteuō*) in the letters of John. From now on it occurs frequently (4:1, 16; 5:1, 5, 10, 13), as the subject of the epistle shifts more to issues of faith (and love) in the last two chapters. The tense of **believe** is aorist, signifying an initial, decisive act of commitment to Jesus Christ, though there can be no doubt that the Elder also understands the necessity of ongoing, continuous faith (4:1; 5:1, 5, 10, 13). The object of faith in the Johannine writings is predominantly Jesus (cf. John 1:12; 2:11, 22–23; 3:15–16, 18, 36; 4:39; 6:29, 35; 7:31, 38; 8:30; 9:35; 10:42; 11:25–27, 48; 12:11, 42, 44, 46; 14:1, 12; 17:20; 20:31; 1 John 5:1, 5, 10, 13), though occasionally it is faith in the one who sent him (John 5:24; 12:44; 14:1; cf. 11:42; 17:8, 21).

In v. 23 this faith is **in the name of his Son, Jesus Christ**. The **name** means the person, character, and authority of the one trusted. The full name **Jesus Christ** and the title **his Son** are nearly creedal statements, similar to John 20:31 (cf. 2:22; 4:2, 15;

5:1, 5). Jesus as the Son of God is a favorite expression of Johannine Christology (John 1:49; 3:18, 35; 5:20, 23, 25; 10:36; 11:4, 27; 14:13; 17:1; 19:7; 20:31; 1 John 1:3, 7; 2:23–24; 3:8, 23; 4:9–10, 14–15; 5:5, 9–13, 20; 2 John 3, 9). It signifies the Son's divine origin and the continuing intimate union of the Father and Son whom he sent. The secessionist false teachers could not accept that the Christ, the Son of God, was the incarnate human, Jesus (2:22–23; 4:2–3; 2 John 7).

Love for one another within the Johannine community has been a prominent theme in 1 John (2:10; 3:10–11, 14, 16–18), and it will continue to be (4:7–8, 11–12, 19–21; 5:2). It derives from God's command (the first and last phrases v. 23 form an *inclusio*; cf. 2 John 4), given through Jesus (John 13:34; 15:10, 17), and, along with believing in Jesus, exhibiting **love** for **one another** distinguishes the faithful followers of the Elder from the secessionists.

3:24 / The closing verse of chapter three completes the teaching on keeping God's **commands** and returns to the main subject of this section of 1 John, assurance. The Elder makes the point that the obedient Christian has the indwelling presence of the Spirit of God as the assurance of knowing God.

Those who obey his commands, i.e., who believe in Jesus and love one another (v. 23), receive what they ask for in prayer (v. 22) and abide in God (v. 24, *menei*; NIV, "live in him"). The indwelling is mutual (the first time this has been expressed in 1 John; cf. 4:13, 15–16), for God also abides **in them**. This Johannine tradition (cf. 2:6; 4:15) is based on Jesus' teaching in the Farewell Discourses of the Fourth Gospel on the coming of the Paraclete, the Holy Spirit. In John 14:16–17, the Father will give to Jesus' disciples a "Counselor" (*paraklētos*), "the Spirit of truth" (cf. 1 John 4:6), who will live in them and be with them forever. Jesus and the Father will come and make their home in those who keep Jesus' teaching (14:23). Jesus urges his followers to "remain (*meinate*) in me, and I will remain in you" (15:4). As in vv. 22–23, the **commands** are God's commands, although it is quite possible that the author intends the reader to infer both God and Jesus. The interpreter faces the same problem in 2:3–4 and 2:26–29. Obedience results in ongoing, personal communion with God (the meaning of *menō*, "abide"; see the discussion of this important concept in 1 John 2:6).

This fellowship with God is mediated by **the Spirit he gave us**, and it is **how we know that he lives in us**. The secessionists were making claims about their relationship to God through the Spirit (4:1–3, 6). They claimed to be God's inspired prophets. But the Elder maintains that only **those who obey his commands** (faith in Jesus and love for one another) receive the Spirit and live in communion with God. This the opponents do not do. The faithful Johannine Christians may rest assured that God lives in them and not in their opponents, because they have the Spirit, and the disobedient secessionists do not, despite their claims. The evidence for possessing the Spirit is in the confession of Jesus as the Christ, the Son of God (v. 23; John 20:31), and in the fruit of the Spirit (esp. love, vv. 16–18; cf. Gal. 5:22–23).

Additional Notes   §8

3:19–20 / There is a detailed study of these verses in Brown, *Epistles*, pp. 248–49.

3:23 / Believing is very important in Johannine theology. It usually means a total personal commitment to Jesus or complete confidence in the object of one's believing. The Gospel and letters of John strongly prefer the verb to the noun (107 times to one, 1 John 5:4), since faith is active and personal, not static and creedal. See Brown, *Gospel, I–XII*, pp. 512–15 and O. Michel, "Faith," *NIDNTT*, vol. 1, 602–3. On the concept of "command" in 1 John, see U. C. von Wahlde, *The Johannine Commandments: 1 John and the Struggle for the Johannine Tradition* (New York: Paulist, 1990).

3:24 / This is the first time the Spirit has been mentioned explicitly in 1 John, though "the anointing" in 2:20, 27 is an indirect reference. **And this is how we know**: cf. "By this we know that we have come to know him" (1 John 2:3); "By this we know that we are in him" (2:5); "By this we have come to know love" (3:16); "By this we shall know that we are of the truth" (3:19); "By this we know that he lives in us" (3:24); "By this we know the Spirit of God" (4:2); "By this we know the Spirit of truth" (4:6); "By this we know that we abide in him" (4:13); and "By this we know that we love the children of God" (5:2). These nine expressions all begin with *en toutō* and contain a form of the verb *ginōskō* in the first person plural, a remarkable witness to the community's need for assurance in the face of the secessionist threat.

In a style typical of the Elder, a subject introduced at the end of the previous section (the Spirit, 3:24) becomes the main issue at the beginning of the next. Throughout 4:1–6 the Elder is concerned to help his readers correctly discern truth from error (4:6b) and true prophetic speaking (4:2) from false (4:1a, 3). This effort is part of the writer's larger project to strengthen the Johannine Christians and to assure them of their right standing with God (4:4, 6) in the face of the continuing attacks on his community by the secessionists (2:19; 4:3; 2 John 7–11).

4:1 / For the fourth time in 1 John, the Elder addresses his readers as **Dear friends** (*agapētoi*; 2:7; 3:2, 21; cf. 4:7, 11; 3 John 1, 2, 5, 11). It is out of his deep love for them that he writes to warn and encourage them.

Two commands, one negative, the other positive, form the heart of the author's teaching in v. 1 and in the section as a whole: **do not believe** (lit., "do not be believing," perhaps implying that some already were) and **test** (lit., "be testing," *dokimazete*; a continuous examining is called for). The objects of these verbs are **every spirit** and **the spirits**. As the end of v. 1 reveals, the Elder has in mind occasions of prophecy when someone would claim to be speaking by the Spirit of God.

The OT was familiar with "lying spirits" or false prophets (1 Kgs. 22:22–24; Jer. 23:16; 27:10, 14–15; 29:8–9; Ezek. 13:1–9), and in the NT, Jesus warns his followers against the rise of false prophets before the end of the age (Matt. 7:15; 24:4–5, 11, 24), as do Paul in Acts 20:28–31, the author of 2 Peter (2:1), and John in the Revelation (16:13; 19:20; 20:10). The apostle Paul lists "distinguishing between spirits" among the gifts of the Spirit (1 Cor. 12:10; cf. 14:29), and he urges the Thessalonians not to "treat prophecies with contempt" but to "test everything" (1 Thess. 5:20–21). Apparently a false prophet had misled them concerning the Day of the Lord (2 Thess. 2:2). The problem with false prophets continued after NT times, as is seen in Didache 11:7–12 and Shepherd of Hermas, *Mandates* 6.2.1.

In the world view of early Christian and other first-century writers, there were many supernatural spirits to contend with, good and evil angels, demonic powers, and a host of invisible beings variously named (e.g., Rom. 8:38; Eph. 1:21; 3:10; 6:12; Col. 1:16; 2:10, 15; Heb. 1:4, 14). In the Dead Sea Scrolls, especially in the Manual of Discipline (1QS) and the War Scroll (1QM), and in the Testaments of the Twelve Patriarchs, references to opposing spiritual forces abound. In this world of spiritual conflict, the readers must not be naive and gullible and **believe every spirit** (meaning every person claiming to speak by "the Spirit"); there are other spirits abroad. The same warning is relevant to the church today, especially with the rising interest in the occult and "new age" religions.

Among the secessionists were people who were claiming to prophesy by the Spirit of God. The Elder calls them **false prophets**, "the spirit of antichrist" (v. 3; cf. 2:18, 22), and "deceivers" (2 John 7; cf. 2:26; 3:7). They have "defected" (Smalley, *1, 2, 3 John*, pp. 219–20) from the community and **gone out into the world**. The same thing is said about "the deceivers" in 2 John 7. First John 2:19 states that they "went out from us," but they were never true members of the community. Yet they continue to try to win over the remaining Johannine Christians who are loyal to the Elder (2:26; 3:7; 2 John 10).

Given this situation, the readers are to **test the spirits**, the purpose of the test being to determine **whether they are from God**. Previously, the Elder had divided his followers and the opposition into two camps: the children of God and the children of the devil (3:1–2, 8–10). If the prophets do not meet the test, they belong to the world (4:5) which is under the control of the evil one (5:19). Ultimately, the Elder sees behind all prophecy either God's Spirit or the devil, the Spirit of truth or the spirit of falsehood (4:6).

4:2 / Having told his readers to "test the spirits," the Elder now gives them the decisive test, in this particular situation, to **recognize**, to discern the presence of, **the Spirit of God** in a person who was claiming to speak prophetically. Literally, he writes, "By this you know the Spirit of God." The test takes the form of a doctrinal confession (lit., "every spirit who confesses";

homologei). The content of this confession is a christological affirmation: **Jesus Christ has come in the flesh**. This is what the
secessionists have denied. They have refused to be believe that
God's Son, the Christ, is Jesus (2:22–23; cf. John 20:31), the one
who was an incarnate, i.e., in-the-flesh, human being. What the
opponents deny is Jesus, the fully human expression of God's
Son, the Word (4:3, 15; John 1:14). This is also the point of 2 John
7: has Jesus Christ come in the flesh; was he fully human? The
Elder's opponents, with their apparent denial of physical human
nature as a possible vehicle for the presence of God, said no. They
could not accept that the divine Christ, the Word, the Son, had
taken on human form and become the man from Nazareth, Jesus
(John 1:46; 7:42; cf. Phil. 2:6–8).

But if a prophetic speaker, one who claims the influence of
the Spirit of God, affirms and confesses the full humanity of
Jesus Christ, a title which combines his human name with his
saving function (cf. John 20:31; 11:27; 1 John 2:22), then that
"spirit-speaker" is **from God**. In a situation, torn by conflict and
competing spiritual claims, one must decide "who is on the Lord's
side" and who is not. The secessionists are claiming to be **from
God** and may be denying that origin to the Elder and his group.
The writer must then repeatedly affirm the secure spiritual standing of his threatened readers ("our fellowship is with the Father
and with his Son, Jesus Christ," 1:3; "we have come to know
him," 2:3; "we are in him," 2:5; "you have an anointing from the
Holy One, and all of you know," 2:20; you know the truth, 2:21;
"we are the children of God," 3:2; "we belong to the truth," 3:19;
"you are from God," 4:4; "we are from God," 4:6; "we live in him
and he in us," 4:13; "you have eternal life," 5:13; "we are of God,"
5:19; "we may know him who is true," 5:20).

This intense social conflict has fostered in the writer and
his community a dualistic view of Christian life in the world as is
reflected throughout these letters in their highly antithetical
language, e.g., light/darkness, truth/error, love/hate, God/world,
children of God/world, us/them, Christ/antichrist, life/death, right-
eous/sinful, God/evil one, of God/of the devil, children of God/
children of the devil, from God/not from God, believe/deny,
Spirit of truth/spirit of error, true God/idols.

4:3 / The doctrinal test, then, has an opposite use, as
well. It may be applied positively (v. 2) or negatively (v. 3). **Every**

spirit, again, means every person claiming to speak by the Spirit (who may in fact be speaking by another, not-from-God spirit). **That does not acknowledge** (lit., "who does not confess"; *mē homologei*) implies a statement of faith which the opponents cannot make. They cannot confess **Jesus**, the name for his full humanity (cf. 4:2b; 2 John 7).

There is a major textual issue in this passage. Many scholars believe that the original text of 4:3a read: "and every spirit that annuls (Gk., *lyei*, 'destroy, abolish, annul'; BAGD, pp. 483–84) Jesus." To annul Jesus would mean to deny the significance of Jesus, or to "negate the importance of Jesus" (see Brown, *Epistles*, pp. 494–96 for a thorough defense of this alternative reading). They think that the Greek text was altered very early in the transmission process by scribes who wanted to make v. 3 parallel to v. 2. Furthermore, they think that the original reading was *lyei*, or its Latin equivalent *solvit*, preserved in the fourth-century Latin Vulgate and in nearly all Old Latin MSS and possibly also in the Greek writers, Irenaeus, Clement, and Origen. While these scholars could be right, there is no denying that the textual evidence for "does not confess" is much stronger. But in the present context it means what *lyei* would have conveyed more forcefully: the heretics want to deny any significance to the human Jesus; for them, as for some modern Christians, the divine Christ is enough.

Such a view, the Elder contends, is **not from God**, but is the antithetical opposite of **from God** in 4:2b. In fact, such a **spirit**, who rejects **Jesus**, is **the spirit of the antichrist**. The Elder made a similar point in 2:22 (the person "who denies that Jesus is the Christ . . . is the antichrist") and does so in 2 John 7 ("deceivers, who do not acknowledge Jesus Christ as coming in the flesh . . . any such person is the deceiver and the antichrist"). That he has the secessionists firmly in mind is shown by 2:18–19.

In both 4:3b and in 2:18 the Elder describes the antichrist(s) in similar language:

> you have heard that the antichrist is coming (2:18b)
> **which you have heard is coming** (4:3b)
> even now many antichrists have come (2:18c)
> **even now is already in the world** (4:3c)

Both passages remind the readers that the subject of "antichrist" is not new; they had heard about it previously in early Christian teaching about the age to come. (See the discussion on "anti-christ" at 2:18.) What is new is that this "antichrist," or **the spirit of the antichrist**, has now appeared in history, in the present, in the actual spiritual conflict of the author and his community. "The last hour" (2:18) has come.

The author's reference to **the spirit of the antichrist** maintains the theme of contrast in this section between the Spirit of God and a spirit or spirits "not from God." Here it is **the spirit of the antichrist**; later it is "the one who is in the world" (v. 4) and "the spirit of falsehood" (4:6). Satan is behind the activities of the schismatic "false prophets" (v. 1). They are **already in the world**, which is the dominion of the evil one (5:19). This is further evidence that the opponents are "the children of the devil" (3:10).

4:4 / The Elder makes two assertions here about his followers. They are **from God**, i.e., as those who are born of God and God's children (2:29—3:2; 3:9–10), they have their origin in God and, therefore, belong to him. Secondly, they **have overcome** the false teachers who deny Jesus. In 2:13, 14 the "young men" of the community are said to "have overcome the evil one." Now, the faithful Johannine Christians have defeated the evil one's representatives, the secessionist teachers, by not accepting their teaching or authority. They have resisted the temptation to accept false doctrine. It may have been this crisis of belief that drove the schismatics from the community (2:19); they rejected both the authority of the Elder and his teaching regarding the full humanity of Jesus.

But this victory over the heretics is ascribed to the power of the Spirit, **the one who is in you** (cf. John 14:16–17). God is given the glory. Just as in 2:27, where "the anointing" which "remains in you" and which "teaches you," is the power to defeat "those who are trying to lead you astray" (2:26), so here "the Spirit he gave us" (3:24d), "the Spirit of truth" (4:6d), enables the community to be spiritually victorious over **the one who is in the world**, "the spirit of falsehood" (4:6d). The author has already said that "the spirit of antichrist" is in the world (4:3), and he will go on to describe the world as the dominion of the evil one (5:19). The devil, the power behind the opponents, has been **overcome** by God's Spirit at work in faithful Christians. In moral and spiritual conflict today, it is still true that "greater is he who is in you than he who is in the world," a strong incentive to rely on the indwelling Spirit of God.

4:5 / While the members of the Johannine community are "from God" (v. 4), their opponents are **from the world**; it is the source and origin of their thinking, values, and actions. They love the world and all that is in it (2:15–16). Having seceded from the community, they have "gone out into the world" (4:1; 2 John 7). The world is now their base of operations, but it is territory of "the evil one," "the spirit of the antichrist," who is in the world (4:3–4) and who controls the world (5:19). From a Johannine perspective, there are just two realms, the Christian community and the world. The Christian community is the sphere of spiritual security, and outside it is Satan's dominion (cf. John 12:31; 14:30; 16:11), in which there is no salvation (cf. Col. 1:13; 1 Cor. 5:2, 5; Cyprian, *On the Unity of the Church*).

Though the opponents claim to be God's representatives (1:6; 2:4, 6), the world's values have so permeated their thinking and beliefs that they **speak from the viewpoint of the world** (lit., "from the world," *ek tou kosmou*). **The world** is not only their physical location, since they have left the community (2:19; 4:1; 2 John 7), but it is the locus of their proclamation. Their words are worldly. Therefore, **the world listens to them**. Whereas the Elder's followers rejected the false teaching of the secessionists and in so doing "have overcome them" (cf. 5:4), the heretics are getting a hearing from those outside the church. Their "ministry" is "successful." Their teaching is popular; it has accommodated to what **the world** wants to hear (cf. 2 Tim. 4:3: "For the time will come when men will not put up with sound doctrine. Instead, to suit their own desires, they will gather around them a great number of teachers to say what their itching ears want to hear").

4:6 / Including himself this time, the author repeats his affirmation of 4:4: **we are from God**. He reemphasizes that his community and its opponents have a different origin and allegiance (cf. v. 5). A second point of contrast is the audience who **listens** (*akouei*). While "the world listens to" the false teachers, **whoever knows God** (lit., "the one who knows God") **listens to us**. In John 10 God's people, the sheep of Jesus the good shepherd, listen to and know his voice (10:3–4, 16). They follow him, and he gives them eternal life (10:27–28). So, the Elder's teaching, especially concerning Jesus, is heard and believed by those **who**

know God. The world and the opponents, i.e., those who are **not from God**, reject the orthodox message. They do "not continue in the teaching of Christ," but they bring a different teaching (2 John 9–10; cf. 2 Cor. 11:4; Gal. 1:6–9). There is almost a predestined flavor to these mutually exclusive categories, as in John 10:26: "you do not believe because you are not my sheep," and John 8:47: "He who belongs to God hears (*akouei*, 'listens to') what God says. The reason you do not hear is that you do not belong to God." This theological self-understanding helps the community to explain the "success" of the heretical movement and why some people have rejected the truth about Jesus Christ having come in the flesh (4:2).

The final point of contrast in v. 6 returns to the opening theme of this section (4:1–3): the opposing spiritual forces behind the secessionists and the Elder's followers. **This is how** (lit., "by this," *ek toutou*) refers to all of the previous instruction in vv. 1–6, including the necessity of testing the spirits by their confession of the full humanity of Jesus Christ (vv. 1–3) and the radical differences between "them and us," as to origin, values, spiritual empowerment, worldliness, audience, and relationship with God (vv. 4–6a). All these help the community discern (*ginōskomen*, "we know") and distinguish **the Spirit of truth** from **the spirit of falsehood**.

The former is the Holy Spirit, the Paraclete, promised to Jesus' followers in the Gospel of John, **the Spirit of truth**, whom the world cannot accept and does not know (14:17), who testifies about Jesus (15:26), and who will guide his disciples into all truth (16:13). The latter, **the spirit of falsehood** (*planēs*, "error," "deception," an expression unique in the NT), is the motivating force behind "the deceivers" (*planoi*, 2 John 7), who deceive themselves (*planōmen*, 1 John 1:8), and who are trying to lead the community astray (*planōntōn*, 1 John 2:26; *planatō*, 3:7). It is the "spirit . . . not from God," "the spirit of the antichrist" (4:3), "the one who is in the world" (4:4). These contrasting good and evil spirits, divine and demonic in their origin and functioning, are closely paralleled in the Dead Sea Scrolls, especially in 1QS 3:13—4:26.

Additional Notes §9

4:1 / Besides **Dear friends**, the Elder's other favorite terms of address are: (1) *teknia*, "dear children" (NIV; "little children," RSV, NASB), occurring at 2:1, 12, 28; 3:7, 18; 4:4; and 5:21; (2) *paidia*, "dear children" (NIV; "children," RSV) at 2:13 and 2:18; (3) *neaniskoi*, "young men" (NIV, RSV, NASB) at 2:13–14; and (4) *pateres*, "fathers" (NIV, RSV, NASB) at 2:13–14. See above on 2:12–14 for further discussion of these titles.

This verse contains the only use of *dokimazō* (**test**) in the Johannine writings.

On the subject of prophecy in early Christianity, see D. Aune, *Prophecy in Early Christianity and the Ancient Mediterranean World* (Grand Rapids: Eerdmans, 1983) and C. H. Peisker and C. Brown, "Prophet," *NIDNTT*, vol. 3, pp. 74–92.

4:2 / This doctrinal test was meant by the author to help his community, faced with the secessionists and their particular views, to find the right path. It was not intended as a universal test for all controversies in which spiritual discernment is called for.

For a study of all of the antithetical language of the letters of John and an interpretation of it that arises out of the social setting of the Johannine community, see Johnson, *Antitheses*.

4:3 / For a more complete discussion of these textual alternatives see Brown, *Epistles*, pp. 494–96; and Marshall, *Epistles*, pp. 207–8.

4:5 / On the Johannine concept of "the world," see above on 2:2 and 2:15; Brown, *Epistles*, pp. 224–26, 323–27; Brown, *Community*, pp. 63–65, 143–44; Stott, *Letters*, pp. 106–8; and R. Kysar, *John, the Maverick Gospel* (Atlanta: John Knox, 1976), pp. 47–64.

4:6 / On the relationship between the Johannine writings and the Dead Sea Scrolls, see Charlesworth, *John and Qumran*.

There is little agreement among those who have made a serious study of 1 John as to how to divide 1 John 4:7—5:4, but most have understood 4:7–12 to center around God's love for us and, in response, our love for one another. It is likely that the opponents of the Elder had stressed their love for God (cf. 4:10, 20), their devotion, piety, and mystical spirituality (cf. 1:6, 8, 10; 2:4, 6, 9; 3:18; 4:1). But the Elder thinks that it is God's love for human beings which is foundational. It is the basis of love for one another and of any claim to love for God.

4:7 / **Love** for **one another** was the writer's theme in 2:9–11 and 3:11–18, and it will be treated one more time in 4:19—5:4. The writer's style is to return often to his main topics for further exploration. This is also a key to understanding and interpreting 1 John. (See Introduction, "Outline or Structure.")

In v. 7, the Elder urges his "beloved" (*agapētoi*; NIV, **Dear friends**) to keep on loving **one another** (*agapōmen*, a present tense hortatory subjunctive). The reason given for this command (cf. 3:23b) is that **love comes from God** (*ek tou theou*; just as the Spirit which confesses Jesus is "from God," 4:2; and the readers and the author are "from God," 4:4, 6; cf. 3:9: "born of God"). Because **love** has its origin in God, those who belong to God (4:4, 6) should demonstrate **love** in their relations with one another. It is the proof of their divine origin (cf. John 13:35, for love as a proof of being Jesus' disciples), which v. 7 underscores by describing those who **love** as people who have **been born of God** (cf. 2:29—3:2, 9–10, where this term was first used of the Johannine Christians, and John 3:3, 5, 7).

Everyone who shows this kind of **love** (*agapē*) in action also shows that he or she **has been born of God**. The author wants to keep the issue of being God's children a matter of practice, but he is not introducing, as some have tried to see here, some new way of becoming a Christian that operates outside of faith in Jesus Christ, the Son of God (cf. John 20:31; 1 John 2:22–23; 4:2–3). For the author, *agapē* love can occur only among those who have come to know God's love in Jesus Christ, which has made them God's children (3:1–2, 16; 4:9–10, 19). So, those who **love** their brothers and sisters in the community of faith show not only that they are members of God's family but that they **know** God as well. This knowing is not knowing about, informational or doctrinal, but is personal, relational knowing, the knowing among members of the same family (cf. 2:3–4, 13–14; 4:6; cf. 2:5; 3:24).

4:8 / Verse 8 sets up a strong antithetical contrast to the affirmations of v. 7 and recalls the sharp polemic of v. 6:

> Everyone who loves . . . knows God (v. 7)
> **Whoever does not love does not know God** (v. 8)

Human beings are divided into two groups: people who know God (i.e., those who live in a right personal relationship with God through Jesus and have eternal life [4:15; 5:11–12; cf. John 14:5–9; 17:3]) and those who do not. The aorist tense of **not know** (*ouk egnō*) points not to the past but to the decisive and absolute character of the opponents' not knowing God. The Elder is thinking primarily about those who claim to be Christians (there is no reflection in these verses on general human morality), like the former members of his community who seceded (2:19). His main point is that having or not having this relationship with God is clearly seen in how people treat each other: they either **love** with the love that comes from God (v. 7), or they do not. *Agapē* love is the evidence of authentic spirituality.

The most striking statement in v. 8 is the description of God's essential nature as **love**: **God is love** (*ho theos agapē estin*; the same phrase occurs again in v. 16). The use of the predicate noun, **love**, points to a deeper reality than the use of predicate adjectives, such as "faithful and just" (1:9). It is more like the statement in 1:5, "God is light" (*ho theos phōs estin*), in which holiness or justice is viewed as central to the character of God, and not as a secondary attribute (cf. John 4:24: "God is spirit," *pneuma ho theos*). All of God's activity is characterized by righteousness and love. Since **God is love**, those who claim to **know God** should be actively and visibly at work for the highest good and well-being of others, and especially, as far as the Elder is concerned, of their brothers and sisters in the Christian community.

4:9 / The profound affirmation "God is love" prepares the readers for the teaching in the rest of this section, but the theme shifts from God's nature to God's actions in history. "The God who is love (8) 'loved us' (10) and expressed his love by sending his Son to earth" (Stott, *Letters*, p. 164).

Verse 9 begins with another **This is how** (*en toutō*, "by this") statement, which occurs twelve times in the letters of John (2:3, 5; 3:10, 16, 19, 24; 4:2, 9, 10, 13, 17; 5:2). Literally translated, v. 9a reads, "By this was manifested the love of God among us." God, who is love, concretely and specifically **showed his love** in an event in history. God is "the God who acts," and who always acts in a way consistent with his nature as holiness and love (1:5; 4:8). God's act of **love** took place **among us**, i.e., in the living memory of those associated with the Elder and his community (see the "we" and "us" affirmations concerning the coming of the Word in 1:1–4). More broadly, God's love was demonstrated on the plane of human history, as a public event. Therefore, v. 9b says that God sent his Son **into the world** (*eis ton kosmon*).

The specific activity which manifested God's **love** was that **He sent his one and only Son into the world**. The sending was an act which began in the past and whose consequences extend into the present and beyond (*apestalken*, perfect tense; NASB: "God has sent"). "Sending" implies preexistence, that **the Son** has come from the Father into the human dimension of existence. This is a point Jesus made repeatedly in the Gospel of John, and which the Elder will make again in 4:10, 14. The **Son** is described as **his one and only** (*autou ton monogenē*). The term means "unique," one of a kind (BAGD, p. 527). While there are many "children of God," there is only one "Son of God."

The **love** of God was seen not only in the sending of his Son into the world, but especially in the purpose for which the Son was sent: **that we might live through him**. Again, the "we" refers primarily to the members of the author's community. While God loves the world (John 3:16) and has sent the Son to be its Savior (1 John 4:14) and "the atoning sacrifice . . . for the sins of the whole world" (2:2), God's intention is realized only in those who believe in him and thereby gain eternal life (John 3:16). The world hated and rejected Jesus and his disciples (John 15:18–19;

1 John 3:13). This is the only use of the verb *zaō*, **live**, in the letters of John; it occurs frequently in the Fourth Gospel (e.g., 6:51, 57–58; 11:25–26). Here its aorist tense (*zēsōmen*) connotes "come to life," the start of a lifelong process (Smalley, *1, 2, 3 John*, p. 242). **Through him** means "by means of him," through who he is and what he has done.

4:10 / **This is love** is literally, "in this is love" (*en toutō estin hē agapē*). That is, "this is the essence of love," or "love consists in this." God's action defines what authentic love is. But first the Elder must say that real **love** is not defined by our love for God. It is **not that we loved God** (*ēgapēkamen*, perfect tense, "we have been loving"). The opponents have claimed to love God, know God, live in God, walk in the light, etc. They have flaunted their "superior spirituality" (they don't even sin; 1:8, 10) before the remaining Johannine Christians. **But** proud human love for God, even "Christian love" (note the "we") is a poor model. The only true standard of love is God's love; it is **that he loved us** (*ēgapēsen*, aorist tense, "decisively, once and for all, loved"), and, as the proof and expression of his love, **sent** (*apesteilen*, aorist tense) **his Son**. This is the definitive expression of **love**. While the primary reference of **we** and **us** in this verse is to those who claim to be Christians, the context supports a broader, secondary application to humankind generally (v. 9, "world"; 2:2; 4:15; John 3:16). On the sending of the Son, see v. 9.

The key word in the last phrase of v. 10 is *hilasmon* (NIV, **atoning sacrifice**). It was used before in 2:2 with respect to Jesus' effective provision for our sins. Given the reference to "the blood of Jesus" in 1:7, *hilasmos* must refer to Jesus' death on the cross as a sacrifice for sins, analogous to OT **atoning sacrifice**s. Such a sacrifice cleanses the beneficiary from the guilt of **sin** and effects reconciliation, or a restored right relationship with God, by averting God's judgment on sin. It is, of course, as 4:9–10 make perfectly clear, **God** who has taken this action. God **loved us and sent his** own **Son** to reconcile us to himself through the Son's atoning death **for our sins**. **For our sins** points to the need for **an atoning sacrifice**; without it we would be under God's judgment and outside the sphere of life and salvation. We would not "have passed from death to life" (John 5:24; 1 John 3:14).

4:11 / Now the Elder draws the ethical consequences from God's great act of love, of which he has been writing since

v. 7. **Dear friends** (lit., "Beloved," *agapētoi*) reminds the readers that they are loved, not just by the author but by God. **Since** is the correct translation of *ei*, not "if"; the case has been demonstrated in vv. 9–10. **God loved**: the aorist tense indicates the absolute and definitive quality of God's love. As above, **us** is, for the Elder, primarily "we" who have come to know God's love, without forgetting that God does love the whole world. The little word **so** (*houtōs*) deserves special attention. It can mean both "in this way" (as seen in God's love in the previous verses) or "so much, excessively." Both are true and make good sense in the present context. God's love, not human love, is the model of authentic love (v. 10), and God's gift of his only Son is an extreme act of love. **God so loved us**, both as to manner and as to intensity. This verse closely resembles John 3:16, and the entire passage (vv. 7–11) may be read as a commentary on it (Brown, *Epistles*, p. 519).

With God's manifested (v. 9) love as the model and motivation, the community's mandate is clear: **we also ought to love one another**. This resumes the thought of v. 7 and applies the lesson of vv. 7–10 to the relationships expected among God's people. While those who have not experienced God's love in Christ cannot be expected to **love**, **we**, the believing community, can and are. The verb **ought** (*opheilomen*) emphasizes **love** as our Christian obligation; we owe it as a debt (Rom. 13:8).

4:12 / Verse 12 is concerned with the reality of God in daily life. This was an important consideration to the Elder's readers. The secessionist false teachers were claiming a vital relationship with God (1:6; 2:6), intimate knowledge of God (2:4), ability to speak as a prophet by God's Spirit (4:1–2), and love for God (4:10). They may even have claimed to have had visions of God, as later gnostic enthusiasts did. This undoubtedly left the Elder's loyal followers wondering about the reality of their own relationship with God. But just as the author has proved false the schismatics' earlier claims to be spiritually superior (1:6–10; 2:3–6; 2:9–11; 4:1–3; 4:7–8, 10), so in v. 12 he points his readers to the way to authentic spirituality. It is the theme of this section of 1 John: **if we love one another**.

The invisibility of God (**No one has ever seen God**; *theon oudeis pōpote tetheatai*) is affirmed five times in the Johannine writings (4:12, 20; John 1:18; 5:37; 6:46). The sentence in John 1:18 is nearly identical to 1 John 4:12a. The word order is different, and the writer uses a different, but synonymous, verb for "see" (*theon oudeis heōraken pōpote*). The word order is significant. **God** comes first, as if to say, "God, as God truly is, I am who I am." God as invisible was also a common concept in the OT (e.g., Exod. 33:20) and in Judaism. But, just as in the Fourth Gospel, where Jesus makes the invisible God known (1:18; 14:7–9), so here in 1 John, **love** for **one another** brings the unseen God to concrete expression in everyday life. **No one has ever seen God**, it is true, but **if we love one another**, we and others experience the presence of God.

Verse 12 expresses this result of **love** for **one another** in two ways (i.e., the "if clause" in v. 12 has a double "then clause"): (a) **God** comes to dwell among us, and (b) God's **love** is perfected among us. First, when **we love one another** (the author continues to have in mind primarily love among Christians within the community, which his opponents do not have, 2:9–11; 3:10b, 14–18; 4:8), **God** dwells (NIV, **lives**, *menei*) among us (NIV, **in us**, *en hymin*). The intimate relationship between the Christian and God has been frequently expressed in 1 John already: "Our fellowship is with the Father and with his Son, Jesus Christ" (1:3). "We are in him" (2:5), and we "live (*menō*) in him" (2:6). "The word of God lives (*menei*) in you" (2:14). Faithful Johannine Christians "remain (*meneite*) in the Son and in the Father" (2:24). "The anointing [the Holy Spirit] you received from him remains [*menei*] in you" (2:27). The readers are urged to "remain (*menete*) in him" (2:27–28). "Those who obey his commands live (*menei*) in him, and he in them," and "we know that he lives (*menei*) in us . . . by the Spirit he gave us" (3:24). There is a mutual abiding of the believing community and God, and the point of 4:12 is that the presence of the unseen God among us is the result of our love for one another.

The second result of love among Christians is that God's **love is made complete** among us. The same expression was used in 2:5, and we face the same problem in understanding exactly what the author meant. Does **his love** (*hē agapē autou*, lit., "the love of him") mean God's love for us, our love for God, or God's kind of love? In 2:5 the last fits the context best. Here God's love for the community has been the main theme in vv. 7–11, so God's love for his children may be uppermost in the author's mind, but the qualitative definition (God's kind of love) is not far from it. If the former is correct, then the Elder means that, though God is unseen, God is not unfelt. Our sense of the reality of God's love for us grows and moves toward perfection. The Greek, *teteleiō-menē estin*, can mean "is being perfected," with the emphasis, then, on the process of a maturing apprehension of God's love.

Additional Notes §10

Within 4:7–12, the following divisions between verses have been suggested:

10/11: Brown, *Epistles*; Culpepper, *1 John*; C. Haas, et al., *Letters*; Schnackenburg, *Johannine Epistles*; Smalley, *1, 2, 3 John*; Westcott, *Epistles*; Nestle; TEV

12/13: Brooke, *Epistles*; Bruce, *Epistles*; Bultmann, *Epistles*; Dodd, *Epistles*; Grayston, *Epistles*; Jackman, *Letters*; Kysar, *I, II, III John*; R. Law, *The Tests of Life* (Edinburgh: T. & T. Clark, 1914, 3d ed.; Grand Rapids: Baker, 1968), p. 16; Marshall, *Epistles*; Smith, *First John*; Stott, *Letters*; M. M. Thompson, *1–3 John*; A. N. Wilder, "Epistles"; UBS, NEB, NIV, NRSV, TEV

16a/16b: Brooke, *Epistles*; Brown, *Epistles*; Culpepper, *1 John*; Perkins, *Epistles*; Westcott, *Epistles*; Nestle; UBS, NEB, NIV, NRSV, TEV (16b begins, "God is love")

16/17: Bultmann, *Epistles*; Grayston, *Epistles*; Haas, *Letters*; Law, *Tests*; Schnackenburg, *Johannine Epistles*; Smalley, *1, 2, 3 John*; Stott, *Letters*; Thompson, *1–3 John*

18/19: Bultmann, *Epistles*; Dodd, *Epistles*; Kysar, *I, II, III John*; Schnackenburg, *Johannine Epistles*; Thompson, *1–3 John*; Wilder, "Epistles"; NIV, TEV

19/20: Brown, *Epistles*; Thompson, *1–3 John*

20/21: Smalley, *1, 2, 3 John*

21/5:1: Brooke, *Epistles*; Bruce, *Epistles*; Culpepper, *1 John*; Grayston, *Epistles*; Houlden, *Epistles*; Jackman, *Letters*; Perkins, *Epistles*; Plummer, *Epistles*; Smith, *First John*; Stott, *Letters*; Westcott, *Epistles*; Nestle; UBS, NEB, NIV, NRSV, TEV

5:2/3 Schnackenburg, *Johannine Epistles*

As to what is the last verse of the unit, the following suggestions have been made:

5:3a: Law, *Tests*

5:4a: Brown, *Epistles*

5:4: Brooke, *Epistles*; Bultmann, *Epistles*; Culpepper, *1 John*; Haas, *Letters*; Marshall, *Epistles*; Smalley, *1, 2, 3 John*; Schnackenburg, *Johannine Epistles*; Nestle

5:5: Bruce, *Epistles*; Dodd, *Epistles*; Grayston, *Epistles*; Jackman, *Letters*; Kysar, *I, II, III John*; Perkins, *Epistles*; Smith, *First John*; Stott, *Letters*; Thompson, *1–3 John*; Westcott, *Epistles*; UBS, NIV, NRSV, TEV

5:12 Plummer, *Epistles*

Our divisions within this unit are based on the understanding that God's love and our response to it unify vv. 7–12, that the chief issue in vv. 13–18 is assurance or confidence, and that 4:19—5:4a revolve around the theme of love among God's children. As to ending the unit after the first half of v. 4, the justification is that v. 4b begins a new theme of faith and Christology with the announcement, "This is the victory that has overcome the world, even our faith."

Further, consistent with the author's typical style, "overcoming the world" is the concept that overlaps or links the two sections.

4:8 / On **God is love,** see Dodd, *Epistles*, pp. 107–10, for a profound discussion of God's nature in Hebrew and Greek thought. The Swiss theologian, Emil Brunner, put love and holiness at the heart of his understanding of God's essence; see E. Brunner, *The Christian Doctrine of God* (Philadelphia: Westminster, 1949), pp. 157–204.

4:9 / See G. E. Wright, *God Who Acts: Biblical Theology as Recital*, SBT 8 (London: SCM, 1952).

For God's sending of the Son used with *apostellō*, see, e.g., John 3:17, 34; 5:36; 6:29; 8:42; 10:36; 17:3, 8, 18, 21, 23, 25; 20:21; with *pempō*, used in John without distinction from *apostellō*, see, e.g., 4:34; 5:24, 30, 37; 6:38–39, 44; 7:16, 18, 28, 33; 8:16, 18, 26, 29; 9:4; 12:44–45, 49; 13:20; 14:24, 26; 15:21; 16:5; 20:21.

On *monogenēs*, see Marshall, *Epistles*, p. 214 n. 8.

§11 Confidence Because of God's Love
(1 John 4:13–18)

In this section of 1 John the Elder's aim is to strengthen the spiritual confidence of his readers. "The writer passes from the facts to Christian consciousness of the facts" (Brooke, *Epistles*, p. 121). He appeals to the indwelling Spirit (v. 13), to the Father's sending of the Son to save them (v. 14), to their confession of faith in Jesus as the Son of God (v. 15), to God's love for them (v. 16), all as the means by which love is perfected among them (v. 17a). The result will be fearless confidence on the day of judgment (vv. 17b–18).

4:13 / The original readers of this letter needed, almost desperately, to be assured of the authenticity of their relationship with God. They were under attack from a group of "super-spiritual" opponents, Christian (so they would have considered themselves) elitists who had seceded from their fellowship (2:19), whose claims about their own relationship with God were of the highest order (1:6, 8, 10; 2:4, 6, 9; 4:10), including the assertion that they spoke by God's Spirit (4:1–3).

Under these circumstances (Grayston calls it "the dissidents' religious browbeating"; *Epistles*, p. 129), the Johannine Christians needed reassurance (to **know**) **that we live in him and he in us**. The idea of living or abiding (*menomen*) in God was the closing topic of v. 12 and is the typical Johannine "link" between two separate sections. In v. 13, then, the author presents a second way to **know** that we have a mutually indwelling relationship with God. The first was by loving one another (v. 12). Here it is by **his Spirit** which **he has given us**. The same ground was also cited in 3:24. In 3:24 the aorist verb emphasized the once-for-all nature of the gift of the Spirit. In 4:13 the perfect verb emphasizes the Spirit's continuing presence. The writer's concern is not so much individual but community assurance. See the genuine plurals in 4:4, 6 ("you," "we," "us,"), 9 ("among us"), 12 ("in" or among "us"), and 13 ("in us," or among us). It is at the corporate level that confidence has broken down.

4:14 / Another reason to be confident is the historical fact that **the Father sent his Son to be the Savior of the world**. It is as if the Elder were saying, "Remember the incarnation! Remember John 3:16!" The verbs **seen** and **testify** are meant to ground the community's assurance in the historical tradition of the Johannine community and of its eyewitness, the disciple whom Jesus loved (John 21:24). Our faith is based on an actual event, personally experienced ("heard," **seen**, "looked at," "touched," "appeared to us"; 1 John 1:1–3), not on wishful thinking or on projected hopes. When the writer says, **we . . . testify**, he is standing with his mentor, the beloved disciple, and with the other elders and apostles, who witnessed "the Christ event."

What they claim to have **seen** and the burden of their testimony is **that the Father sent his Son to be the Savior of the world**. Two elements are present here: (a) the relationship between Jesus and his *"Abba,"* and (b) the Son's mission of universal salvation. That Jesus was uniquely conscious of his special relationship of Sonship with the Father is witnessed to by the Synoptic Gospels (e.g., Matt. 11:27) and throughout the Gospel of John (e.g., 5:17–23; 6:43–46; 8:28–29, 42, 54–55; 10:29–38; 11:41–42; and most of chaps. 14 and 17). The disciples of Jesus saw, remembered this, and told others about it, so that it came to be recorded in the Gospel tradition. The Son's message was the coming of the kingdom of God, entered into by allegiance to Jesus (Synoptics), or eternal life through believing in Jesus (John). In either case, in whatever language, the **Son** came to be **the Savior of the world** (cf. John 3:16–17). The Elder had already said that he was the "atoning sacrifice" "for the sins of the world" (2:2) and that the Son was sent "into the world that we might live through him" (4:9). The Son is the world's **Savior**, in that he is the means by which its sins are forgiven, and he gives it eternal life.

4:15 / The Elder's third argument for strengthening the spiritual confidence of his readers is their own confession of faith in Jesus and its results. Verses 14 and 15 are linked together by their christological focus. While in v. 14 the community's assurance rests upon the apostolic tradition's witness to Jesus as God's agent for salvation, in v. 15 it is their own response to God's act in Christ that brings them into fellowship with God. That the latter is the author's concern is shown by the repeated use of the language of mutual indwelling (v. 12: "God lives in us"; v. 13: "we live in him and he in us"; v. 15: **God lives in him and he in God**; v. 16: "lives in God, and God in him"). The readers require assurance of this fact, especially in the face of the attempted "spiritual imperialism" of the secessionist false teachers.

The way to assurance, then, is to confess (NIV: **acknowledges**; *homologēsē*) **that Jesus is the Son of God**. The emphasis is on the human name, **Jesus**. The gnostically influenced false teachers would have believed in the **Son of God**, a divine being from heaven. But that this supernatural figure was the fully human, come-in-the-flesh **Jesus**, they could not affirm (4:2; 2 John 7). We encountered the same pattern in 2:22, where the opponents might accept "the Christ" (defined their way, as a spiritual being), but they denied that this "Christ" was Jesus. In so doing, the Elder maintains, they deny the Son (and the Father as well; 2:23). But faith in the **Son of God** brings **God** to abide (*menei*) in the believer and the believer in God. In this verse the corporate assurance of vv. 12–14 is now also personal and individual.

4:16 / In v. 16, the Elder returns to the topic of **love**, and in so doing he lays the fourth stone in the foundation of support for the community's confidence in their spiritual standing. They can be confident because they are **loved**. This is something they have come to **know** (perfect tense, *egnōkamen*) and have come to **rely on** (perf. tense, *pepisteukamen*) over time and by experience (cf. John 6:69). This is the **love** which **God has for us**. The phrase **for us**, *en hymin*, can also be translated "in us," emphasizing our consciousness of God's love. Love from other sources may prove undependable; even brothers and sisters from one's own community can turn in hatred and rejection (2:9–11; 3:10b–15, 17; 4:8a, 20), but God's **love** can reassure our self-condemning (cf. 3:19–20) and uncertain (see the emphasis on "knowing" in 2:3, 5, 13–14; 3:19, 24; 4:2, 6, 13) hearts. God's **love** is not turned on and off, present one day but gone the next, because **God is love** (cf. 4:8). **Love** is God's essential nature. All that God does toward us all the time arises out of God's love for us (cf. Rom. 8:35–39).

Therefore, **whoever** abides (NIV, **lives**; *menei*) **in love**, that is, in the same *agapē* love God is and has for us, **lives in God, and**

God in him. Note the continuing emphasis on mutual indwelling and on assurance of fellowship with God that we have seen in this entire section (4:12b, 13a, 15b). God's love and a life lived in that love ought to be ample assurance against our own doubts and the contradictions of others.

4:17 / Verses 17–18 are a conclusion and an application of the Elder's teaching on spiritual confidence. "First and foremost these verses extol the possibility of the gift of *parrēsia* ('confidence')" (Bultmann, *Epistles*, p. 74). **In this way** (*en toutō*) refers to the whole unit above (vv. 13–16) and all its grounds of assurance of fellowship with God. By the means described above, and especially by abiding in love (16b), God's **love** is perfected (NIV, **is made complete**) **among us**. God's **love** comes to completion or perfection when it realizes its objective in the believing community, and that aim is the full assurance that does not doubt acceptance and communion with God. For the author the ideal of **complete** or perfect **love** (2:5; 4:12, 17–18) is primarily a matter of the community's (**among us**) sense of its being right with God, as they are being undermined by the attacks of the schismatic opponents.

The remainder of v. 17 and v. 18 apply the teaching on spiritual confidence to the coming **judgment**. The result of perfected or completed **love** to give us **confidence** (*parrēsia*, "boldness") **in the day of judgment**. Because "we live in him and he in us" (vv. 12b, 13a, 15b, 16b), because we have the Spirit (13b), because we have the apostolic testimony to God's sending his Son to save us (14), because we do confess Jesus as God's Son (15), and, above all, because of God's love for us (16), Christians can be assured that God's **day** of eschatological **judgment**, like the coming of Christ, will find them "confident and unashamed" (2:28).

One way of summarizing this is to say that we have **confidence** as we anticipate God's **judgment**, because **we are like** Christ (lit., "as he is so also we are"). All six uses of *ekeinos* (**him**) in 1 John refer to Jesus (2:6; 3:3, 5, 7, 16). Being **like him** (cf. 3:2) means walking as he did (2:6), being a beloved child of God yet unknown by the world (3:1–2), not practicing sin and being righteous (3:5–7), laying down our lives for one another (3:16), and being born of God (5:18). In all these passages a direct likeness is drawn between Jesus and the Christian. Because we are like Christ, God's beloved and obedient Son, we who are also born of God, loved, and obedient, can be confident in the **judgment**. **In this world** is mentioned in contrast to the coming era of judgment. If **we are like him in this world**, then we can be assured that on **the day of judgment** we will have nothing of which to be afraid.

4:18 / The mention of the coming final judgment could cause some to be afraid. But **fear** is no part of **love**. If we know that, like Jesus, we are loved by God (3:1; 4:9–11, 16), then there is no cause for any **fear** before God, even though we will be judged. In fact, **perfect love** throws fear away (*exō ballei ton phobon*). **Love drives out fear**; the two are completely incompatible and cannot co-exist in the same consciousness. The reason for this is that **fear has to do with punishment**, and, although we will be judged (4:17; Rom. 14:10; 2 Cor. 5:10; Heb. 9:27), we will not be punished or condemned (John 3:18; Rom. 8:1). In Johannine theology, the believer in Jesus has already passed from death (spiritual death and its concomitant punishment) to life (John 5:24; 1 John 3:14). If members of the community still harbor **fear** in their hearts, they have progress yet to make in being **made perfect in love**. The Elder urges perfection in love as a goal for spiritual growth, because (a) it is the result of obedience to God's commands (2:5), (b) it comes from loving one another (4:12), and (c) it will provide the believer with assurance not only "in this world" (4:17) but in the world to come.

Additional Notes §11

4:13 / The author feels the need to return to the subject of assurance frequently: 2:3–6; 2:12–14; 3:1–2; 3:19–24; 4:4–6; 4:13–18; 5:13–15; 5:18–20. It is one of the main themes of 1 John. See Introduction, "Outline or Structure," for the others.

4:14 / On the authorship of these letters and on the relationship between the Elder and other apostolic figures, see the Introduction.

On Jesus' unique relationship with God there is a vast amount of literature. See V. Taylor, *The Person of Christ in New Testament Teaching* (London: Macmillan, 1958), chaps. 13 and 14; O. Cullmann, *Christology*, pp. 270–90; G. Kittel, "*abba*," *TDNT*, 1964, vol. 1, pp. 5ff.; J. Jeremias, *The Central Message of the New Testament* (London: SCM, 1965), pp. 9–30; *New*

Testament Theology, Vol. 1: The Proclamation of Jesus (London: SCM, 1971), pp. 61–68; Schnackenburg, *Gospel*, vol. 2, pp. 172–86; Ladd, *Theology*, pp. 159–72; Dunn, *Christology*, pp. 22–33.

An exposition of the contrasting yet often complementary approaches to Jesus and his message in the NT are found in various works of NT theology: Dunn, *Unity and Diversity*, pp. 11–59, 203–31; L. Goppelt, *Theology of the New Testament* (Grand Rapids: Eerdmans, 1981), vol. 2, pp. 16–30, 65–106, 176–78, 186–88, 216–24, 247–57, 280–84, 296–300; W. G. Kümmel, *The Theology of the New Testament* (Nashville: Abingdon, 1973), pp. 22–95, 255–333; Ladd, *Pattern*, pp. 41–86; Ladd, *Theology*, parts 1–2; L. Morris, *New Testament Theology* (Grand Rapids: Zondervan, 1986), pp. 39–55, 98–106, 120–27, 157–71, 225–47, 288–89, 293–94, 302–6, 317–19; J. Reumann, *Variety and Unity in New Testament Thought* (New York: Oxford, 1991), chaps. 4–5; and E. Schweizer, *A Theological Introduction to the New Testament* (Nashville: Abingdon, 1991), chaps. 25–27, 29.

The term "savior" occurs only twice in the Gospel and letters of John, here and in John 4:42, appropriately on the lips of non-Jews, the Samaritans. The latter text also calls Jesus, "the Savior of the world" (cf. 1 Tim. 4:10). The Emperor Hadrian, A.D. 117–138, was called "the Savior of the world." See Cullmann, *Christology*, pp. 238–45; and W. Foerster, "*sōzō, etc.*," *TDNT*, vol. 7, pp. 980–1012.

Kosmos appears 22 times in 1–3 John. It has a "neutral" sense only in 1 John 2:2, 4:9, 14. "Material possessions" (*ton bion tou kosmou*) in 3:17 may be also, but the sense of *bios* in 2:16 is decidedly negative. Like Luke, the author of the Johannine letters may have viewed wealth as negative, not neutral. It might be used for good, but it is spiritually dangerous. The other occurrences of *kosmos* in 1, 2, and 3 John are 2:15–17; 3:1, 13; 4:1, 3–5, 17; 5:4–5, 19. On *kosmos* in the Johannine writings, see H. Sasse, "*kosmos*," *TDNT*, vol. 3, pp. 867–98; Brown, *Gospel, I–XII*, pp. 508–10; *Epistles*, pp. 222–24, 323–27; and Ladd, *Theology*, pp. 225–27.

4:15 / This language goes back to Jesus' teaching on the vine and the branches (John 15:1–8), on the coming of the Holy Spirit (14:16–17), on his and the Father's coming to live within the disciples (14:20, 23), and to his prayer in John 17 (vv. 21, 23, 26).

The verb *homologēsē* is aorist subjunctive, pointing to "the (single) basic public confession of faith that makes one a Christian" (Brown, *Epistles*, p. 524).

For the confession of faith in Jesus as the Son of God in the Fourth Gospel, see 1:34, 49; 11:27. For Jesus' own teaching about himself as the Son, see 5:19–27; 6:40; 8:36; 10:36; 11:4; 14:13; 17:1; 19:7. For the Fourth Evangelist's teaching about Jesus as the Son, see 3:16–17, 35–36; 20:31. The title is even more prominent in 1 John: 1:3, 7; 2:22–24; 3:8, 23; 4:9–10, 14–15; and 5:5, 9–13, 20. In 2:23, 3:23, 4:15, 5:5, 5:10, and 5:13 allegiance to the Son of God is presented as a confession of faith.

4:16 / It is better not to break v. 16 into two parts and start a new section as many do. The thought is continuous from v. 13 through v. 18. It is all on spiritual confidence.

4:17 / Earlier editions of the NIV did not contain the phrase **In this way**.

In v. 17, the grammatical construction, *hina* with the subjunctive, can be either a purpose or a result clause. The latter is more appropriate here, since it is the consequence of perfect love which is foremost in the author's mind.

Verse 17 contains the only Johannine reference to "the day of judgment." See Matt. 10:15; 11:22, 24; 12:36, 41–42; Luke 10:14; 2 Pet. 3:7; Jude 6. In the early church writers, see 2 Clement 16:3, 17; Epistle of Barnabas 11:7; 19:10; 21:6. F. H. Klooster, "Judgment, Last," *ISBE*, vol. 2, pp. 1162–63; L. Morris, *The Biblical Doctrine of Judgment* (Grand Rapids: Eerdmans, 1960), and W. Schneider, "Judgment," *NIDNTT*, vol. 2, pp. 361–68.

In the Gospel of John, *ekeinos* is used broadly of many people: John the Baptist (1:8; 5:35), Moses (5:46–47), Judas (13:26–27, 30), Peter (18:17, 25), and of the disciple whom Jesus loved (19:35; 21:7, 23). It also occurs in reference to the devil (8:44), to God (1:33; 5:37–38; 6:29; 8:42), to the Spirit (14:26; 15:26: 16:8, 13–14), and to Jesus (1:18; 2:21; 3:28, 30; 5:11, 19; 7:11; 9:12, 28, 37; 19:21; cf. 4:25). The term completely lacks the distinctive usage of 1 John.

On the relation between the believer and Christ in this passage, see Dodd, *Epistles*, pp. 119–20.

Culpepper thinks that the Elder's opponents did not think there would be any future judgment and that this led them to neglect the love command. The opponents criticized the Elder's group for still living in fear of judgment and charged that they had no confidence in God (*1 John*, p. 93). Culpepper may be correct (Grayston holds a diametrically opposite view of the opponents' eschatology; *Epistles*, pp. 95–97, 130) but 1 John gives us little evidence for the opponents' eschatological views.

4:18 / The only other use of "punishment" (*kolasis*) in the NT is in Matt. 25:46, at the end of the parable of the sheep and the goats with reference to eternal or eschatological punishment. On the relationship between fear and punishment, "the point of the author is that fear arises out of anticipation of one's destiny in the final judgment" (Kysar, *I, II, III John*, p. 102).

Brown points out that in the Johannine writings there is no positive use of the term "fear" in relation to God. *Phobos* seems to have lost its positive connotations of reverence and awe (*Epistles*, pp. 530–31).

The 1984 edition of the NIV correctly changed "the man who fears" to **the one who fears**. Such corrections could have been made much more consistently throughout the NIV.

§12 Love among God's Children
(1 John 4:19—5:4a)

While the theme of love continues in this new section, there is a definite shift of focus away from the concern for assurance (4:13–18) to the practice of love among God's children, a message the Elder has proclaimed before (2:9–11; 3:11–18; 4:7–12). The tone of the unit is that of logical argument, in which the author compares and contrasts claims of love for God and love for one's brothers and sisters in the faith, or the lack of it. The opponents are in mind throughout, as they have been in every earlier discussion of love. That the secessionist false teachers have proved their lack of love for their brothers and sisters in the community is the writer's overarching assumption.

4:19 / There is a strong contrast between v. 18 and v. 19, between fear and **love**. The **we** with which v. 19 begins is emphatic: "as for us, **we** do not fear, **we** love." The author includes himself with his readers, urging them to positive action toward others (**love**), instead of self-preoccupying fear. By stating this ideal as if it were a present accomplishment, the Elder assumes the best of his community, and, as a result, motivates and encourages them to realize it. The verb for **love**, *agapōmen*, can be present indicative (**we love**) or a hortatory subjunctive ("let us love"). They are not much different in this context, and one's choice depends on one's view of the writer's rhetorical strategy—to command or to encourage.

Does the author have in mind **love** for God or **love** for one another, when he says **we love**? He means both, all active love on the part of the believing community, whether for God or others. In fact, the absolute **we love** may both point back to v. 18, contrasting fear as our response to God, and point ahead to vv. 20–21, in which love for other Christians is in view.

How is it possible for us to have lives characterized by **love**? **Because he first loved us** is the author's answer. The aorist tense of **loved** points to God's once for all, decisive act of love in sending Jesus Christ as our Savior (vv. 9–10, 14; cf. John 3:16). It is God's **love** which enables authentic *agapē* **love** among Christians. (While it is a worthy sentiment, the Elder does not have in mind generic, human love; he limits his argument to what is or ought to be happening among those who claim to be Christians). The self-sacrificing nature of divine **love** calls forth among believers the same grateful response of costly **love** (cf. 3:17–18) in return, both to God and to one another.

4:20 / The phrase **if anyone says** is one of the Elder's ways in this letter of referring to the claims of the secessionists (cf. 1:6, 8, 10; 2:4, 6, 9; cf. 4:2–3; 5:10). The "super-spiritual" false teachers were celebrating their love for God; they were claiming a level of intimate knowledge of and fellowship with God which the readers had not attained. **I love God** was on their lips (cf. 3:18), but their actions gave a contrary testimony. They thought it possible to **love God**, without raising the issue of **love** for others, especially other Christians. For them, the two matters were completely separable. Jesus did not find it possible to separate them. When he was asked what was the greatest commandment, he gave a double answer, including, inseparably, love for God with love for neighbor (Matt. 22:34–40). The Elder does not believe that they can be divided either. He argues that anyone who claims to **love God** is **a liar**, if such a person, at the same time, **hates his brother**. Note that, with this author, there is no middle ground of indifference to one's brother nor merely inadequate love (Westcott, *Epistles*, p. 161). It is typical Johannine dualism to contrast absolutely **love** and **hate**. The latter means "to have no love for." In 2:9 the Elder rejected the claim "to be in the light," if the boaster "hates his brother." Such a person is a child of the devil (3:10), a murderer (3:15), and **a liar**. One cannot both **love God** and simultaneously **hate his brother**, as the Elder's opponents are doing. A claim to do so is patently false.

Why? Because, the Elder argues, it is easier to love the **seen brother** than the unseen **God**. At least it is easier to test the former than the latter. There is very little evidence possible for whether one **loves God**. Even worship, devotional practices, and commandment-keeping may be done for other motives. But there is abundant evidence possible for the authenticity of **love** for one's **brother**, and it is more difficult to falsify, since **love** is primarily, not an interior state of the heart, but the visible commitment in action, going "out of one's way," to advance the highest good and well-being of others. The **love** is in the deed, first and foremost, and secondarily in its purpose. So, when the Elder looks at the opponents and sees them disregarding the well-being of his needy community (cf. 3:17–18), and, indeed, aggressively attacking them, this is *prima facie* evidence for the absence of any *agapē* **love** at all. If it is not there for the **brother**, it is not there for **God**. The very nature of *agapē* **love** demands that it include one's brother or sister as well as God.

On God as **not seen**, cf. 4:12 and John 1:18. The verb for **see** is in the perfect tense indicating that the secessionists have known well, over a period of time, the needs of the brothers and sisters they are rejecting. The textual variant, substituting "how is he able to love" for "he" **cannot love** arose due to the copyists' desire to make this verse conform more closely in style to 3:17. **Cannot love** is also the better attested text.

4:21 / Verse 21 reinforces the teaching of v. 20 by citing a divine **command** which links **love** for **God** with **love** for one's **brother**. Literally translated, v. 21a reads: "And this commandment we have from him." Does "him" (NIV, **he**) refer to Jesus' own linking of these commandments in Matthew 22:34–40 (par. Mark 12:28–31; Luke 10:25–28), or perhaps to the "new commandment" of John 13:34? Or is the Elder referring to God as the origin of this teaching on love for God and neighbor in the Torah (Deut. 6:5; Lev. 19:18)? While the author does not always separate clearly between God and Jesus in his writing, as we noted earlier in several passages (e.g., 1 John 1:5–7; 2:3–6; 2:26–29; 3:2–3; 4:17), the context here points to **God** as the source of the **command** to **love** one's **brother** or sister. Indeed, it is God's teaching which Jesus cites in the Synoptics and on which the "new commandment" (John 13:34) is based.

Whoever loves God recalls the claims of the opponents, as implied in 4:10 and stated explicitly in 4:20. They have touted their love for God, but the Elder warns that this profession is invalid when not accompanied by visible, active, practical **love** for one's brothers and sisters in the community. Because they have not done this (2:9–11; 3:10b, 14–18; 4:8, 20), the secessionists' claim to **love God** must be rejected, along with their claim "to be in the light" (2:9).

5:1 / The opening verse of chapter 5 does not begin a new topic, but it continues the theme of the inseparability of love for God and for God's children among those who claim to be Christians. That the Elder is speaking of love among Christians, and not of the broader concern of love for neighbor, is evident in the confessional language of v. 1: **Everyone who believes that Jesus is the Christ**.

This description of the Christian as a believer in **Jesus** as **the Christ** is very Johannine (John 11:27; 20:31; cf. 7:30–31; 10:24–25). We have seen it previously in the summary of Johannine faith in 3:23a: "to believe in the name of his Son, Jesus Christ," in the Spirit-inspired confession, "Jesus Christ has come in the flesh" (4:2), and in the community's affirmation that "Jesus is the Son of God" (4:15; 5:5; cf. 2:23). Further, it is implied in the opponents' denial that Jesus is the Christ (2:22) and in the refusal of the "spirit of antichrist" to "acknowledge Jesus" (4:3).

To believe that **Jesus is the Christ** is to believe that the one who came in the flesh (John 1:14), the fully human Jesus, is also the divine Son of God (John 20:31), the one who came from heaven (John 13:3; 16:28) as Revealer (John 1:18) and Redeemer (John 3:16–17). The Elder's opponents do not accept this Christology.

Those who do accept and confess it are **born of God**. This description of the community as God's children or **born of God** appeared earlier in 2:29—3:2 and 3:9–10 (cf. 4:4, 6). It serves to differentiate the true Johannine Christians from the children of the devil (3:10; cf. John 8:44), who have seceded (1 John 2:19).

The Elder uses of the concept of **born of God** as a way of showing why it is only logical to love both one's brother and God. The author's point depends on the sense of three forms of the verb *gennaō* in this verse. First, believers in Jesus are described as **born of God** (*ek tou theou gegennētai*, perf. pass.; lit., "has been begotten of God"). Next, God is "the one who begat" (*ton gennēsanta*, aor. act.). Finally, the expression, **his child**, is actually "the one who has been begotten of him" (*ton gegennēmenon ex autou*; perf. pass.). The Elder's point, then, repeats the theme of 4:21 in different words: since every believer has been begotten of God, those who authentically love the one who begat (God) also love the one who has been begotten (one's brother or sister in

Christ). It would not make any sense to do otherwise, to claim to love the father while refusing to love his children. Yet this is precisely what the schismatics do. What Jesus said about husband and wife may also be said of love for God and for one's fellow believer, "What God has joined together, let man not separate" (Mark 10:9).

5:2 / This verse begins with the last of the writer's eight **This is how we know** statements (2:3, 5; 3:16, 19, 24; 4:2, 13). They reassure the readers of their spiritual standing before God (we know him, 2:3; we are in him 2:5; we belong to the truth, 3:19; he lives in us, 3:24; we live in him, 4:16), to discern the presence of the Spirit of God (4:2), and to understand the nature of love (3:16; 5:2).

Specifically in v. 2, the object of our knowledge is **that we love the children of God**. All along the Elder has been urging his readers to love one another (2:10; 3:11, 14, 16, 18, 23; 4:7, 11–12, 21; 5:1), and he has made love for one's brothers and sisters a criterion for distinguishing between his own faithful community and the misbelieving secessionists (2:9, 11; 3:10, 15, 17; 4:8, 20). But how does one know whether one is authentically loving **the children of God** (3:1–2, 10)? A variety of answers from within the epistle is possible: when we "lay down our lives for our brothers" (3:16), by having pity on our brother when he is in need (3:17), when we love "with actions and in truth" (3:18), and when we love like God does (4:10–11). Verse 2 adds: **by** (lit., "whenever," at the same time, we are) **loving God and carrying out his commands**. One test of true Christian love is whether it comes from a heart that loves and is obedient to God. This, of course, is the reverse of the point made in 4:20—5:1, in which authentic love for God is seen in love for God's children, one's fellow believers. The two truths are complementary.

But we should also note that **carrying out his commands** (lit., "doing his commandments"), and not just **loving God**, is the evidence required. We are to "walk in the light" (1:7), keep his commands and obey his word (2:3–5; 3:24), "walk as Jesus did" (2:6), do what is right (2:29; 3:7), purify ourselves (3:3), not keep on sinning (3:9; 5:18), and keep ourselves from idols (5:21). But above all the **commands** of God are to believe in Jesus Christ and to love one another (3:23). There is also a certain circularity in the Johannine thinking about love and obedience (cf. 2 John 5–6).

Those who truly love their comrades in the community will evidence this by a morally consistent and Christ-like character, one of the signs of which is love.

5:3 / In v. 3 the author gives a reason for connecting loving God and keeping God's commands, as he did in v. 2. He argues that **love for God** is expressed in obedience; that is how it is demonstrated. Jesus taught the same: "If you love me, you will obey what I command" (John 14:15); "Whoever has my commands and obeys them, he is the one who loves me" (14:21); "If anyone loves me, he (or she) will obey my teaching" (14:23); and "If you obey my commands, you will remain in my love" (15:10). The proof, perhaps the Elder would even say, the essence (**this is**), of **love for God** is **to obey his commands**. Compare 2 John 6: "And this is love: that we walk in obedience to his commands." It is also the evidence of knowing God (1 John 2:3–5). The Elder believed that the heretical teachers could not produce this evidence of the authenticity of their relationship with God.

The last clause of v. 3 is an encouragement **to obey his commands**: they are not **burdensome** (lit., "heavy, difficult," *bareiai*). Similarly, the yoke of Jesus (in contrast to the heavy yoke of the Torah), which disciples are called to take upon them, is "easy and my burden is light" (Matt. 11:30). The "teachers of the law and the Pharisees" (Matt. 23:2), in contrast, were accused of putting heavy (*barea*) loads upon the people's shoulders, while being unwilling to help them (Matt. 23:4). **His commands**—the writer always has primarily in mind the love command—**are not burdensome**, because he strengthens us to carry them out, by his power (Phil. 4:13) and by his love (1 John 4:7, 19).

5:4a / Directly continuing the thought of v. 3, the first clause of v. 4 gives the Elder's reason for considering God's commands not to be a heavy burden to the believer: **everyone born of God overcomes the world**. The description of the Christian as **born of God** (lit., "the one having been born from God," *to gegennēmenon ek tou theou*) recalls v. 1. Membership in God's family means having become God's children by God's will (John 1:12–13). The power of the new birth is present within them as they seek to "obey his commands." Indeed, the neuter phrase "everyone begotten by God" points to the quality and inherent power of everyone who is **born of God** (Brown, *Epistles*, pp. 541–42). Doing what is right (2:29), not continuing to practice sin (3:9;

5:18), and loving one another (4:7) also arise out of the power of the new birth. What would be impossible in their own strength is "not burdensome" for those **born of God**.

Indeed, so powerful is the reality of the new birth that the believer (with the community of which the Christian is a part) **overcomes the world**. Here, **the world** is that hostile environment in which the Johannine Christians live, but which they are not of (John 17:11, 14, 16). Though God loves it (John 3:16), and Christ died for it (1 John 2:2; 4:9, 14), it has rejected and hates both Jesus and the disciples (John 15:18; 17:14; 1 John 3:13). It is where the false prophets, those deceivers and antichrists, went when they seceded from the community (1 John 2:19, 4:1, 3; 2 John 7), and there they found a sympathetic audience who listened to their views (1 John 4:5). Believers **overcome the world** by not loving the world "or anything in the world" (1 John 2:15); instead, they do "the will of God" (2:17) and rely on the Spirit of God who is in them and who "is greater than the one," the spirit of antichrist (4:3) and of falsehood (4:6), ultimately, the evil one (5:19), "who is in the world" (4:4). Like Jesus (John 16:33: "Take heart! I have overcome the world"), and because his Spirit is in them (4:13), they too have **overcome** (lit., "conquered," *nika*) **the world**.

The next section of 1 John, beginning with v. 4b, leaves the themes of love and obedience (4:19—5:4a) and emphasizes faith and Christology (5:4b–12).

Additional Notes   §12

4:19 / After **we love** some ancient MSS add either the word "God" (Sinaiticus and some versions) or "him" (K and L, ninth century, and the Byzantine witnesses). But they are attempts to improve the original reading, the absolute **we love**, as well witnessed by Alexandrinus, Vaticanus, and the Vulgate. See Metzger, *Commentary*, p. 714.

4:20 / For the opponents as liars, see 1:6; 2:4, 21–22; and cf. 1:8, 10; 2:26; 3:7; 4:1, 6c; 5:10; John 8:44, 55; see also Stott, *Letters*, p. 173.

On the superior attestation of **cannot love**, see Metzger, *Commentary*, p. 715. This reading is witnessed by Sinaiticus and Vaticanus over Alexandrinus, K, and L.

5:3 / On v. 3c, cf. Deut. 30:11–14; Philo, *Spec. Laws*, 1.55, 299. Herm. *Man.* 12.4: "those who have the Lord in their hearts can also be the lord of . . . every one of these commandments. But to those who have the Lord only on their lips, but their hearts are hardened, and who are far from the Lord, the commandments are hard and difficult."

5:4a / The 1984 edition of the NIV changed "has overcome" to **overcomes** to reflect the Greek text more accurately.

§13 *Faith in Jesus and the Testimony of God (1 John 5:4b–12)*

This section of 1 John opens with a celebration of victorious faith (v. 4b), describes that faith in relation to Jesus (vv. 5–6a), and undergirds it with teaching about the testimony of the Spirit (vv. 6b–8) and of God (vv. 9–11). Faith in that testimony has eternal consequences (v. 12).

5:4b / In the author's typical style, **overcoming the world** is the "link concept" between the previous passage (4:19—5:4a) and the new one. On the meaning of **overcoming the world**, see the comment on 5:4a above. The Elder begins with an announcement, a joyful proclamation: **This is the victory** that has conquered **the world**. Victory (*nikē*, the only time this noun occurs in the feminine form in the NT) comes from the same root as **overcome**, *nikaō*. It emphasizes "the means for winning a victory," such as an emperor's power that causes him to be victorious (BAGD, p. 538). So in 5:4b, the Elder implies that **our faith** is the power that has enabled believers to defeat the evil assault of the **world**. The tense of **overcome** in v. 4b is aorist; the victory of the believing community (**our faith**) was decisively accomplished in its rejection of the false teachers. In vv. 4a and 5 the same verb is used in the present tense, since the victory, once won, must be continuously realized as new attacks occur (Stott, *Letters*, p. 177).

Our faith could be understood as an abstract noun meaning "Christianity," or "the content of what we believe," and there can be no doubt that the content of faith is crucial for the author. His emphasis here certainly also includes the act of believing or trust, as both the verb in v. 5b and the importance of accepting/believing God's testimony in vv. 9–10 show. It is the fact that the community actively believes God's testimony concerning the identity of his Son that enables it to **overcome the world** and the schismatic false teachers who have gone out into it (2:19; 4:1;

2 John 7). For the Elder, believing and the right, or orthodox, content of belief are inseparable.

5:5 / The relationship between belief and the right content of belief is also evident in v. 5. The question with which the verse begins focuses on the person **who** conquers or defeats **the world**. That spiritually victorious individual is the one who presently and continuously **believes that** (note the emphasis on **that**, not on "believing in") **Jesus is the Son of God.** Both the activity of faith and its object are included. This christological affirmation recalls others in 1 John. Jesus is "his Son" (1:3, 7; 3:23; 4:10, 14; 5:9–11, 20), "his one and only Son" (4:9), "the Son" (2:22–24; 5:12), "the Son of God" (3:8; 5:10, 12–13, 20), and "Jesus is the Christ" (2:22; 5:1). And it is identical to the confession in 4:15. For Johannine Christians **Jesus** as **the Son of God** implies a great deal: his divine nature (John 3:16, 18; 5:18; 10:30; 1 John 4:9), his being born of God (1 John 5:18), his preexistence (John 3:17; 10:36; 17:3, 5; 1 John 4:9–10, 14; cf. John 8:58), his union with the Father (John 3:35; 5:16–23; 10:30; 1 John 2:23), and, in fact, his deity (John 1:18; 1 John 5:20; cf. John 5:18; 10:33).

The emphasis in nearly all of the christological statements in 1 John falls on the name **Jesus**. The primary issue between the Elder and the false teachers who seceded is whether the human, "come in the flesh" (4:2; 2 John 7) **Jesus** is the same person as the divine **Son of God.** To confess that **Jesus is the Son of God** is to possess a faith that **overcomes the world**. This kind of faith clearly separates one from the heretical opposition which denies and rejects **Jesus** (2:22–23; 4:3; 2 John 7; cf. 3:1; 5:10).

5:6 / Again, the Elder emphasizes the human name **Jesus Christ. This is the one** of whom he is writing, a specific, historical human being. He describes him in a way that the gnostically inclined opponents would have found repugnant, as **the one who came by water and blood.** Some MSS substitute "spirit" for **blood**, in order to make this verse more parallel with John 3:5; other MSS just add "spirit" to **water and blood**, but **water and blood** alone is well attested and is surely the original reading (Metzger, *Commentary*, pp. 715–16).

Understanding the text's meaning has been a more difficult problem. **Came by** refers either to Jesus' incarnation or to the whole course of his earthly life as one sent from God. **Water** may point to his birth or his baptism, or to the **water** that flowed from his side on the cross. **Blood** may refer to his death on the cross or to the "sacrament" of the Lord's Supper. The pair of terms, **water and blood**, then, (a) may be sacramental, including both baptism and the Eucharist, (b) may comprise the whole of Jesus' earthly ministry, from his birth or baptism to his death, or (c) may both refer to his death, when **water and blood** came from his wounded side (John 19:34).

While we cannot know fully what was in the author's mind, the clues contained in the rest of v. 6 and in the Fourth Gospel incline toward some form of solution (b). Clearly, in the remainder of v. 6, the Elder is arguing against his opponents, who could affirm that the Son of God, the **Christ, came by water only**. They denied that the divine Son of God, the **Christ, came by blood** as well. While **water** can refer to birth (one possible interpretation of John 3:5–6), it is more likely a reference to Jesus' baptism (John 1:29–34; the event itself is never narrated in John's Gospel due to the continuing conflict with disciples of John the Baptist). One early Christian tradition identifies the opponents of the Elder with Cerinthus and his followers, who believed that "the Christ" came upon Jesus at this baptism but left him before the cross. They denied that the divine Christ could be truly human or suffer. Both the Elder and his secessionist adversaries accepted that the baptism of Jesus, **the water**, witnessed to his being "the Son of God" (John 1:34), but the Elder, and emerging orthodox Christianity with him, against the schismatic heretics, also affirmed that the Son of God **came by**, i.e., was divinely and savingly present through, his suffering and death on the cross, **the blood**.

To this **the Spirit testifies**. In the Fourth Gospel, **the Spirit** came down upon Jesus at his baptism, confirming to John the Baptist that "this is the Son of God" (John 1:32–34). At the cross, "the disciple whom he loved" saw the flow of blood and water from the side of Jesus and testified to it, "and we know that his testimony is true," just as the Elder now emphasizes that **the Spirit is the truth** (John 19:34–35). This suggests that the Johannine community understood **the Spirit** to be giving testimony through the beloved disciple (Brown, *Epistles*, pp. 579–80). Note also that **testifies** is in the present tense, implying that the witness of **the Spirit** was not merely historical, in relation to Jesus' career, but is ongoing, in relation to the life of the believing community, in fulfillment of Jesus' promise in John 15:26, "he will testify about me." The **Spirit** is "the anointing" which teaches the community all things, just as Jesus promised that "the Spirit of truth" would do (John 14:17, 26; 1 John 4:6). The Johannine writings consider all three persons of the Trinity, to use a phrase from later theology, to be **the truth** (God, John 4:24; Jesus, John 14:6; the Spirit, 1 John 5:6).

5:7–8 / The **For** with which v. 7 begins shows the direct connection with v. 6. Jesus came by **water** and **blood**, and the **Spirit** testifies to this. That means **there are** really **three that testify**. There is no reason to interpret the significance of the three neuter nouns any differently than in v. 6. **The water and the blood** denote Jesus' baptism and his death, the beginning and the end of his public ministry. To these saving, historical events **the Spirit** bore and bears witness. See the exegesis of v. 6. A minor motif here may be the requirement of the Jewish law for "two or three witnesses" to attest the truth (cf. Matt. 18:16; cf. Deut. 19:15). All three witnesses, **in agreement** (lit., "the three are unto the one"), point to Jesus and to his authentic identity as the Son of God and the Christ (vv. 5–6), in contradiction to the false teachers, who, while claiming to speak by **the Spirit** (4:1, 3), and perhaps also affirming the testimony of his baptism to his Sonship, denied the witness of **the blood** of the cross, which testimony **the Spirit** confirms (v. 6b). The witness of **the Spirit** may be mentioned first in the list of **three**, because it is through **the Spirit** that the community of faith recognizes the truth (v. 6) about Jesus (John 14:26).

The AV contains the following words which are not in any of the early MSS of the NT. They appeared first in some copies of the Old Latin version in the fourth century, probably as a marginal note which later found its way into the text. The added words, following **testify** (NIV; "bear record," AV) are: "in heaven, the Father, the Word, and the Holy Ghost, and these three are one. And there are three that bear witness in earth. . . ." None of the best MSS of the letters of John include these words. All modern translations omit them or note that they are not original. See Metzger, *Commentary*, pp. 716–18.

5:9 / Verse 9 begins a section (vv. 9–11) on **the testimony of God** concerning **his Son**. The NIV solves an awkward Greek construction by eliminating the first word of v. 9, "if." Literally, this verse reads, "If the testimony of people (*tōn anthrōpōn*) we are accepting, the testimony of God is greater, because this is the testimony of God which he has testified concerning his Son." The author's point is logical, a form of the *a fortiori* argument: God is greater than his creation, humanity; therefore, if **we accept** human **testimony** about something, we ought also, or perhaps instead, to accept God's. A secondary implied argument is that **God's testimony** is **testimony** concerning his own **Son**; therefore, it deserves higher, or perhaps sole, priority.

What human testimony does the author have in mind? One clue is that it is testimony which **we** are **accept**ing. In John 19:34–35 "the disciple whom Jesus loved" (cf. John 19:26) saw and gave testimony to the flow of blood and water from Jesus' side. "His testimony is true," and "he knows that he tells the truth, and he testifies that you may believe," the editor/author of the Fourth Gospel says to the reader. The Johannine community itself was founded upon the witness and work of the beloved disciple. The community says of him in John 21:24: "This is the disciple who testifies to these things and who wrote them down. We know that his testimony is true." Clearly, the Johannine Christians, including the Elder, **accept the testimony of** the beloved disciple. Yet even his reliable **testimony** is not to be compared with **the testimony of God**, a witness given concerning **his** own **Son**.

What does the author mean by **God's testimony**? It is **testimony** which has already been given and which continues in force (the tense of the verb *martyreō* is perfect). Yet while the divine **testimony** has a past referent (what God has already said through the Spirit, the Paraclete, cf. vv. 6–7), it also looks forward in this passage to vv. 10–11 which explicitly explicate **God's testimony**.

Behind this passage, to which it is the background, is John 5:31–47, a discourse of Jesus concerning valid testimony to his identity. John the Baptist (vv. 33–35), Jesus' own work (v. 36), the Father (vv. 37–38), the Scriptures (v. 39), and Moses (vv. 45–46) are all witnesses to his identity and authority.

5:10 / Verse 10 continues the subject of God's testimony begun in v. 9 and focuses on the human response to it. The passage contains three comparisons. First, the one **who believes** is contrasted, in typically Johannine antithetical style, with the one **who does not believe**. Second, there is a comparison of the objects of belief and of unbelief. The Elder contrasts believing in (*pisteuōn eis*) **the Son of God** with not believing (*mē pisteuōn tō*)

God. Whereas we might have expected the contrast to be identical, instead, the author goes beyond the simple contrast to draw out its implication: the opposite of believing in **the Son of God** is not just denying the Son, but it is really unbelief in **God**.

Third is the comparison of consequences. For the one **who believes in the Son of God**, that person **has this** (lit. "the") **testimony in his heart** (lit., "in himself"). The **testimony** is the witness of God "about his Son," just spoken of in v. 9. For the one **who does not believe God**, the result is that such a person **has made** God **a liar**. The same charge was leveled in 1:10 against those who claimed "we have not sinned." Clearly, the Elder has his opponents in mind in both places, and he elsewhere calls them liars in 2:4, 2:22, and 4:20 (cf. also 1:6; 2:21, 27). The last element of the "logic" of v. 10 is the writer's reason for claiming that the unbeliever **has made him** (God) **out to be a liar**: it is **because he has not believed** (lit., "has not believed in"; *ou pepisteuken eis*) **the testimony God has given** (lit., "has testified") **about his Son**.

The author claims, in v. 10, that people who believe in the Son of God, which includes the belief that the Son of God is Jesus (5:5b), have in themselves God's testimony about his Son. This testimony includes the witness of the Spirit in vv. 6–7, but it primarily looks ahead to v. 11, where the content of God's testimony is stated explicitly. Those who believe in God's Son are inwardly assured by God's Spirit that their faith is justified, that the one to whom they have committed themselves in faith is trustworthy, that they were "right to trust in Christ" (Stott, *Letters*, p. 184). The Elder's opponents, denying what God has said about his Son, Jesus, miss God's inward confirming testimony and remain "in the darkness" (1:6; 2:9, 11).

5:11 / What is **the testimony** of God, which the writer has spoken of since v. 9? It is "testimony . . . about his Son" (vv. 9c, 10c). It certainly includes the idea that the Son of God is Jesus (v. 5), the one who came by both water and blood (vv. 6–8), which statements his opponents, the secessionists, deny. But the principal proposition in God's testimony concerns the connection between **his Son** and **life**. **This is the testimony** presents the content of God's witness, though, of course, it is not the whole content of what God has said concerning Jesus.

The testimony is contained in two closely linked affirmations: **God has given us eternal life**, and **this life is in his Son**. In 1 John 1:2 and 5:20 "his Son, Jesus Christ" is called **eternal life** (*zōēn aiōnion*). In 2:25, **eternal life** is what God has promised to those who acknowledge the Son (2:23) and remain faithful. "No murderer has eternal life in him," but those who love their brothers and sisters "have passed from death to life" (3:14–15; cf. John 5:24). In the Johannine writings **eternal life** is a present spiritual reality, the qualitatively different life of the realm of God present in human beings who believe in Jesus. John 17:3 describes it as "that they may know you, the only true God, and Jesus Christ, whom you have sent." It is a gift from God (also from Jesus, John 10:28; 17:2); in fact, v. 11 speaks of it as **given** (*edōken*, aorist) at a definite time in the past, undoubtedly in the "Christ event." Yet it also continues to be **given** in the present in response to faith in Jesus. It is **given**, the Elder says, to **us**, i.e., to those who have remained in the community of the faithful, not to the secessionists; they have not remained (1 John 2:19, 23–27), and they do not have eternal life (1 John 3:14–15).

The second part of the content of God's testimony is the connection between the **life** and the **Son**: **this life is in his Son** (cf. John 1:4; 5:26). It is **in the Son** for two reasons: because the **Son** is **life** (1 John 1:2; 5:20; John 11:25; 14:6), as are his words (John 6:63, 68). He also is "the bread of life" (John 6:35, 48), and, as "the light of the world," he is "the light of life" (John 8:12). **Eternal life** is also **in the Son**, because it is through faith in the **Son** (or by coming to him, John 5:40; or by looking to him, 6:40; or by eating his flesh and drinking his blood, 6:54) that one receives the gift of **life** (cf. 2:25; John 3:15–16, 36; 6:47; 20:31). God's free gift of an eternally right relationship with God is inseparable from knowing and trusting Jesus Christ.

5:12 / Having spelled out the nature and content of God's testimony about his Son in vv. 9–11, the Elder in v. 12 makes clear the personal implications, positive and negative, of God's decision to tie the gift of life to **the Son**. They are absolutely antithetical:

has	the Son	has	life
not have	**the Son of God**	**not have**	**life.**

The concept of "having the Son" (v. 12; 2 John 9), "having the Father" (2:23; 2 John 9), or "having God" (2 John 9) is unique in the NT. It connotes a close and secure relationship with God, but it also dangerously borders on possessing God for one's own purposes, including polemic against one's opponents. The idea of "having God" did occur in the intertestamental writings as a way of expressing the covenantal confidence of the Jewish people (see 3 Macc. 7:16; T. Dan 5:2).

In the letters of John, **the Son** is the single term of God's covenant with his people, so that one's relationship with him is decisive, both for one's relationship with God and for whether one has or is bereft of eternal life. The same point is made in equally antithetical terms in John 3:36:

> "Whoever believes in the Son has eternal life,
> but whoever rejects the Son will not see life,
> for God's wrath remains on him."

Note that in v. 12 the writer uses **Son** and **Son of God** synonymously. The second title reminds the readers that **the Son** and **life** both come from God.

Additional Notes   §13

5:4b / The link concepts in other passages are: "Son of God" and "life" in 5:12–13, "love" in 4:18–19, "living" in 4:12–13, "from God" in 4:6–7, "spirit" in 3:24—4:1, "truth" in 3:18–19, "love" in 3:10–11, "remain . . . continue" in 2:27–28, and the end of the age in 2:17–18. New sections clearly begin at 1:5, 2:3, and 2:12 without the use of linking ideas or phrases.

5:6 / A full discussion of the various alternative interpretations of this verse may be found in Brown, *Epistles*, pp. 575–78.

5:7–8 / See Brown, *Epistles*, pp. 581–85 for a thorough discussion of the history of exegesis of this passage and a comprehensive presentation of "The Johannine Comma," the additional words added to some early Latin MSS that made their way into the AV; "Appendix IV: The Johannine Comma," *Epistles*, pp. 775–87.

5:9 / Brown argues (*Epistles*, p. 586) that the human testimony in the Elder's mind is that of John the Baptist, to which the secessionists are appealing. While that is certainly possible, and John's testimony is one of the witnesses to whom Jesus' refers in John 5:33–35, much more directly stated in the Johannine writings is the witness of the Spirit through the testimony of the beloved disciple. In this passage, the author is not attacking the secessionists as much as he is reminding his readers of both human and divine witnesses to Jesus as the Christ and the Son of God.

On the concept of "witness" in the NT, see L. Coenen and A. Trites, "Witness," *NIDNTT* vol. 3, pp. 1038–51; A. A. Trites, *The New Testament Concept of Witness* (Cambridge: Cambridge University, 1977), and J. M. Boice, *Witness and Revelation in the Gospel of John* (Grand Rapids: Zondervan, 1970).

5:10 / The variation in the use of the Greek prepositions with the verb for **believe** does not yield any difference in meaning. It is typical of this author to vary his style of writing with no significance to the variation; Brown, *Epistles*, p. 589.

This verse, along with the rest of 5:6–11, John 15:26, and Rom. 8:16, formed the basis for the Reformation teaching on "the internal witness of the Holy Spirit." Though the Reformers came to associate the witness of the Spirit with the authority of Scripture as God's Word, the passage in 1 John does not do so, but emphasizes God's witness in the believer concerning Jesus. On the "witness of the Spirit," see G. W. Bromiley, *ISBE*, vol. 4, pp. 1087–88.

5:11 / On the Johannine concept of eternal life, see Ladd, *Theology*, pp. 254–69; Schnackenburg, "The Idea of Life in the Fourth Gospel," *Gospel*, vol. 2, pp. 352–61; Brown, *Gospel, I–XII*, pp. 505–8; O. Piper, "Life," *IDB*, vol. 3, pp. 124–30; Dodd, *Interpretation*, pp. 144–50.

For an alternative view of God's **testimony**, see Marshall, *Epistles*, p. 242 and Smalley, *1, 2, 3 John*, p. 287.

§14 Assured by the Certainties of Faith (1 John 5:13–21)

The Elder concludes his message of exhortation to the remaining faithful members of his community by assuring them of several certainties of the Christian life, with regard to possessing eternal life (13), asking and interceding in prayer (14–17), not sinning (18), being God's children in an evil world (19), and knowing Jesus Christ, the true God (20). In the light of these great realities comes a final warning (21).

5:13 / Continuing his style of linking the beginning of a new section with the end of the previous one (see the note on 5:4b), the writer carries over the concepts of **eternal life** and the title, **the Son of God**, into his concluding statement of purpose for writing this letter. **I write** (lit., "I wrote"; *egrapsa*, an example of the epistolary aorist; see also 2:13c, 14, 21, 26) forms an *inclusio* with "we write" of 1:4: just as the latter looks forward to the entire epistle, so **I write** looks back on the whole of it. Verse 13 bears a close resemblance to the concluding statement of purpose in the Gospel of John, 20:31: "But these are written that you may believe that Jesus is the Christ, the Son of God, and that by believing you may have life in his name." Both verses come at the end of their document (chap. 21 of the Gospel is an epilogue), state a purpose for writing, use the demonstrative pronoun "these things," address the need for continuing faith on the part of those who are already Christians, use the title **Son of God** in describing faith's object, and assure the readers of having **eternal life** through faith in his **name**.

Against the dark backdrop of the denial of Jesus (2:22–23; 4:2–3; 2 John 7), of schism within the community (1 John 2:19; 2 John 7–11), and of claims to superior spirituality by these secessionist false teachers (1:6, 8, 10; 2:4, 6, 9; 4:10a, 20a), the Elder has written to assure his readers (**that you may know**) of their abiding spiritual inheritance: they have **eternal life**. They have it now (3:14; cf. John 5:24), based on God's gift of **eternal life** in his **Son** (5:11). To **believe in . . . the Son** is to "have the Son" (5:11–12); to "have the Son" is to **have eternal life**. **The name** is the person and the authority associated with that person. See 2:12 ("your sins have been forgiven on account of his name") and 1 John's "summary verse," 3:23.

5:14 / Continuing the theme of assurance, the writer addresses **the confidence we have**. Confidence (*parrēsia*) was his theme in 2:28, 3:21, and 4:17. In 2:28 it was **confidence** before Christ at his coming (*parousia*); in 3:21 it was the **confidence** before God which leads to expectant prayer, and in 4:17 it was **confidence** with respect to another eschatological event, God's judgment. **In approaching God** translates the phrase *pros auton* (lit., "toward him," or "in his presence"). That the "him" refers to God is not readily apparent, since "the Son of God" is the closest referent. The NIV also adds the word "God" at 5:16, where the Greek has only the verb *dōsei*, "he will give." But that God is intended is likely, given that the subject is prayer, the parallel passages using *pros ton patera* (before the Father) in 1:2, 2:1 (cf. 3:21: *pros ton theon*, before God), and that **his will** later in v. 14 is best understood as God's will (cf. 2:17).

The content of the **confidence** is expressed in the rest of v. 14 and in v. 15. It is the assurance that our prayers are heard and fulfilled, when they are in accordance with God's will. First, the Elder says that God **hears us** ("listens to us"; *akouei hēmōn*), i.e., God listens with approval, when we **ask anything according to his will**. There are two points to consider here. **Anything** may be asked. This is emphasized in v. 15's "whatever we ask." There are no restrictions on the community's (**we, us**) supplications and intercessions.

Secondly, we must ask **according to his will**. That is the only condition attached to this momentous promise, and it is the general condition of all prayer. "Your will be done" was not only in Jesus' teaching model of prayer (Matt. 6:9–13), it was a condition to which he subjected himself (Matt. 26:39, 42; John 4:34; 5:30; 6:38–40). In the Gospel of John prayer must be in Jesus' name (14:13–14; 15:16; 16:21–24, 26), and the praying disciples must abide in Jesus and his words in them (15:7). In 1 John 3:21–22, prayer is answered because "we obey his commands and do what pleases him." The commands are then defined as believing in his name and loving one another (3:23). All of these are ways of describing what it means to pray **according to** God's **will**. This condition is not meant to deter prayer (except selfish prayer) but to encourage it! God will do what we ask in good faith.

5:15 / Verse 15 constitutes the second half of the "confidence" expressed in v. 14. Literally, the difficult conditional sentence reads, "And if we know that he hears us, whatever we ask, we know that we have the things asked which we have asked from him." The first clause of v. 15 refers back to the assurance of v. 14 that prayers prayed according to God's will are prayers heard. The next step, then, is the assurance that prayers heard are indeed prayers answered. The writer adds **whatever we ask** as an encouragement to prayer and to establish even more firmly the readers' shaky confidence (note the double **we know**) in the face of the secessionists' assaults. No subject, inside God's will, need be excluded. The Elder says **we have** (not "we will have") **what we asked** him for. The realization of our prayer has already begun when we have asked in faith for something, no matter what it is, that is God's will for us. This is the uniform testimony of the New Testament (e.g., Matt. 7:7; 18:19; 21:22; John 14:13–14; 15:7; 16:23–24; Jas. 1:5–8; 4:2–3; 5:16b; 1 John 3:22).

5:16 / The theme of prayer continues in vv. 16–17, but now the author treats a specific issue, or perhaps a question, that has arisen in the Johannine fellowship in view of the schism (2:19): should we pray for our brothers who practice sin? That the writer first thinks of *intercessory* prayer after his encouragement to pray in vv. 14–15 demonstrates the unselfish nature of true prayer. Authentic prayer reaches out to others in their need; it does not primarily grasp for things for oneself. The most serious problem affecting the community is the split between those who have remained loyal to the Elder and his teaching and those who have followed the false teachers and seceded. How does one pray in this situation?

The Elder's answer is that one **should pray** (lit., "she/he will pray") if one happens to **see** (aorist tense) a **brother** or sister "sinning a sin" (lit.) "not unto death" (*mē pros thanaton*). The sin must be obvious or visible. It may also be habitual, as the use of the present tense suggests, and it must be only **for those whose**

sin does not lead [or has not already led] **to death**. The NIV
translation implies the phrase "not unto death" means **a sin** that
does not lead to death, but it may also mean "a sin that has not
led to death." The issue of when the **death** occurs is not resolved
in the phrase itself, but the Elder's refusal to authorize prayer for
those whose sin is unto death (v. 16cd) suggests that he thinks of
the death as having already occurred. Like the author of Hebrews, he may believe that it is impossible for them, "if they fall
away, to be brought back to repentance" (Heb. 6:4–6; cf. Heb.
3:12–19; 6:1–8; 10:26–31).

The matter of primary importance is prayer for one's err-
ing colleague in the community. Such a prayer, the author believes, is clearly according to God's will, and it will be heard and
answered. **God** (lit., "he") **will give him life**. The NIV's insertion
of **God** is an interpretation, since it is believed that the Elder
would not say that Christians, through their prayers for each
other, give **life** to each other. But the latter is the most natural
translation of the Greek text and is not invalid within Johannine
theology, provided that one understands that God is the source
and giver of life by means of the prayers of one's co-members in
the community.

The thorniest question of interpretation in this passage has
been the meaning of the phrase *mē* (v. 17 has *ou*) *pros thanaton*,
"not unto death." To what is the author referring? There have
been several alternatives in the history of the understanding of
these verses. Some think that the main distinction is between
serious and less serious sins, between so-called mortal and venial
sins (a distinction from later moral theology), or between deliberate and unintentional sins (an ethical distinction from Judaism
not made elsewhere in the Johannine writings). Others raise the
possibility that "sin unto death" means sins whose result is the
actual physical death of those who had sinned (e.g., Ananias and
Sapphira in Acts 5:1–11; cf. 1 Cor. 11:29–30). In this case the writer
would be prohibiting prayers for the dead (Bruce, *Epistles*, pp.
124–25), but this seems unlikely.

More possible is the understanding that the Elder is referring to the apostasy from the community of those who had been
believers. They now rejected the faith in Jesus, God's Son, which
they had formerly espoused (Plummer, *Epistles*, p. 122; Dodd,
Epistles, p. 136). They have committed the unpardonable sin (cf.
Matt. 12:32; Luke 12:9–10) of blaspheming against the Spirit's

witness to the full humanity and deity of Jesus. They used to be true Christians; now they are not (cf. Heb. 6:4–6; 10:26–29). The problem with this solution is that the Elder thinks of his opponents as never having been true members of the community (2:19: "They went out from us, but they did not really belong to us. . . . their going showed that none of them belonged to us").

It is more probable that the real distinction in vv. 16–17 is the same distinction we have observed all along in 1 John (and which continues in 2–3 John), i.e., between the Elder's faithful followers, who "believe in the name of [God's] Son, Jesus Christ, and . . . love one another" (3:23) and the antichrist, false prophet, secessionist, worldly, lying and deceiving children of the devil, who deny Jesus and hate their brothers (2:18–19, 22–23; 3:10, 15; 4:1–3, 5; 2 John 7). The Elder never states that a **brother** commits a "sin unto death," only the sin "not unto death." **There is a sin that leads** [or has led] **to death**, and it is that sin, i.e., rejection of Jesus as God's Son, the Christ, that the schismatics have committed. The author holds out no hope of effective prayer for them.

5:17 / Completing the discussion of prayer for those who have sinned, the Elder reminds his readers that all sin is to be taken seriously, a point he has made repeatedly from the beginning (1:6—2:2; 3:4–10; 5:16–18). The Johannine community does not take sin lightly. **All wrongdoing is sin**, and it should not seem less significant because it can be prayed for and forgiven (v. 16ab). This encouragement to pray for **all wrongdoing** applies, of course, only to **sin that does not lead** [or has not already led] **to death** (see the discussion on v. 16 above).

5:18 / In v. 18 the author resumes affirming his concluding list of certainties of the Christian life (v. 13: "that you may know"; v. 14: "the confidence we have"; v. 15: "we know . . . we know"; v. 16: "he will pray and will give him life"; v. 18: **we know**; v. 19: "we know"; v. 20: "we know" and "we are in him"). By these he intends to end his message of exhortation on a note of assurance and encouragement.

The principal assurance in v. 18 is this: true Christians do not keep on sinning. Perhaps he felt the need to reemphasize this teaching in view of his admitting in vv. 16–17 that a "brother" or sister can commit sins which are "not unto death." In 1 John 3:3, 9 the Elder based his argument that authentic Christians do not practice sin on their close personal relationship (abiding in him) with Christ (3:6) and on the fact that the new birth or new nature makes continuing in sin an impossibility (3:9). Here his argument is similar: the term **born of God**, *ho gegennēmenos ek tou theou*, as a description of the child of God, occurs in both verses, and the relationship with Christ is again decisive. But the Christian's victory over sin is given a new setting: the cosmic-moral battle between Christ (**the one who was born of God**, *ho gennētheis ek tou theou*) and Satan (**the evil one**). This description of Christ is unique in the Johannine literature, though the verb *gennaō* is used of Christ in John 18:37. The writer has changed his verb tenses to make clear the distinction between the Christian (perf. pass. ptcp.) and Christ (aor. pass. ptcp.). This is much more preferable than the view that both verbs refer to the Christian, with the result that the Christian keeps himself. In Johannine theology, it is Jesus who keeps the believer (John 17:11–12, 15). The alternative view would also require the pronoun to be the reflexive "himself" (*heauton*), rather than **him** (*auton*; a later reading in the Greek MSS did introduce the reflexive pronoun; see Metzger, *Commentary*, p. 719).

The practice of sin as a way of life (*hamartanei*, present tense) is ruled out, because the Son of God protects Christians or **keeps** them **safe**. That is, as the remainder of the verse explains, Christ guards his followers from the attack of **the evil one**, the personification of all of the spiritual forces which oppose God (cf. John 17:15; 1 John 2:13–14; 3:12; 5:19). **Harm** is literally "touch, or lay hold of" (*haptomai*; cf. John 10:28: "No one can snatch them [My sheep] out of my hand"). The Elder has already told his readers that "greater is He who is in you than he who is in the world" (NASB; 1 John 4:4b), a reference to "the spirit of antichrist" (4:3).

5:19 / As with vv. 18 and 20, this verse begins with **We know** (*oidamen*), a verb of affirmation and assurance. The certainty here is that the loyal followers of the Elder truly belong to God (lit., "we are of God," *ek tou theou esmen*, cf. 4:4, 6; NIV: **we are children of God**), no matter what the secessionists might be saying about them or what claims the false teachers were making for themselves. The schismatic false prophets, the "deceivers, who do not acknowledge Jesus Christ as coming in the flesh" (2 John 7), "have gone out into the world" (4:1; 2 John 7), where the "spirit of antichrist" is (4:3). In fact, they are now "of the world" (*ek tou kosmou*), in contrast with the readers who are "from God" (4:4, 6;

ek tou theou). But **the world** is a spiritually dangerous place to be, because **the whole world is under the control of** (lit., "lies in," *keitai*) **the evil one**; cf. John 12:31.

Just as in v. 18, where Christ keeps the believer safe from harm in the battle with the evil one, so in v. 19 the antithetical conflict continues between opposing spiritual forces. The two sides are delineated: **we**, the **children of God**, and **the whole world**, which lies in Satan's **control**. Despite the facts that Jesus is "the atoning sacrifice . . . for the sins of the whole world" (2:2), that "the Father sent his Son to be the Savior of the world" (4:14), and that God loved the world (John 3:16), the world has rejected Jesus (John 1:10; 15:18) and his followers (John 15:18–19; 1 John 3:13). Therefore, Christians are not to "love the world or anything in the world" (2:15), because "everything in the world . . . comes not from the Father but from the world" (2:16). The Johannine community's view of their relation to **the world** was, sociologically speaking, sectarian.

5:20 / The Elder continues elucidating the concluding certainties of faith with which he encourages his dear community in crisis. Verse 20 contains several such assurances. It begins with the writer's familiar **We know** (*oidamen*), which occurs five times in vv. 15–20 (also 3:2, 14). What **we know** are theological and experiential truths which have been challenged by the separatists. First, **the Son of God has come** (*hēkei*). The secessionists denied that Jesus was **the Son of God**. (On **Son of God** in 1 John see the commentary and notes on 1:3, 7; 2:22–24; 3:8, 23; 4:9–10, 14–15; 5:5, 9–13; 2 John 3, 9.) They believed that the divine **Son of God** could not have taken on flesh and blood in the person of Jesus (4:2; 2 John 7), which is why the Elder has repeatedly emphasized Christ's humanity and used his human name, Jesus (1:1–3, 7; 2:1, 6, 22; 3:23; 4:2–3, 10, 15; 5:1, 5–6; 2 John 3, 7). If Jesus was not **the Son of God**, then **the Son of God** has not come, and it is likely that this is what the schismatics had told the remaining Johannine Christians who were loyal to the Elder. The Elder flatly denies it. In John 8:42, Jesus tells his interlocutors, "I proceeded forth [*exēlthon*] and have come [*hēkō*] from God" (NASB).

One result of the coming of God's Son is that he **has given us understanding** (*dianoia*). This is the only occurrence of *dianoia* in the Johannine writings. It was a term widely used by later Gnostics, who claimed a special insight and illumination into spiritual matters. Perhaps in this pre-gnostic period, the opponents of the Elder were already using it in this way. In the LXX it was used to translate the Hb. *qereḇ* and *leḇ*, "inward being" and "heart." "We do have *dianoia*. Jesus gave it to us," the Elder assures his readers, much as he says in 2:20: "You have an anointing from the Holy One, and all of you know" (cf. 2:26–27).

The purpose of this **understanding** is experiential and christological: **that we may know**—in a continuing and progressive way (Westcott, *Epistles*, p. 196)—**him who is true**. Jesus enabled his followers to know God (John 1:14, 18; 14:6–11; 17:2–3, 6, 26; cf. John 8:32; 10:38). That God is meant is seen later in v. 20 where Jesus is called **his Son**. All along the Elder has been assuring his readers that they do know God/Christ (often indistinguishable; 2:3–4, 13–14; 4:7–8; cf. 3:19, 24; 4:2; 5:19). **Him who is true** (*ton alēthinon*), as a substantive adjectival description of God, is unique here, though it occurs elsewhere as an adjective modifying the noun "God" (Isa. 65:16; 3 Macc. 6:18; John 17:3; 1 Thess. 1:9; 1 John 5:20; Rev. 6:10; cf. John 7:28). More often in the NT it describes Jesus (Rev. 3:7, 14; 19:11; John 1:9, the true light; 6:32, the true bread; 15:1, the true vine).

Not only do **we . . . know him who is true**, but **we are in him who is true**. This emphasizes the intimate, saving fellowship that true Johannine Christians enjoy (1:3; 2:5–6, 24; 3:24; 4:13, 15–16; cf. John 17:21), in contrast with the secessionists, who are not **in him** (1:6; 3:6). The NIV introduces the word **even** to suggest that the relationship between the two prepositional phrases, the "in" clauses, is ascensive, as if there were a climactic *kai* between them. Another possibility is that the second clause is modal: it explains how **we are in him who is true**, i.e., by being **in his Son Jesus Christ**.

Verse 20 concludes with the declaration, "This" [NIV, **He**; *houtos*] **is the true God and eternal life**. The referent of the demonstrative pronoun is unclear. Does it refer to all that the author has been saying heretofore about God and Christ (Dodd, *Epistles*, pp. 140–41; Kysar, *I, II, III John*, p. 117)? Such a summary abstraction, while logical to us, is unlike the author. Does it refer to God (Brooke, *Epistles*; Smalley, *1, 2, 3 John*; Stott, *Letters*; Westcott, *Epistles*)? The author has called God **him who is true** twice in this verse, so that the climactic announcement, "This" **is the true God** would be considerably redundant. It is more likely that *houtos* refers to its immediate antecedent, the last named person,

Jesus Christ, as the NIV implies (Brown, *Epistles*; Bruce, *Epistles*; Bultmann, *Epistles*; Culpepper, *1 John*; Marshall, *Epistles*; Schnack-enburg, *Johannine Epistles*; Smith, *First John*; Thompson, *1–3 John*). Elsewhere the Johannine writings call Jesus "God" (John 1:1, 18; 20:28) and treat him as equal with God (e.g., John 5:18; 8:58; 10:30; 14:7–9; 17:11, 22–23). The second predicate of *houtos*, **eternal life**, is also more likely to be a description of Jesus (John 11:25; 14:6; 1 John 1:2). Finally, it is more likely that the Elder would end his exhortation with a resounding affirmation of the full deity of the human Jesus, the key truth denied by the secessionist false teachers, and with the assertion, against them, that to know this Jesus is to have **eternal life** itself (cf. 5:11–13).

5:21 / That the threat of the secessionists and their teaching has been in the Elder's mind all along in this epistle, and especially as he has penned these concluding certainties of the faith, is revealed clearly in the warning with which 1 John ends. For the last time he calls his readers his **Dear children** (*teknia*; 2:1, 12, 28; 3:7, 18; 4:4), a term which Jesus had used for his disciples in John 13:33. The imperative verb for "guard" or **keep** (*phylaxate*) is in the aorist tense, connoting a decisive action, though not necessarily once-for-all, since the need for protecting themselves **from idols** will presumably continue. "We are to 'keep ourselves,' even if the Son of God 'keeps' us" (Smalley, *1, 2, 3 John*, p. 309; cf. 5:18, using *tērei*; cf. Jude 21, 24).

What are the **idols** from which the writer wants his readers to defend themselves? The answer must be sought in the context of 1 John itself, since it is unlikely that the Elder would introduce a warning against pagan idolatry in the last verse of a closely unified exhortation. Westcott defines idolatry as anything which takes the place rightly due to God and sees the warning as against any well-known object of false devotion (*Epistles*, p. 197). But this can be made more contextual: the Elder considers the secessionists' views of God, their "images," especially their rejection of the come-in-the-flesh Jesus as the divine Christ, idolatrous. They are a denial of "him who is true" and of "the true God," even "his Son Jesus Christ" (5:20). This false teaching is not the true faith, taught by Jesus, and preserved for the community by the beloved disciple in the Fourth Gospel.

Additional Notes   §14

5:13 / That **believe**, in John 20:31, refers to continuing faith assumes that *pisteuēte* is the original reading, not *pisteusēte*. The textual evidence is evenly balanced, but the usual use of the present subjunctive with a Johannine *hina* clause (cf. 19:35) and the more likely purpose of the Fourth Gospel as written to strengthen believers makes *pisteuēte* the better choice. See Metzger, *Commentary*, p. 256.

On the significance of "name" in the Johannine writings, see Brown, *Epistles*, pp. 302–3; *Gospel, I–XII*, pp. 754–56.

5:14 / The 1984 edition of the NIV changed "assurance" to **confidence**.

5:16 / The Elder does not actually forbid such prayer, but he has no confidence that it will be heard and answered, in contrast to the confidence he feels about God responding in a life-giving way to all of the other prayers of the believing community (cf. vv. 14–16ab).

On the phrase "not unto death," see D. M. Scholer, "Sins Within and Sins Without: An Interpretation of 1 John 5:16–17," in *Current Issues in Biblical Interpretation*, ed. G. F. Hawthorne (Grand Rapids: Eerdmans, 1975), pp. 230–46.

The best resources for working through the various exegetical problems in this difficult passage are Brown, *Epistles*, pp. 610–19, 635–37; Culpepper, *1 John*, pp. 109–11; Jackman, *Letters*, pp. 162–67; Marshall, *Epistles*, pp. 245–51; Scholer, "Sins," pp. 230–46; Stott, *Letters*, pp. 188–93; and Thompson, *1–3 John*, pp. 140–45.

5:18 / Some interpreters think that *ton gegennēmenon* (NIV, "his child"; lit., "the one having been born") in 1 John 5:1 refers to Jesus rather than to the Christian.

The 1984 edition of the NIV changed "does not touch him" to **cannot harm him**.

5:19 / The core definition of sectarianism involves a strong sense of separation from the world, as well as the conviction that one's community possesses essential truth which others do not have. See Johnson, *Antitheses*, pp. 260–300.

5:20 / On Jesus as God in the NT, see R. E. Brown, *Jesus, God and Man* (New York: Macmillan, 1972); Cullmann, *Christology*, pp. 306–14; Dunn, *Christology*, pp. 258–68; W. Pannenberg, *Jesus—God and Man* (Philadelphia: Westminster, 1968), pp. 115–58; and R. Scroggs, *Christology in Paul and John* (Philadelphia: Fortress, 1988), pp. 63–77.

5:21 / In addition to *teknia*, the Elder has used the similar term *teknon*, pl. *tekna*, to refer to his readers' status as "children of God" (3:1–2, 10; 5:2). In 2 and 3 John he uses *tekna* to refer to the members of the house churches to whom and from whose fellowship he is writing (2 John 1, 4, 13; 3 John 4). The Elder's other terms of familiar address for his community are *paidia* ("children," 2:14, 18), which Jesus also used for his disciples in John 21:5, *adelphoi* ("brothers [and sisters]," 3:13; cf. 3 John 3, 5, 10), which Jesus called his disciples in John 20:17 (cf. 21:23), and *agapētoi* ("beloved ones," 2:7; 3:2, 21; 4:1, 7, 11; 3 John 1, 2, 5, 11). The Elder's usage is based, in part, on Jesus' terms for his disciples in the Fourth Gospel (cf. also 3 John 15 and John 15:14–15).

On the range of possible identifications of **idols** which have been given in the history of interpretation, see Brown, *Epistles*, pp. 627–28. Idolatry may also be related to sin, and this is not far from understanding "idols" as the heretical views of the opponents, since "the sin unto death" of 5:16–17 is disbelief in, or rejection of, Jesus. Sin is also the subject of 5:18, from which "the one who was born of God" keeps the Christian safe. Sin and idolatry are also closely related in the Dead Sea Scrolls (1QS 2:11–12, 16–17; 4:5; 1QH 4:9–11, 15; 4QFlor 1:17).

2 John

§1 Salutation (2 John 1–3)

Second John begins with a greeting or salutation similar in form to other NT letters. The writer and recipients are identified, followed by a wish for God's blessing. But this introduction also contains material that fits the writer's and readers' specific situation and recalls the controversy in which all three letters of John are set. The Elder quickly reveals the two main concerns which are on his mind, and they correspond to the two principal themes of the letters of John as a whole: truth and love.

1 / Instead of his name, the author gives his title: **the elder**. This is the closest we ever come to any identification of the author of these letters (cf. 3 John 1). Literally, **the elder** (*presbyteros*) means "the old man," but it is used here, as in early Christianity generally, for an authoritative teacher and leader, usually, though not always (1 Pet. 5:1), distinguished from an apostle (Acts 15:2, 4, 6, 22–23; 20:17; 1 Tim. 5:17; Titus 1:5; Jas. 5:14). Since he was well known to his readers, he did not need to use his name.

The elder's loving yet commanding tone reveals him as the ruling teacher of a region which included many congregations or house churches. He sent his emissaries to visit them (3 John 5–10), and he himself planned to do so (2 John 12, 3 John 14). We also hear of the schismatic false teachers sending out their traveling representatives to the remaining churches still loyal to the Elder in his territory (2 John 7, 10).

The chosen lady and her children is the author's way of referring to a church and its members. We see this also at the end of the letter in the greeting from **the elder**'s own congregation, whom he calls "the children of your chosen sister." These two house churches are part of the same family of congregations in the same geographical area. They are known as the Johannine community because of their connection with the apostle John (see the section on authorship in the Introduction).

This family is in crisis. They have recently suffered a wrenching schism (1 John 2:19), and **the elder** in these letters calls the remaining members closer together to ward off the threat to their spiritual well-being (2 John 8) and perhaps to their survival. Therefore, he expresses his greeting in terms of **love** and **truth**, the two commitments most essential for their unity and strength. **The elder** and **all who know the truth** love this congregation. Commitment to the **truth** that is being threatened by the schism delimits the circle of **love**, at least in this crisis situation. **Truth** is the sphere which determines who are the real Johannine Christians (as opposed to those false teachers who have left the community) and, therefore, the area in which "brotherly love" is to be exercised. Those **who know the truth** are the remaining members of the community who are agreed on the basic christological doctrine under fire in the schism.

Truth (*alētheia*) occurs five times in the first four verses, a striking redundancy unless the author is deliberately emphasizing it, and that is precisely his intent. He writes to a house church in the midst of a "truth crisis," as was happening throughout the Johannine churches at this time. **Truth** means, generally, the Johannine way of seeing things, but in these letters, it has to do with a most fundamental matter, the identity of Jesus Christ (cf. v. 7; 1 John 2:22; 4:2; 5:1, 5; who is the truth, John 14:6). Because the false teachers pose a threat to its central teaching, the community must close ranks in an intimate fellowship that minimizes the danger of the continuing secession (1 John 2:19; 2 John 8–10). This personal bond that keeps churches in crisis together is **love**.

In the New Testament **love** (*agapē*) is voluntary, self-sacrificing, positive regard for and action on behalf of other people. In the Johannine writings **love** is God's essential nature (1 John 4:8, 16), and it is defined by God's **love** for humanity, especially in the sending of the Son for human redemption (John 3:16; 1 John 4:9–10). That same self-giving **love** is to characterize the relationship among Jesus' disciples: "since God so [in this way] loved us, we also ought to love one another" (1 John 4:11).

2 / Verse 2 gives a reason for the love which the Elder and "all who know the truth" have for "the chosen lady and her children." It is **because of the truth** which they share in common. This verse provides further evidence for the limitation of love in the Johannine epistles to those who have remained, amid the

controversy, loyal disciples of the Elder. It is not that the letters of
John reject the broader concepts of love for neighbor or love for
the enemy; it is, rather, that these more inclusive concepts are not
at issue in the conflict with the secessionists and that the Elder is
concerned to heighten commitment among those who remain.

The truth is described in two ways: it **lives in us**, and it **will
be with us forever**. **Lives** translates the theologically important
Johannine term *menō* (RSV, NASB, "abides"). Not only do faithful
disciples remain in **the truth**, but **the truth** remains in them.
Similarly, Jesus **lives** in the believer, and the believer **lives** in him
(John 15:4, 7). In John 14:17 the Spirit of truth **lives** with the
disciples and will be in them, but the Elder's opponents, who
claim to be without sin, do not have **the truth** in them (1 John
1:8). This "personal **truth**" will continue with the faithful Johannine Christians into eternity. It is one source of their confidence
and spiritual security (cf. 1 John 3:19–24). Note the Elder's identification of himself with his readers, evident in the use of **us** (cf.
vv. 3–6; 1 John 1:3).

3 / **Grace, mercy and peace** are common in salutations
of NT letters. First Timothy 1:2 and 2 Timothy 1:2 have precisely
this trio. But the form of this blessing is unique. Literally, it begins,
"There will be with us grace, mercy, peace. . . ." Only 2 John
(a) uses the phrase **will be with us**, (b) calls **Jesus the Father's Son**,
and (c) delimits the sphere of the blessing as **in truth and love**.

Grace is God's free, unmerited favor to the world and
especially to those who belong to Christ (John 1:14, 16–17). **Mercy**,
unique here in the Johannine literature, is God's forgiving good-
ness, and **peace** (John 14:27; 16:33; 20:19, 21, 26) is the condition
of believers, who have received God's **grace** and **mercy** in Jesus
Christ, who himself has overcome the world.

These blessings come to God's people from **God the Father
and from Jesus Christ, the Father's Son**. The family/relational
terminology and the linking of **Father** and **Son** with the Elder's
community subtly underscore the unity of the loyal Johannine
Christians with God, a point that is elsewhere made explicit
(1 John 4:6).

But how does one come to enjoy these divine blessings?
The Elder says that they **will be with us in truth and love.** The
use of the future tense may imply that not all of the house
churches in the Elder's orbit are actively enjoying God's blessing:

some have joined the schismatics; others are in conflict, perhaps divided about whether to remain with the Elder or to side with the "new wave" (2 John 9) secessionists. The threefold blessing will belong to those who remain **in truth and love**.

In truth, as we have already seen, means "doctrinally correct when it comes to the basic truth about Jesus Christ," i.e., in agreement with the Elder that Jesus Christ is fully human (1 John 4:2; 2 John 7). In **love** means "not part of the secession." Those who left the community (1 John 2:19) broke the **love** command, and thereby demonstrated that they were not really Jesus' disciples, since the latter are to be characterized by **love** for one another (John 13:34–35; 1 John 3:11, 16–18, 23; 4:7, 11, 21). The Elder's community is a fellowship of both **truth and love**. Neither can be minimized; both are at the core of what it means to be Christian. These two concepts are explored further in vv. 4–11.

Additional Notes   §1

---

1 /   2–3 John are the only letters in the NT which do not name their author (Hebrews is not a letter), and 2 John is the only NT letter to use a title for its readers rather than a proper name. On the epistolary form of 2–3 John, see the Introduction and Brown, *Epistles*), pp. 788–95.

On **elder** (*presbyteros*), see L. Coenen, "Bishop, Presbyter, Elder," *NIDNTT*, vol. 1, pp. 192–201, with extensive bibliography; and G. Bornkamm, "*presbys, presbyteros, etc.*," *TDNT*, vol. 6, pp. 651–83.

Metzger, *Commentary*, p. 721, notes that although **chosen lady** (*kyria*) can be a proper name, it is used here metaphorically of a local congregation.

On **truth** in the Johannine writings, see Brown, *Gospel, I–XII*, pp. 499–501, and Thiselton, "Truth," pp. 889–94.

F. F. Segovia examines **love** in the Gospel of John and 1 John in *Love Relationships in the Johannine Tradition*.

2 /   In the Gospel and letters of John the love command is restricted to those who are within the community, i.e., to disciples. The subjects of love for neighbor (Luke 10:27) and love for enemy (Matt. 5:44) do not occur. On the limitation of love in the Johannine writings, see Brown, *Epistles*, pp. 269–72 and, to the contrary, J. A. T. Robinson, *The Priority of John* (London: SCM, 1985), pp. 329–39.

On the term **lives** (*menō*, "abides"), see Brown, *Epistles*, pp. 259–61 and E. Malatesta, *Interiority and Covenant*.

3 / **Grace, mercy and peace** are uncommon Johannine vocabulary. **Grace** is not used elsewhere in the letters of John, and in the Gospel it appears only in the prologue in combination with "truth" (*alētheia*) as a description of Jesus Christ (John 1:14, 16–17). **Mercy** occurs only here in the Johannine corpus, and **peace** appears here, in 3 John 14, and in the Fourth Gospel as a gift and greeting from Jesus to his disciples (14:27; 16:33; 20:19, 21, 26).

Twelve times in the New Testament the greeting which opens a letter is from both **God the Father** and (usually, the Lord) **Jesus Christ**. This is the only verse in the Johannine writings in which **God the Father** occurs, and it is the only place in the entire NT in which Jesus is called "the Son of the Father" (**the Father's Son**; Brown, *Epistles*, p. 659).

§2 *Walking in the Father's Commands (2 John 4–6)*

We were introduced to the dual themes of truth and love in the salutation (vv. 1–3); now the Elder expands on them in vv. 4–6. The common concern which unites these verses is walking in obedience to the Father's commands. Verse 4, which reveals the occasion of the epistle, i.e., the immediate circumstance or event that caused him to write the letter, centers on the command to walk in the truth, while vv. 5 and 6 focus on the command to walk in love.

It is customary in ancient letters to begin with words of thanks or commendation to the readers. Our author keeps the custom, though his concern for containing the schism and its effects cannot be concealed.

4 / **It has given me great joy** (lit., "I rejoiced greatly") reflects the author's relief and happiness at the news he has heard about this congregation. Given the crisis created by the secession (1 John 2:19), any positive report is an occasion for rejoicing, and it is also the occasion for the epistle. The Elder, having heard a good word about this house church, writes to commend (v. 4), teach (v. 5), and warn its members (v. 6).

He commends them—or rather, **some** of them—for **walking in the truth**. But what has given him **great joy** has also had an underside of pain. The most he can say is that he found *some* **of your children** doing what he wishes *all* of them would do (cf. 3 John 4). **Some** have continued in loyal obedience to God (and in harmony with the Elder); others have not. Not all of them are **walking in the truth**, for some have joined the secession.

The expression **walking in the truth** recalls the emphasis on truth in vv. 1–3 and foreshadows the commendation of Gaius in 3 John 3 for **walking in the truth**. The phrase, in its Johannine epistles context, means more than Christian behavior, though this is certainly included in it. It emphasizes holding to the truth of the gospel, the truth about Jesus Christ, which has been denied by those who have left the community (cf. 1 John 2:21–23; 4:2–3).

Those who have remained loyal to the Elder and to the truth of the gospel are living **just as the Father commanded us** (lit., "even as we received a command from the Father"). The word "command," or "commandment(s)" (*entolē*), is used frequently in 1 and 2 John, most often with reference to God's commands (cf. 1 John 2:3–4, 7–8; 3:22–24; 4:21; 5:2–3). All of **us**, that is, the Elder and his followers, received a divine order which they are to obey. **Some** are doing this, and some are not. To leave the community and to follow another "rule" is to disobey not just the Elder, but God!

First John 3:23 summarizes the Father's command in terms of believing in Jesus Christ and walking in love toward one another. The double theme of walking in truth and love is a "rule of life" for the Christian community (cf. John 14:15, 21; Eph. 4:15; Col. 1:4–5; 1 John 3:18; 2 John 1, 3; 3 John 1).

5 / The NIV divides into two clear sentences one longer, more complex sentence in the Greek. The Elder again refers to the congregation of his readers as **dear lady** (lit., "lady," *kyria*; cf. vv. 1, 13). It is the feminine form of the common address to Jesus as "lord" (*kyrie*; cf., e.g., John 4:11, 15, 19, 49; 5:7; 6:34, 68; 9:36, 38; 11:3, 12, 39; 12:21). He asks this house church, simply but profoundly, **that we love one another**. This request is not a **new command**, and, therefore, it is not to be rejected either as novel or as imposing an additional burden. This has been the community's ethic **from the beginning** (John 13:34–35; 1 John 2:7; 3:11). The **we** includes not only the members of **dear lady**'s congregation, but also the Elder himself and the house church he represents. It is the unity of this **we**, the Johannine community, that has been broken by the schism. **Love** is the vital power to keep Christians together amid controversy and conflict. It can heal old wounds and keep new ones from opening. In this crisis, what the Johannine world needs now, to cite an old song, is **love**, the commitment to work together sacrificially for each other's highest good. Again, as is characteristic of the Johannine writings, the author is thinking of love within the community, among those who are supposed to belong to the truth. This is what he writes to teach them (1 John 3:11, 14, 16–18, 23; 4:7–8, 11–12, 20–21).

6 / Yet it is impossible to claim to practice **love** without also obeying God's **commands**. **Love** is not just a feeling; it is seen concretely in the lives of those who obey God's word (1 John 2:5). It is made visible "with actions and in truth" (1 John 3:18). Jesus taught his disciples the same: "If you love me, you will obey what I command" (John 14:15); "Whoever has my commands and obeys them, he is the one who loves me" (John 14:21); "If you obey my commands, you will remain in my love" (John 15:10). Not all those who say, "Lord, Lord," will enter the kingdom, but only those who do the will of the Father (Matt. 7:21).

While **love** is defined by walking according to **his commands** (v. 6a), the heart of all God's **commands** is **love** (v. 6b; Matt. 22:37–40; Rom. 13:8; Gal. 5:14; 1 Tim. 1:5). Each of the Ten Commandments, for example, is a specific instance of what it means to love God or neighbor. The Elder also reminds his readers that God's **command**, given through God's Son (John 13:34–35), is one they have had **from the beginning** of their life as a Christian community (cf. 1 John 1:1; 2:7, 24; 3:11; 2 John 5). Both love and obedience to God's commands were commodities in short supply in some sections of the Johannine community. It was vital to the well-being of the remaining Johannine Christians that they become top priorities.

Additional Notes   §2

---

4 / The Father's commands as seen by the Johannine community are the subject of Urban C. von Wahlde's excellent study *The Johannine Commandments*. See esp. pp. 49–73, 105–37, 199–225.

5 / The phrase "from the beginning" is a favorite of the author's. He uses it ten times in the epistles. See the extended discussion of it in Brown, *Epistles*, pp. 155–58. Here it means "when you first received the teaching which we received from Jesus."

6 / The NIV attempts to make an awkward and repetitive Greek sentence clearer by introducing the word **love** at the end of v. 6. Literally translated the second half of v. 6 says, "This is the commandment, even as you heard from the beginning, that you should walk in it." The NIV, along with several recent commentators (Bruce, Dodd, Marshall, Smalley, and Stott, but not Brown), interprets the **it** at the end of v. 6 as a reference to **love**, rather than as a reference to its closer antecedent **commandment**. See the discussion in Brown, *Epistles*, pp. 666–68.

This is the longest section of the letter and is primarily a warning against those who have seceded from the community and who hold a false doctrine concerning the person of Christ. It makes explicit the Elder's implied claim (v. 4) that some of the (former) members of the community are not walking in the truth. After describing the false teachers in four ways (v. 7), he warns the readers not to follow them but to continue to be faithful, lest they suffer great spiritual loss (vv. 8–9). He concludes this section with orders on how to treat these itinerant "heretics" (vv. 10–11).

7 / The reason for the Elder's dual emphasis on truth and love (vv. 4–6) is that **many deceivers . . . have gone out into the world**. There are five descriptors of the false teachers in verse 7. (1) They are **many**. How many is unknown, but a substantial section of the Johannine community has seceded from the remaining believers loyal to the Elder (1 John 2:19). They are gaining in popularity (1 John 4:5), and they constitute a serious threat to the spiritual well-being of the Elder's followers, as the writing of 1–2 John shows.

(2) They are **deceivers** (*planoi*), because they lead the community astray with their claims (cf. 1 John 2:26 and 3:7, where the same Greek verb is used; cf. also 1 John 4:6, where the opponents are said to be inspired by "the spirit of error," *planēs*; see the Introduction for a discussion of the claims of the opponents), and because they deceive themselves as well (1 John 1:8).

(3) They **do not acknowledge** (lit., "confess"; *homologountes*; cf. 1 John 2:23; 4:2–3, 15; it is a fundamental "confession of faith" issue for the Elder) **Jesus Christ as coming in the flesh**. The same doctrinal defect was cited in 1 John 4:2 as the criterion by which to distinguish true and false prophets. These false teachers denied Jesus' full humanity. They are the forerunners of the Doce-

tists who claimed that Christ only seemed to be human. They also have similarities with later Gnostics for whom the human body was inherently evil and who, therefore, could not consider the Son of God to have been actually in the body. At issue is the claim of the Gospel of John: "The Word became flesh and made his dwelling among us" (John 1:14). In other passages in 1 John it is put as the issue of whether the human, crucified, Jesus is the divine Christ, the Son of God (1:7; 2:2, 22; 3:23; 4:3; 5:1, 5–7, 20–21).

(4) They **have gone out into the world**. They have left, or have seceded from, the Johannine community, of which they were once a part. The key passage is 1 John 2:19a: "They went out from us, but they did not really belong to us." **Gone out** may, from the opponents' standpoint, also mean "in the spirit of missionaries, to win over others to their . . . beliefs" (Smalley, *1, 2, 3 John*, p. 328). First John 4:1 also says that "many false prophets have gone out into the world." For in early Christianity, including the Elder's churches, there were only two spheres of spiritual reality: in Christ, or in Johannine terms "in the truth" (i.e., in the believing fellowship), and in **the world**. The latter is the realm of the evil one (1 John 5:19). To leave the Christian community in the Elder's day was not to establish a new denomination. It was to be lost in the darkness of the devil's domain! (See Col. 1:13; 1 Cor. 4:5.)

(5) **Any such person is . . . the antichrist**. Our author has already called them **deceivers**, a term he repeats in the singular with the definite article (**the deceiver**). **The antichrist** recalls the description of these opponents in 1 John 2:18, the first use of the term **antichrist** in any literature. The term is used only in 1–2 John as a description of the Elder's opponents and nowhere else in the NT (1 John 2:18, 22; 4:3). The reference is to a figure of the end times, an apocalyptic character, like Paul's "man of lawlessness" in 2 Thess. 2:3–9, who opposes Christ (hence **antichrist**; the prefix *anti* may also mean "instead of" or "substitute") and his coming reign. The Elder sees in these false teachers a harbinger of the end of this age (cf. 1 John 2:8). In the book of Revelation "the beast" is described as "like a lamb" (13:11). He "deceived" (*plana*) the inhabitants of the earth (13:14), and his number, a "man's number," is 666 (13:18). The author of Revelation referred to the entire Roman Empire of his day as the **antichrist**.

8 / Having completed his description of them, the Elder now warns the community against following them. **Watch out**

(lit., "be looking out for yourselves")! The reason for this command of concern is the serious consequences of going the way of the false teachers. Down that road is: (1) the loss of all that has been accomplished so far in their Christian lives (v. 8a), (2) ultimate failure to obtain the **full** eschatological **reward** God has prepared for those who remain faithful (v. 8b), and also (3) the loss of a vital relationship with God (v. 9), and thus, forfeiture of eternal life itself (1 John 5:11–12).

There is an interesting textual problem in v. 8. Some MSS have **Watch out that you do not lose what you have worked for** (*eirgasasthe*), and the NIV has followed that reading. Other MSS have **Watch out that you do not lose what** *"we* have worked for*"* (*eirgasametha*). Metzger prefers the latter because it is the reading which best explains the origin of the other, since it is deemed more likely that a copyist would have changed the verbal endings to make them all the same (second person plural) rather than to introduce the more "delicate nuance" **that you do not lose what** "we, your apostles and teachers, have wrought in you" (*Commentary*, p. 721). What has been accomplished in our Christian lives is a group effort; we owe much to our pastors, teachers, and mentors.

The verb which the NIV translates **lose** (*apolesēte*) may also be translated "destroy." There is a sense in which to follow **the deceivers** is not just to lose passively what has been achieved, but to destroy actively all that God, working through them and their leaders, has done in their lives.

9 / The secessionists have not only "run out" on the rest of the Johannine Christians, thus breaking the unity of the community in love, but they have also **run ahead.** The Greek word here (*proagōn*) means to "go too far" or "to walk ahead of those who are going slowly" (BAGD, p. 702). The secessionists may think of themselves as "progressives," "modern," or philosophically and theologically "up-to-date." But to the Elder, they have left authentic Christianity and no longer **have God.** They do not enjoy an ongoing right relationship with God (cf. 1 John 2:23).

The opposite of **runs ahead** is to **continue in the teaching of Christ.** Here we see that the issue over which the false teachers and their followers have left the community and thus jeopardized their salvation is Christology. One can understand the phrase **the teaching of Christ** in two ways. Either it means **Christ's** own **teaching**, a subjective genitive grammatically, or it means the **teaching** about **Christ**, an objective genitive. While the former is not impossible, especially if Jesus' love command is in mind, it is more likely that the Elder means the correct doctrine about **Christ**, i.e., that he came in the flesh (v. 7). One who **continues** (*menōn*, "abides" or "remains") faithful to this **teaching has both the Father and the Son**, since it is through **the Son** that **the Father** is accessed (John 14:6; 1 John 2:23; cf. Heb. 4:14–16; 7:25; 10:19–22), and since **the Father** and **the Son** are one (John 10:30). Doctrinally faithful Johannine Christians continue to enjoy a vital relationship with God, unlike the "progressive" secessionists.

10 / In view of vv. 7–9, the community needs to understand how to treat the false teachers when they come to the remaining Johannine house churches bringing their heretical Christology and attempting to win them over to the schism and away from the Elder. **If anyone comes to you** refers to the practice of both the false teachers and the Elder's friends of visiting around the circuit of the several congregations in the Johannine orbit for which the Elder is responsible. Third John also refers to this practice (3 John 3, 5–8, 10).

The Didache, an early Christian writing virtually contemporary with the letters of John, also mentions itinerant teachers: "Now, you should welcome anyone who comes your way and teaches you all we have been saying. But if the teacher proves himself a renegade and by teaching contradicts all this, pay no attention to him. . . . Welcome every apostle on arriving, as if he were the Lord. But he must not stay beyond one day. In case of necessity, however, the next day too. If he stays three days, he is a false prophet. . . . If he asks for money, he is a false prophet" (Did. 11:1–2, 4–6; cf. also Did. 12:1–5). The days of itinerant evangelists did not end with the apostles, and there was a continuing necessity to guard against charlatans.

The test of those who **come to you** is whether or not they **bring this teaching**, i.e., the **teaching** of Christ, that Jesus Christ indeed came in the flesh. If they do not, then the readers are not to (1) **take him into your house** or (2) **welcome him** (lit., "be saying to him, 'Greetings!' "). What the author here prohibits is not petty but serious. Follow his counsel, and it will be very difficult for the schismatics to continue their destruction. The Elder prohibits showing hospitality to the opponents, that is, the practical provision of the material and financial assistance ("aid and comfort to the enemy") they need to travel from place to place. Deprived of "room and board," the false teachers may make no further in-roads into the Johannine community, or so the Elder hopes. **House** may also mean "house church," in which case the Elder is intending to prevent the schismatics from teaching (Thompson, *1–3 John*, p. 155). As the readers were warned previously against false doctrine, here they are warned against "false charity" (Plummer, *Epistles*, p. 139).

11 / **Anyone who welcomes him** implies more than just a greeting; it includes cooperation in and help with the mission of those who have divided the community. Such actions by the secessionists are **wicked work** (lit., "his works, the evil ones"). The Elder does not want "the chosen lady and her children" to have *koinōnia* (NIV **shares**, Gk. *koinōnei*) with those who practice evil. While the Elder's advice may sound unloving, he is not advocating hatred for the opponents, only a plan to prevent them from perpetrating a teaching that would eviscerate the heart of Christianity. Kysar rightly asks, "How flexible can the perimeters of Christian belief be without sacrificing the integrity of faith itself?" (*I, II, III John*, p. 132). The Christian church has the responsibility to draw lines which "exclude teaching and practice it deems out of harmony with the revelation of Scripture" (Thompson, *1–3 John*, p. 156). Yet it must always teach this truth in love (Eph. 4:15), a verse which has proved easier to quote than to enact.

Additional Notes   §3

---

7 / The NIV does not translate the opening Greek word of v. 7, *hoti*, "for," which shows the relation between vv. 4–6 and vv. 7–11. The schismatic false teachers have motivated the Elder's concern for **truth** and **love**.

The author uses the pres. ptcp. *erchomenos*, "coming," for Jesus' incarnation (cf. 1 John 4:2, where the perf. ptcp. "having come" was used). The use in 2 John 7 may be influenced by Ps. 118:26, "Blessed is he who comes in the name of the Lord" (cf. John 12:13). See also John 1:15, 27.

On the christological views of the opponents, see the Introduction to this commentary and Brown, "Origin of I and II John in a Struggle with Adversaries," *Epistles,* pp. 47–68.

On the term **antichrist**, see E. Kauder, "Antichrist," *NIDNTT,* vol. 1, pp. 124–26, and J. E. H. Thomson, "Antichrist," *ISBE,* vol. 1, pp. 139–41.

For a comparison of the eschatology of the Gospel and letters of John, see Brown, *Community,* pp. 135–38 and Brown, *Epistles,* pp. 27–28, 99–100, and 420–26.

8 / What are the readers at risk of losing? In v. 8, the key term is **reward.** Their salvation does not seem to be at risk. But in v. 9, the author states that those who forsake the true "teaching" about "Christ" do "not have God," either "the Father" or "the Son." Would he say that if they forsake the truth, they never really knew it? That is what he says of the secessionists in 1 John 2:19: they were never really part of the true community; if they had been, they would have stayed. Or, does he think that "losing God" is a genuine possibility? See I. H. Marshall, *Kept by the Power of God,* pp. 186–90.

9 / Brown argues in favor of the subjective genitive on the grounds that "**Christ**'s own **teaching** is the Johannine way of thinking about the continuing teaching of the Paraclete in the community." See *Epistles,* pp. 674–75, 687–89.

On the expression "having God," see H. Hanse, "*echō,*" *TDNT,* vol. 2, pp. 822–24 and J. Eichler, "Fellowship," *NIDNTT,* vol. 1, pp. 637–38.

10 / On hospitality in the early church and in the Johannine epistles, see Brown, *Epistles,* 728–32, A. J. Malherbe, "The Inhospitality of Diotrephes," pp. 222–32, and R. H. Stein, "Entertain," *ISBE,* vol. 2, 105–7. This is a subject that more directly concerns 3 John.

11 / The harsh tone of the Elder is discussed at length in Brown, *Epistles,* pp. 690–93, in Smalley, *1, 2, 3 John,* pp. 333–34, and in Barker, "1 John, " pp. 365-66. Dodd expresses strong reservations at the Elder's plan of action (see *Epistles,* pp. 151–53 and Thompson's response, *1–3 John,* pp. 155–56).

§4 *A Final Greeting (2 John 12–13)*

Having completed his main purposes (instructing the readers to walk in truth and in love [vv. 4–6] and warning them against the false teachers [vv. 7–11]), the Elder closes the letter with his hope for a personal visit to this congregation (v. 12) and greetings from his own house church (v. 13).

12 / Much more needs to be said, about the secession, the false teaching, the importance of standing for the truth in love, and so forth. But the Elder defers any further communication in writing (**paper and ink**) until he can make a personal, **face to face** (lit., "mouth to mouth," in Greek idiom) visit. Apparently the chosen lady's (2 John 1) group is not close by, but in a neighboring town or at some distance. See the Introduction for the view that the Elder is writing to a group of churches in his sphere of authority in the vicinity of Ephesus. The Elder has, or believes he has (this is, of course, contested by the secessionists and by Diotrephes; see 3 John 9–10), pastoral responsibility for "the care and oversight" of these congregations.

The reason for, or perhaps the anticipated result of, the visit is **that our joy may be complete**. The same hope for fulfilled **joy** occurs in 1 John 1:4 (cf. John 15:11). There it is one of the reasons for writing (cf. 1 John 2:1). In both cases, **joy** is a characteristic of Christian communication and fellowship (cf. 1 John 1:3).

13 / Just as the readers' congregation and its members were called "the chosen lady and her children" (v. 1), so the author's church and its members are called **the children of your chosen sister**. Thus, the two verses form an *inclusio* which frames this epistle. Such designations reflect the intimate, "Christian family" (cf. John 1:12; 19:25–27) relationships among Johannine Christians and their self-understanding as God's **chosen** people (John 15:16, 19).

While the wording of this closing (and its companion verse in the salutation) is unique in the NT, ending a letter with a greeting is a common practice in first-century Greek letters.

Additional Notes   §4

---

12 / Given the geographical spread of the churches in Revelation 2—3, assuming they were part of the Johannine circle of influence, the Elder's church and the chosen lady's church could be many days' journey apart.

13 / These close relationships, described in family language among non-blood-related people, are called "fictive kin" relations by cultural anthropologists. See, e.g., B. Malina, *Christian Origins and Cultural Anthropology* (Atlanta: John Knox, 1986), p. 39.

The adjective, **chosen** (*eklektē*), occurs in the Gospel and letters of John elsewhere only at John 1:34, in a disputed MS reading, though likely the original one, in which John the Baptist says of Jesus, "You are the chosen one of God." The verb from which the adjective comes occurs in John 6:70, 13:18, and 15:16, 19; in every case it refers to Jesus' choice of the disciples. Thus, believers in Jesus are his **chosen** ones, as the Elder calls these two Johannine congregations.

On the literary characteristics of 2 and 3 John, see R. Brown, "General Observations of Epistolary Format," Appendix V, *Epistles*, pp. 788–95.

3 John

§1 Salutation and Good Wishes (3 John 1–2)

Third John is the shortest letter in the NT. The opening passage of 3 John identifies the writer and the reader, and includes, as was common in ancient personal letters, a health wish. Unlike 2 John, in which "the chosen lady and her children," a local congregation, are addressed, 3 John was written to an individual. Third John 1, with its mention of love and truth, closely parallels 2 John 1, but the health wish (3 John 2) appears in place of the more traditional Christian greeting (2 John 3).

1 / The author's only identification of himself in the letters of John is **The elder** (cf. 2 John 1). This self-description literally means "old man," but it was commonly used in early Christianity as a title for authoritative leaders and teachers (Acts 15:2, 4, 6, 22, 23; 20:17; 1 Tim. 5:17; Titus 1:5; Jas. 5:14; 1 Pet. 5:1, 5). No further name was necessary since his readers already knew his identity well, as the tradition-bearer who connected them with the life and teaching of Jesus and with their founder, the disciple whom Jesus loved (1 John 1:1–3; John 21:20, 24; cf. 3 John 12). See the Introduction for a discussion of the authorship of these letters.

The elder writes to his **dear friend** (lit., "beloved") **Gaius**. To call **Gaius** "beloved" (*agapētos*), as he will three more times in this brief letter (vv. 2, 5, 11), is to mark him as one of **the elder**'s loyal followers (cf. 1 John 2:7; 3:2, 21; 4:1, 7, 11), "beloved" because God has first loved them (1 John 4:11, 19). **Gaius** is a common Roman name used of three other individuals in the NT (Gaius of Corinth, Rom. 16:23; 1 Cor. 1:14; a Macedonian Gaius, Acts 19:29; and Gaius of Derbe, Acts 20:4). It is not altogether clear that the use of "beloved" implies that **the elder** knew **Gaius** personally, though the NIV's translation **dear friend** makes it appear so. He may have known of **Gaius** only from the report of "the brothers" (vv. 3, 5).

The elder loves him **in the truth** (cf. 2 John 1, 3). **Truth** and **love** are the two most prominent themes in the Johannine epistles. They reflect **the elder**'s concern for right belief (in Jesus as the incarnate divine Son of God) and for right conduct (obedience to the **love** command which Jesus gave them; John 13:34). First John 3:23 summarized them: "And this is his command: to believe in the name of his Son, Jesus Christ, and to love one another as he commanded."

Love in the New Testament is unmerited, self-sacrificing, positive regard for and action on behalf of others. In the Gospel and letters of John, **love** is God's essential nature (1 John 4:8, 16), and it is defined by God's **love** for the world, especially in the sending of the Son for human redemption (John 3:16; 1 John 4:9–10). Self-giving **love** is to be seen among Jesus' disciples (John 13:34a, 35). Jesus' **love** or God's **love** is the standard or pattern (John 13:34b; 1 John 4:11).

The emphasis on **truth** in the epistles derives from the crisis that threatens the unity and perhaps even the survival of Johannine Christianity. The schism which has divided this community of believers (1 John 2:19; see Introduction) centers upon the **truth** about the nature of Jesus Christ, whether he had really been fully human ("in the flesh"; 1 John 4:2–3; 2 John 7), whether his death on the cross ("his blood") was of essential, saving significance (1 John 1:7; 2:1–2; 4:10; 5:6–8), and whether faithfulness to his teaching and example was morally obligatory for those who are now "in the light" (1 John 1:6–7; 2:3–6, 9–11; 3:16, 24a; 2 John 9).

Those who hold to these **truth**s are the real Johannine Christians, in contrast to the false teachers and their followers who have left the community. Those, like **Gaius**, who are **love**d within the sphere of this **truth**, are the remaining members of the community who hold to **the elder**'s interpretation of the **truth** about Jesus, his life, death, and teaching. This controversy may also involve the true understanding of the Gospel of John, the community's official theological and historical presentation of Jesus, which was written some years earlier (see the Introduction).

2 / The second part of the opening section, besides the salutation in v. 1 , is the health wish (v. 2). Health wishes formed a common part of greetings in the ancient world (Kysar, *I, II, III John*, p. 139), and here the Elder thinks not only about the physical health of Gaius, but about his spiritual well-being too. What the "brothers" have reported (3 John 3, 5–6) has convinced the Elder of the **health** of Gaius' **soul**. What he feels the need to **pray** for, then, is that **all** of the other circumstances of his life (lit., "concerning everything") might **go well** (*euodousthai*; lit., "to be led along a good road"). The author's wish for the general well-being of his **friend** was a customary concern in Hellenistic letters and constitutes no basis for a "right to prosperity" among Christians.

Additional Notes §1

---

1 / On the use of the term **elder** in 2 and 3 John, see G. Bornkamm, *"presbyteros," TDNT*, vol. 6, pp. 670–72; Brown, *Epistles*, pp. 647–51; Coenen, "Bishop, Presbyter, Elder," *NIDNTT*, vol. 1, pp. 192–201; H. von Campenhausen, *Ecclesiastical Authority and Spiritual Power in the First Three Centuries* (Stanford: Stanford University, 1969), pp. 76–123.

2 / On health wishes in antiquity, see the detailed discussion in Brown, *Epistles*, pp. 703–4.

§2 *Gaius Commended for His Faithfulness (3 John 3–4)*

It was common in NT times to begin personal letters with an expression of thanksgiving (cf. 2 John 4; Rom. 1:8f.; 1 Cor. 1:4f.; Phil. 1:3f.; Col. 1:3f.). In these two verses the Elder expresses his great joy at the faithfulness of Gaius, as it has been reported to him by some "brothers" who have visited the congregation. A schism has divided the Johannine churches into two groups ("they," or "them," and "us"; 1 John 2:19), those loyal to the Elder and those who rejected his authority and teaching and have "gone out into the world" (1 John 4:1; 2 John 7). Amid this raging controversy, the Elder is encouraged to discover that Gaius has remained loyal and has not sided with the opposition (1 John 4:1–6). Neither has he attempted to be neutral (see the notes on 3 John 9–10).

3 / In vv. 3 and 4 the Elder expresses **joy** (*echarēn*, v. 3; *charan*, v. 4). He rejoices greatly (NASB, "was very glad") that Gaius is still **in the truth**, and in v. 4 he has "no greater" **joy** than hearing that his followers continue to be loyal to it. Such **joy** is made more poignant by the sadness of the division which has devastated the community. The Elder must have wondered who would defect to the secessionists next. What about Gaius? Would he remain loyal?

Then **some brothers** came and reported that Gaius was still in **the truth** (lit., "when brothers coming and witnessing to your truth"). The NIV's **faithfulness** does not occur in the Greek text. He was still with the Elder and had not gone over to the schismatic false teachers. Gaius' obedience is seen in his consistent Christian life: he **continues to walk in the truth**. The **brothers** were the Elder's friends (cf. v. 14). They may have been traveling at his request to assess the damage the schism had caused and to report to the Elder who was remaining faithful and who was not (Diotrephes, vv. 9–10).

To **walk in the truth** (v. 4: "walking in the truth"; cf. "walk in the day/in the night," John 11:9–10; "walk in the darkness/ light," John 8:12; 1 John 1:6–7; 2:11; "walk according to his commandments," 2 John 6) means to be true to the teaching about Jesus (2 John 9) and to the love command (2 John 5–6; cf. the thematic summary in 1 John 3:23) which are at the center of the Johannine community's tradition and experience. **The truth** is spiritual reality as the Elder and his followers understand it. The schism is so threatening, because it presents a different **truth**, i.e., a different Jesus (cf. 2 Cor. 11:4; Gal. 1:8) and a way of living together as God's people apart from the primacy of love (1 John 2:9–11; 3:11–18).

4 / Literally, the first part of v. 4 reads, "Greater than these, I do not have joy." Given the problems the Elder faces, hearing that his **children** are still on his side, i.e., are still **walking in the truth**, is the best news possible.

The sense of intimacy among the Johannine Christians is evident from the writer's language in vv. 1–4. He calls Gaius his "dear friend" (lit., "beloved," vv. 1–2). He refers to the messengers who have told him of Gaius' loyalty as "brothers" (v. 3). This is a common designation for members of the community in these epistles (1 John 2:9–11; 3:10–17; 4:20–21; 5:16; 3 John 5, 10) and certainly for them goes back to Jesus' post-resurrection reference to his disciples as his "brothers" (John 20:17; cf. John 21:23). The Elder also continues to call his readers **my children**, those for whom he feels a fatherly compassion and responsibility. He uses two different Greek words interchangeably (a common Johannine technique of stylistic variation, cf. John 21:15–17) for them as his **children** (*teknon* or *teknion*, in 1 John 2:1, 12, 28; 3:7, 18; 5:21; 3 John 4; and *paidion*, in 1 John 2:14, 18). Jesus called his disciples *teknia* (John 13:33) in the upper room and *paidia* on the seashore after his resurrection (John 21:5). The author's use of these terms for his community directly reflects Jesus' use of them for his disciples. The Johannine community continues the intimacy which was experienced among the loyal eleven apostles. (See also the note on "fictive kin" relationships in 2 John 13).

Additional Notes   §2

3–4 / Reference to members of a community as **brothers** or **children** certainly pre-dates Jesus' use of the terms for his disciples, though it is his use of them that is of primary importance for the writer and his community. On the use of **brothers** in the Bible, Judaism, and other Hellenistic groups, see J. Guenther, "Brother," *NIDNTT*, vol. 1, pp. 254–58; H. von Soden, *"adelphos," TDNT*, vol. 1, pp. 144–46. On the background of the term **children**, see G. Braumann, "Child," *NIDNTT*, vol. 1, pp. 285–87; C. Brown, "Child," *NIDNTT*, vol. 1, 283–85; A. Oepke, *"pais," TDNT*, vol. 5, pp. 636–54; and O. Piper, "Child," *IDB*, vol. 1, p. 558.

§3 Gaius Commended for His Hospitality (3 John 5–8)

In this section the Elder praises Gaius for the support he has given to the Elder's traveling representatives, "the brothers," in the ongoing conflict with the false teaching secessionists. He urges that Gaius continue this vital ministry, as his part in working for the truth.

5 / For the third time the writer calls Gaius his **dear friend** (*agapēte*, vv. 1–2), for Gaius has demonstrated his **faithful** friendship to the Elder and allegiance to his cause by his kind treatment of the Elder's allies, **the brothers**. Even though they were not personally known to Gaius (NIV, **strangers**), he did not refuse them hospitality, but met their needs, probably with food and shelter as a host. This gave **the brothers** the opportunity to bring the teaching (most likely in support of the Elder's campaign against the false teachers who had left the community, 1 John 2:19; 4:1; 2 John 7) which the Elder had sent them to deliver. "It was a signal feature of Gaius' hospitality that he was prepared to extend it to people who were otherwise unknown to him and had no claims on him except that they formed part of the company of those who like him had come to know the truth" (Marshall, *Epistles*, p. 85). These traveling representatives of the Elder may well have been refused hospitality by the nearby house church of Diotrephes (v. 10).

Note that what Gaius is commended for doing in 3 John, the Elder commands "the elect lady" not to do in 2 John 10–11. It is those loyal to the Elder who deserve support but not those who advocate the secession and its heretical Christology (2 John 9). Both factions are sending itinerant teachers, and the churches must be discerning. That is why in 1 John 4:1–2 the Elder urges the churches to test the prophets (cf. 1 Thess. 5:20–21) and provides for them the test.

6 / The first half of the verse refers to a previous occasion when "the brothers" told the writer's congregation (**church**, *ekklēsia*), the "home base" of Johannine Christianity, of Gaius' **love** (cf. v. 3, where "the brothers" witnessed to his "faithfulness to the truth"). This **love** was practical, "not with words or tongue but with actions and in truth" (1 John 3:18). Now Gaius is encouraged to continue this love-in-action. The second half of v. 6 refers to the future service (**you will do well**) which the author wants Gaius to undertake, consistent with his past conduct: continue to show hospitality. The verb for **send them on their way** (*propempsas*) means to help on one's journey by providing food or money, or by arranging travel (BAGD, p. 709).

The standard for Gaius' provision of hospitality is high: **in a manner worthy of God**. The Elder's allies, "the brothers," represent, not only the one who sent them, but also **God** (cf. 1 John 4:6). Therefore, they are to be treated as one would treat the Lord. The writer wants to motivate Gaius to care for "the brothers" with devotion and sacrifice (cf. Heb. 13:1–2: "Keep on loving each other as brothers. Do not forget to entertain strangers, for by so doing some people have entertained angels without knowing it").

7 / In this verse the writer explains why (*gar*, "for," untranslated in the NIV) Gaius should treat the brothers "well," and "in a manner worthy of God." It is because **they went out** (*exēlthon*; same verb as in 1 John 2:19; 4:1; and 2 John 7 in reference to the secession and mission activity of the Elder's opponents) **for the sake of the Name**. They were advancing its cause, proclaiming its truth, and defending it from attack and misunderstanding. Therefore, they are to be cared for as God's representatives.

This use of the term **the Name** was common in the OT and in Judaism as a reference to God. It was a way of speaking of God without using the sacred **Name** of YHWH itself. In early Christianity it also became a reference to Jesus, into whose **Name** they were baptized (Acts 10:48; 8:16), for whose **Name** the Christians suffered (John 15:21; Acts 5:40–41), and in whose **Name** they were forgiven (Acts 2:38; 1 John 2:12). The Elder includes Jesus in his reference to **the Name**. In 1 John 3:23 the writer describes his readers as those who "believe in the name of his Son, Jesus Christ" (5:13: "who believe in the name of the Son of God"; cf. John 1:12; 2:23; 3:18; 20:31).

He also says that the brothers received **no help from the pagans**. Literally, he says, they were "receiving nothing from the Gentiles" (*ethnikōn*). "The proclamation of Jesus is made without either expecting or begging for support" (Brown, *Epistles*, p. 713). It was common for itinerant "evangelists" for various causes to beg and plead for money from their hearers (and without the benefit of television or professionally prepared fund-raising letters!).

In the Didache, an early Christian church manual contemporary with the letters of John, the readers were instructed to "welcome anyone who comes your way and teaches you all we have been saying" (11:1). But these people "must not stay beyond one day. In the case of necessity, however, the next day too. If anyone stays three days that one is a false prophet" (11:5–6). "But if someone says in the Spirit, 'Give me money,' . . . you must not heed him . . . " (11:12). "Every one who comes to you 'in the name of the Lord' must be welcomed. Afterward, when you have tested him, you will find out about him" (12:1). The passages from the Didache illustrate not only the widespread and necessary practice of hospitality in ancient times but also the need for discernment in providing financial support.

The term *ethnikos* (**pagan**, Gentile) occurs only four times in the NT, once here and three times in the Gospel of Matthew (Matt. 5:47; 6:7; 18:17). It was originally a term of Jewish contempt for non-Jews (Gentiles), and that is how the term is used in Matthew, reflecting that Gospel's strong Jewish origins. But early Christians used it also in reference to non-Christians, and that is its meaning here in 3 John: the Elder's missionaries have accepted no assistance from non-Christians. Whether the Elder's opponents sought aid, as they traveled to the Johannine churches (2 John 10–11), is not known, but the contrast may be intended as further motivation for Gaius to support the brothers.

8 / The **we** at the opening of v. 8 is emphatic: **we**, in contrast with the non-Christians (v. 7). Actually, the Elder has Gaius specifically in mind. He wants him, based upon what he has just said (**therefore**), to fulfill the obligation (**we ought**; *opheilomen*; the Didache passages above [see v. 7] reveal the same sense of duty) of **show**ing **hospitality** (*hypolambanō*) to **such** Christian missionaries. Gaius is to provide them with the necessities for their journey and to support them in any way he can.

Such **hospitality** should be refused to those who come to the Johannine churches and who do not bring the true teaching that Jesus Christ has come in the flesh (2 John 7–10). Such people (the secessionists) are deceivers and antichrists; they do wicked work, and so do those who help and support them (2 John 11).

By contrast, people like Gaius, who aid and strengthen those who have remained loyal to the Elder, share in their **work . . . for the truth.** Gaius is a good example of someone who shows love in practical action. He "has material possessions" and sees and helps his fellow Christian in need (1 John 3:17). Not every Christian has the gifts or opportunity to be an evangelist or a missionary, but nearly everyone can, like Gaius, be a "fellow worker in the truth" (RSV), by supporting those who go forth to bring the gospel to others.

Additional Notes   §3

---

6 /   The word *ekklēsia*, or church, is used in the Gospel and letters of John only in 3 John (vv. 6, 9, 10). It refers to the local congregation or house church of the Elder (v. 6) and of Diotrephes (vv. 9–10). It is unclear whether Gaius belonged to the house church of Diotrephes, hosted his own house church, or belonged to one nearby (perhaps the most likely possibility). For the practice of "witnessing before the congregation," see Matt. 18:17; Acts 4:23; 11:2–4; 12:12–17; 14:27; 15:4; 20:17–35; 21:17–19; 2 Cor. 13:1; Gal. 2:2; 3 John 3, 6.

7 /   On the concept of **Name** in Scripture and especially as a reference to God and Jesus, see R. Abba, "Name," *IDB*, vol. 3, pp. 501–3, 505–8; Brown, *Gospel, I–XII*, pp. 754–56; H. Bietenhard and F. F. Bruce, "Name," *NIDNTT*, vol. 2, pp. 648–56 (with extensive bibliography); and G. F. Hawthorne, "Name," *ISBE*, vol. 3, pp. 480–83.

§4   The Opposition and Inhospitality of Diotrephes (3 John 9–10)

Diotrephes is a starkly contrasting character to the hospitable and loyal Gaius. What the Elder has commended Gaius for, Diotrephes refuses to do, and, beyond that, he stands in active opposition to the author. Verses 9 and 10 contain six descriptive phrases about Diotrephes, and they are all negative.

9 / The Elder **wrote** a letter (Gk. *ti*, "something") to **the church**. Was it 1 John? While it is impossible to know the order of the three letters of John, 3 John 9 may be a reference to 1 John. 1 John was intended to circulate among all the churches for which the Elder felt a pastoral responsibility. Otherwise, it refers to a lost letter, probably destroyed by **Diotrephes**. It is unlikely that 3 John 9 refers to 2 John, since the thrust of 2 John is against the teaching of the schismatics, while 3 John, despite its sixfold criticism of **Diotrephes**, never mentions theological or doctrinal deviation.

This is the second of three uses of **church** (*ekklēsia*) in 3 John, the only uses in the Gospel and letters of John. In 3 John 6, the reference was to the local church of the Elder. In 3 John 10 it is to the house church of **Diotrephes**, and that is its most natural referent here. The language implies that Gaius knows of this **church**, though it is likely not Gaius' own church (otherwise why would he need to be informed by the Elder of what **Diotrephes** is doing?), but one nearby.

Diotrephes (the name means "God-nurtured") has rejected what the Elder **wrote**, and in so doing has also rejected the Elder himself. This is the first of his six criticisms of **Diotrephes**, two of which are in v. 9 and four in v. 10. He **will have nothing to do with us** (lit., "does not accept us"). The use of **us** by the author is not merely the plural of majesty or a stylistic variation of "me." The writer aligns himself with the Johannine tradition, with the apostolic witness to Jesus, on which his own authority is based (cf. 1 John 1:1–5). Therefore, when **Diotrephes** disowns the Elder, he is cutting himself off from the Johannine community's founding authoritative teaching, from the witness of the "disciple whom Jesus loved" (cf. John 21:20–24). The writer is the community's living link with its apostolic past, but **Diotrephes** does not accept his authority.

Diotrephes loves to be first (*philoprōteuōn*). Literally, the author calls him "the loving-to-be-first-among-them Diotrephes." It is a prominent characteristic of his personality (contrast Mark 10:42–45). It also acknowledges **Diotrephes**' assertion of his position as the leader of his own house church. Because **Diotrephes** wants **to be first**, he can acknowledge no other above himself, not even the Elder. He seeks to be independent of his influence and authority.

10 / The Elder anticipates having to do something about this situation **if I come** (cf. 2 Cor. 13:1–2). In v. 14 he hopes to talk with Gaius "soon" and "face to face," just as in 2 John 12 he hopes "to visit . . . and talk" with "the chosen lady and her children." He had already sent his traveling representatives, "the brothers" (3 John 3, 5) and something he had written, but Diotrephes had rejected all these. Next time, he will come himself (cf. v. 13).

His plan is to bring up or **call** to mind (*hypomnēso*) before the congregation the practices (*poiei*, "he is doing"; emphasizing their continuous nature) of Diotrephes. These practices are the subject of the Elder's remaining four criticisms: Diotrephes (a) is **gossiping maliciously about us**; (b) **refuses to welcome the brothers**; (c) **also stops those who want to do so**; and (d) **puts them out of the church.** (See v. 9 for the first two complaints).

The NIV's **gossiping maliciously** misconstrues the sense of the Greek *phlyarōn* here. Literally it means to talk nonsense about someone or to bring false charges against them (BAGD, p. 862). The Elder adds "with evil words." What the author objects to is not attacks on his character (which "gossip" implies) but the unjustified charges that Diotrephes is raising. These charges are not only against the writer personally but against **us**, those who bear the tradition of the Johannine community. Presumably, they include the claim that the Elder is not to be regarded as the authoritative leader and teacher.

Diotrephes is **not satisfied with that**. His fourth affront to the Elder goes beyond speaking to action, even as evil deeds go beyond evil words. **He refuses to welcome the brothers**. Here his inhospitality contrasts most sharply with the actions of Gaius commended earlier (vv. 5–8). Diotrephes, rejecting **the brothers**, rejects the Elder whom they represent. He does not want them or the Elder to control or influence the house church he leads. He seeks complete independence, even from the tradition for which the Elder stands (though he may believe these are separable).

This is not to say, however, that the teaching of Diotrephes is heretical or agrees with that of the secessionists. Remarkably, the Elder never criticizes Diotrephes as a defector from "the truth" (cf. 2 John 1–4), nor does he say that Diotrephes is a "deceiver" or an "antichrist" (2 John 7). Apparently, Diotrephes does "acknowledge Jesus Christ as coming in the flesh" (1 John 4:2; 2 John 7). The position of Diotrephes, therefore, represents a third alternative in the disintegrating Johannine fellowship: the Elder's company, the "new wave" of the secessionists, and Diotrephes' independence movement. The author believes that it is imperative to put a stop to the continuing divisions in his community.

The Elder's fifth criticism of Diotrephes closely follows the previous one. Not only does Diotrephes refuse to support the traveling missionaries (by providing for their needs and advancing their mission), he also refuses to allow other members of his house church to show them any hospitality. **He . . . stops those who want to do so**. He has the authority to do this, perhaps because the **church** is an assembly which meets in his own house or because of his recognized position in his area. Diotrephes tolerates no interference with his leadership, with his desire "to be first" (v. 9).

Finally, Diotrephes will not permit in his house church those who continue to show allegiance to the Elder. He expels them; **he puts them out** (lit., "throws them out") **of the church.** It is not enough that he succeeds in preventing the Elder's representatives from meeting with his **church**; he must also punish those who want to hear them. Diotrephes has a clear policy of avoiding involvement in the schism. He apparently refuses to hear either the Elder or the secessionists, and instead maintains his own preeminent and independent authority. This is one of the first instances of an attempt at complete local church autonomy, exercised, in this case, through a dictatorial leadership style.

Either the Elder's authority is not sufficient to enable him to deal with Diotrephes' defection directly, or he has a very "democratic" concept of the use of pastoral authority. Unlike Paul's use of apostolic authority, especially 1–2 Corinthians, the Elder can, or perhaps he chooses to, only **call attention to what he** [Diotrephes] **is doing.** His authority is primarily his pastoral love and care for his churches and his link with the preceding generation of Johannine apostolic witnesses. The secessionists have withdrawn, contesting his teaching, and Diotrephes has withdrawn, questioning his leadership. It is clear that both groups do not accept his authority.

Additional Notes   §4

---

9 / The Greek text says *egrapsa ti*, "I wrote something." There are other MSS readings, but this one is the most likely (see Metzger, *Commentary*, p. 723). The reference to **church** in 3 John 9 may be broader and encompass all of the house churches under the Elder's oversight, including the congregations of "the chosen lady" (2 John 1), Gaius, and Diotrephes. This wider use would not be the same as Paul's universal **church** in Ephesians (Eph. 1:22; 2:19, 21; 5:23–32). It would refer to the churches in a given region as one **church**.

The Elder's letter (as also the letters of Paul; cf. 2 Cor. 10:11) was a substitute for his presence, as were also the Elder's traveling missionary representatives who came to Gaius (3 John 3, 5), to "the chosen lady and her children" (2 John 1), and to Diotrephes (3 John 10). To reject his letter and his friends was to reject him personally.

10 / The actions of Diotrephes have been set in their historical context by Malherbe, "The Inhospitality of Diotrephes," pp. 222–32. Brown has traced these divisions in Johannine Christianity and their outcome in the early second century in *Community*, esp. pp. 93–99, 145–64.

Was Diotrephes an early bishop with powers of excommunication, as Bultmann (*Epistles*, pp. 101–2) and Käsemann thought? See E. Käsemann, "Ketzer und Zeuge," *ZThK* 48 (1951), pp. 292–311. This goes beyond the evidence of this epistle and reads into the Johannine historical situation the polity of the later patristic era. A masterful summary of the various scholarly views on the relation between the Elder and Diotrephes is found in Brown, *Epistles*, pp. 727–39.

§5 *Exhortation and the Example of Demetrius (3 John 11–12)*

The writer turns from the negative example of Diotrephes to the positive example of Demetrius. Gaius is to imitate the latter. By so doing, he will align himself with God, the truth, and the Elder.

11 / For the fourth time in this brief letter the author calls Gaius **dear friend** (*agapētos*, "beloved"; vv. 1, 2, 5). He is the Elder's true **friend** amid a schism that has torn the Johannine churches apart. His steadfast loyalty makes him all the more beloved. Further, his value is especially evident in the light of Diotrephes' lack of loyalty and his refusal to acknowledge the Elder's authority. Friends like Gaius are crucial to the author in maintaining solidarity among the house churches which are threatened by the secessionists and their teaching.

Gaius is called upon to see the current situation in sharply antithetical categories of **good** and **evil**, of being **from God** or out of touch with **God** (**has not seen God**; cf. 1 John 3:6, 9–10; 4:1–6). The negative, destructive behavior of people like Diotrephes and the false teachers must be avoided, while those who do **what is good**, who thereby show that they are **from God**, are to be emulated. Imitating positive examples of Christian living is a common theme in the NT. Paul urges his readers to follow the example of himself and other Christian leaders (1 Cor. 4:16; 11:1; Phil. 3:17; 4:9; 1 Thess. 1:6; 2 Thess. 3:7, 9; cf. 1 Thess. 2:14) or to **imitate** the Lord (1 Thess. 1:6; Eph. 5:1; cf. 1 Cor. 11:1; Matt. 5:48). The entire eleventh chapter of Hebrews is an exhortation to "imitate those who through faith and patience inherit what has been promised" (Heb. 6:12).

The sentence, **Anyone who does what is evil has not seen God**, is curious. In Johannine theology, "no one has ever seen God" (1 John 4:12; John 1:18); yet Jesus, "God the one and only" (*monogenēs theos*, "only begotten God"), has made him known.

John 6:46 states that "No one has seen the Father except the one who is from God; only he has seen the Father"; yet Jesus also said in John 14:9, "Anyone who has seen me has seen the Father." Seeing God is the equivalent of knowing God, experiencing God, or understanding who God is as revealed in the Son, Jesus. In 3 John 11 the Elder asserts that evildoers do not share this essential spiritual experience.

12 / In v. 11 Gaius was urged to "imitate . . . what is good" and also, by implication, "anyone who does what is good." Now he is given a positive example, **Demetrius**, who was likely the bearer of this letter, and another one of "the brothers," the Elder's traveling representatives (vv. 3, 5). The Elder introduces him as a loyal friend, well attested by the author's supporters (lit., **by everyone**). Unlike the traveling false teachers of 2 John (2 John 7, 9–10) and Diotrephes (3 John 9–10), Demetrius is trustworthy and should be given hospitality, as the writer instructed in 3 John 5–8, not as he prohibited in 2 John 10–11.

What does it mean that Demetrius is **well spoken of** (*memartyrētai*, "has been witnessed") **even by the truth itself**? Verses 3–4 record the testimony (*martyrountōn*, "witnessing") of "some brothers" to Gaius and to other Johannine Christians who "walk in the truth." Their lives reflect the **truth**, both in doctrine (i.e., they accept Jesus as having come in the flesh, 2 John 7) and in practice (they love one another, 2 John 5–6; 3 John 5). If this **truth**, which is opposed by the schismatics, could stand up and testify, it would approve **Demetrius** as a friend and brother.

Demetrius is also well known to the Elder himself and to his community, probably meaning the home-base church in Ephesus (see the Introduction for more on the historical background to these letters). The author's affirmation of **Demetrius** confirms his orthodoxy in the current crisis. He is "one of us, on our side." The Elder adds his own **testimony** to that of **everyone** and of **the truth itself**.

The phrase **you know that our testimony is true** is especially Johannine. Jesus repeatedly "testifies" in the Fourth Gospel, and the truth of his self-testimony or of the testimony of others about him is a frequent topic (John 1:19–23; 3:11–12, 32–33; cf. 4:39; 5:31–39; 7:7; 8:13–18; 10:25–26; 18:23, 37–38). The Johannine community testifies concerning Jesus in John 1:14 and 3:11, and in John 19:35 and 21:24 they (note the "we" in 21:24) affirm that the testimony of the disciple whom Jesus loved is true. The subject of contested testimony is prominent also in 1 John 5:6–12.

This concern for the truthfulness of Jesus and for the Johannine community's witness about him is clear evidence of the setting of conflict and controversy in which the Johannine literature was written. It also points to the Fourth Gospel's Jewish setting in which rules about valid testimony were an important issue (cf. John 5:31–40; 8:12–18).

Additional Notes §5

---

11 / This verse is typical of the moral and theological dualism which permeates every part of the epistles. I have described and evaluated at length the dualistic or antithetical language of the Johannine epistles in *The Antitheses of the Elder*. Some attempt is made there to account for the extreme recourse to such language in the Johannine literature by a study of the historical and sociological setting of the Johannine community.

On the concept of "seeing" in the Gospel and letters of John, see Brown, *Gospel, I–XII*, pp. 501–3.

12 / "We," as a reference to the author and his community, occurs not only in the letters of John, but in the Gospel as well. This is especially evident when Jesus is speaking, but it is also reflected in the testimony of his disciples (John 1:14, "we have seen his glory"; John 3:11, "we speak of what we know"; John 4:22, "we worship what we do know"; John 6:69, "we believe and know that you are the Holy One of God"; John 9:4, "we must do the work of him who sent me"; John 16:30, "we know that you know all things . . . we believe that you came from God" (RSV); cf. John 19:35; John 20:25, "we have seen the Lord"; John 21:24, "we know that his testimony is true"; cf. John 21:25). In the letters, it occurs in the prologue to 1 John (vv. 1–4) and is one of the Elder's most common ways of speaking. He often prefers the first person plural to "I" (1 John 1:5—2:6; 2:18–19; 3:1–3, 14–24; 4:6–7, 9–14, 16–17, 19, 21; 5:2–4, 9, 11, 14–15, 18–20; 2 John 2–6; 3 John 8, 12). Many of these references, especially in 1 John, are to what the community has experienced or to what it knows (1 John 1:1–3, 5; 2:3–4, 18; 3:2, 14, 16, 19–21, 24; 4:6, 13–14, 16; 5:2, 15, 18-20).

The subject of witness or testimony in the Gospel and letters of John was studied by Boice, *Witness and Revelation*, and by Brown, *Gospel, I–XII*, pp. 227–28.

In these final verses of 3 John, the Elder expresses his desire to communicate with his readers in person. He and his friends extend their greetings to each one of them.

13–14   /   There are still many things which the author wants to say to Gaius and to his **friends** about the conflict which has divided the community, about keeping to the truth of Jesus Christ, and about loving one another—the principal themes of the letters of John (cf. 1 John 3:23). Some things, however, are best said **face to face** (*stoma pros stoma*, lit., "mouth to mouth"). For example, the conflict with Diotrephes must be dealt with personally (cf. v. 10, "if I come").

The endings of 3 John and 2 John are quite similar, and that is evidence that the two letters, one to a church, "the chosen lady and her children" (2 John), and one to an individual, Gaius (3 John), were written at the same time. Both express that the author has much left to say, that he is unwilling **to write** further with "paper and ink" (2 John 12; **pen and ink**, 3 John 13), and that he **hopes** to "visit" (2 John 12; **see you,** 3 John 14) and to **talk face to face** (2 John 12; 3 John 14). Third John 14 adds the nuance that is not merely the Elder who will **talk**, but that **we will** both **talk** together.

There is in 3 John, however, a note of greater urgency. The Elder wants to come and see Gaius immediately (*eutheōs;* this sense is not well conveyed by the NIV's **soon**). Given the spread of the schism through the Johannine churches perpetuated by the ongoing efforts of the traveling false teachers (2 John 7–11) and now the defection of the church of the independent Diotrephes, the author must prevent further losses and repair the current damage by an immediate personal visit to the outlying Johannine churches for which he is responsible.

The closing words of 3 John, and of the Johannine epistles as a whole, are not given a separate verse number in the NIV, as they are in the Greek texts (Nestle, 26th ed.; UBS, 3d ed.) and in most modern translations.

The Elder wishes Gaius **peace**. Though these are traditional words of **greeting,** they have special meaning for Gaius and the Elder in this setting of conflict and controversy, spawned by the schism (1 John 2:19). Gaius needs both the inner, spiritual **peace** that comes from God and is the sign of a right relationship with God, and renewed harmony with Diotrephes and the other troubled Johannine Christians of his region. In the Gospel of John Jesus expected that his disciples would have conflict in the world, so he said, "Peace I leave with you; my peace I give to you. . . . In this world you will have trouble. But take heart! I have overcome the world" (John 14:27; 16:33). Now, years later, the "trouble" of the world has invaded the church.

The friends was a phrase which the Johannine Christians used to refer to one another. It probably derives from John 15:13–15: "You are my friends" (John 15:14). "I no longer call you servants . . . I have called you friends" (John 15:15). Jesus also called Lazarus "our friend" (John 11:11). The Quakers, or The Society of Friends, took their name from these passages. The first group of **friends** are those with the Elder, at the home-base church, probably in or near Ephesus.

The Elder's personal concern for each member of the community is seen in his request that each of **the friends**, those supporting and faithful colleagues in Gaius' area, be greeted individually, **by name.**

For Further Reading

The bibliography is restricted primarily to works in English. A few major studies in other languages have been included.

Commentaries on the Johannine Epistles

Barker, G. W. "1 John, 2 John, 3 John." In *The Expositor's Bible Commentary*. Edited by F. Gaebelein. Volume 12. Pages 293–377. Grand Rapids: Zondervan, 1981.

Brooke, A. E. *The Johannine Epistles*. ICC. New York: Charles Scribner's Sons, 1912.

Brown, R. E. *The Epistles of John*. Anchor Bible 30. Garden City, N.Y.: Doubleday, 1982.

Bruce, F. F. *The Epistles of John*. Grand Rapids: Eerdmans, 1970.

Bultmann, R. *The Johannine Epistles*. Hermeneia. Philadelphia: Fortress, 1973.

Calvin, J. "The First Epistle of John." In *The Gospel According to John and the First Epistle of John*. Translated by T. H. L. Parker. Grand Rapids: Eerdmans, 1961.

Culpepper, R. A. *1 John, 2 John, 3 John*. Knox Preaching Guides. Atlanta: John Knox, 1985.

Dodd, C. H. *The Johannine Epistles*. MNTC. London: Hodder and Stoughton, 1946.

Findlay, G. G. *Fellowship in the Life Eternal: An Exposition of the Epistles of St. John*. London: Hodder & Stoughton, 1909.

Grayston, K. *The Johannine Epistles*. NCB. Grand Rapids: Eerdmans, 1984.

Haas, C., M. de Jonge, and J. L. Swellengrebel. *A Translator's Handbook on the Letters of John*. Helps for Translators 13. London: United Bible Societies, 1972.

Houlden, J. L. *A Commentary on the Johannine Epistles*. HNTC. New York: Harper and Row, 1973.

Jackman, D. *The Message of John's Letters*. BST. Downers Grove, Ill.: InterVarsity, 1988.

Johnston, G. "I, II, III John." In *Peake's Commentary on the Bible*. Edited by M. Black and H. H. Rowley. Pages 1035–40. New York: Thomas Nelson, 1962.

Kysar, R. *I, II, III John*. ACNT. Minneapolis: Augsburg, 1986.

Marshall, I. H. *The Epistles of John*. NICNT. Grand Rapids: Eerdmans, 1978.

Morris, L. "1 John, 2 John, 3 John." In *The New Bible Commentary: Revised*. Edited by D. Guthrie, et al. Pages 1259–73. Grand Rapids: Eerdmans, 1970.

Perkins, P. *The Johannine Epistles*. New Testament Message 21. Wilmington, Del.: Michael Glazier, 1979.

Plummer, A. *The Epistles of John*. Cambridge: Cambridge University, 1886; Grand Rapids: Baker, 1980.

Schnackenburg, R. *The Johannine Epistles. A Commentary*. Translated by R. H. and I. Fuller. New York: Crossroad, 1992.

Shepherd, M. H., Jr. "The Letters of John." In *The Interpreter's One-Volume Commentary on the Bible*. Edited by C. M. Laymon. Pages 935–41. Nashville: Abingdon, 1971.

Smalley, S. S. *1, 2, 3 John*. Word Biblical Commentary 51. Waco, Tex.: Word, 1984.

Smith, D. M. *First, Second, and Third John*. Interpretation. Louisville: John Knox, 1991.

Stott, J. R. W. *The Letters of John*. Revised edition. TC. Grand Rapids: Eerdmans, 1988.

Strecker, G. *Die Johannesbriefe*. Kritisch-Exegetischer Kommentar über das Neue Testament 14. Göttingen: Vandenhoeck & Ruprecht, 1989.

Thompson, M. M. *1–3 John*. IVPNTC. Downers Grove, Ill.: InterVarsity, 1992.

Thüsing, W. *The Three Epistles of John*. The New Testament for Spiritual Reading 23. New York: Herder & Herder, 1971.

Vawter, B. "The Johannine Epistles." In *The Jerome Biblical Commentary*. Edited by R. E. Brown, et al. Section 62. Englewood Cliffs, N.J.: Prentice-Hall, 1968.

Westcott, B. F. *The Epistles of St. John*. 3d ed. London: Macmillan, 1892; Grand Rapids: Eerdmans, 1960.

Wilder, A. N. "Introduction and Exegesis of the First, Second, and Third Epistles of John." In *The Interpreter's Bible*. Edited by G. A. Buttrick. Volume 12. Pages 207–313. Nashville: Abingdon, 1957.

Background and Theology

Aune, D. *Prophecy in Early Christianity and the Ancient Mediterranean World*. Grand Rapids: Eerdmans, 1983.

Bauer, W. *Orthodoxy and Heresy in Earliest Christianity*. Translated by Philadelphia Seminar on Christian Origins. Edited by R. A. Kraft and G. Krodel. Philadelphia: Fortress, 1971.

Betz, H. D. "Orthodoxy and Heresy in Primitive Christianity." *Int* 19 (1965), pp. 299–311.

Bogart, J. *Orthodox and Heretical Perfectionism in the Johannine Community*. Society of Biblical Literature Dissertation Series 33. Missoula, Mont.: Scholars, 1977.

Boice, J. M. *Witness and Revelation in the Gospel of John*. Grand Rapids: Zondervan, 1970.

Boismard, M.-E. "The First Epistle of John and the Writings of Qumran." Chap. in J. H. Charlesworth, ed., *John and Qumran*. London: Chapman, 1972.

Borchert, G. L. "Ephesus," *ISBE* (1982). Volume 2. Pages 115–17.

Briggs, R. C. "Contemporary Study of the Johannine Epistles." *RevExp* 67 (1970), pp. 411–22.

Bromiley, G. W. "Witness of the Spirit," *ISBE* (1988). Volume 4. Pages 1087–88.

Brown, R. E. *The Community of the Beloved Disciple*. New York: Paulist, 1979.

_____. *The Gospel according to John, I–XII*. Anchor Bible 29. Garden City, N.Y.: Doubleday, 1966.

_____. *Jesus, God and Man*. New York: Macmillan, 1972.

_____. "The Qumran Scrolls and the Johannine Gospel and Epistles." Chap. in *New Testament Essays*. Garden City, N.Y.: Doubleday, 1968.

Brunner, E. *The Christian Doctrine of God*. Philadelphia: Westminster, 1949.

von Campenhausen, H. *Ecclesiastical Authority and Spiritual Power in the First Three Centuries*. Stanford: Stanford University, 1969.

Carson, D. A. *The Gospel according to John*. Grand Rapids: Eerdmans, 1991.

Charlesworth, J. H., ed. *John and Qumran*. London: Chapman, 1972.

Cullmann, O. *The Christology of the New Testament*. Philadelphia: Westminster, 1963.

_____. *The Johannine Circle*. Philadelphia: Westminster, 1976.

Culpepper, R. A. *The Johannine School*. Society of Biblical Literature Dissertation Series 26. Missoula, Mont.: Scholars, 1975.

_____. "The Pivot of John's Prologue." *NTS* 27 (1980–81), pp. 1–31.

Dodd, C. H. "The First Epistle of John and the Fourth Gospel." *BJRL* 27 (1937), pp. 129–36.

_____. *The Interpretation of the Fourth Gospel*. Cambridge: Cambridge University, 1953.

Dunn, J. D. G. *Christology in the Making*. Philadelphia: Westminster, 1980.

_____. *Unity and Diversity in the New Testament*. London: SCM, 1977.

Filson, F. V. "First John: Purpose and Message." *Int* 23 (1969), pp. 259–76.

Fuller, R. H., ed. *Essays on the Love Commandment*. Philadelphia: Fortress, 1978.

Furnish, V. P. *The Love Command in the New Testament*. Nashville: Abingdon, 1972.

Goppelt, L. *Theology of the New Testament*. Two volumes. Grand Rapids: Eerdmans, 1981.

Gustafson, J. P. "Schismatic Groups." *Human Relations* 31 (1978), pp. 139–54.

Hengel, M. *The Johannine Question*. Philadelphia: Trinity International, 1991.

_____. *Son of God*. Philadelphia: Fortress, 1976.

Howard, W. F. *Christianity according to St. John*. London: Duckworth, 1943.

_____. "The Common Authorship of the Johannine Gospel and Epistles." *JTS* 48 (1947), pp. 12–25.

Jeremias, J. *The Central Message of the New Testament*. London: SCM, 1965.

_____. *New Testament Theology*. Volume 1: *The Proclamation of Jesus*. London: SCM, 1971.

Johnson, T. F. *The Antitheses of the Elder: A Study of the Dualistic Language of the Johannine Epistles*. Duke University diss. Ann Arbor: University Microfilms, 1979.

de Jonge, M. "Who Are 'We'?" In *Jesus: Inspiring and Disturbing Presence*. Nashville: Abingdon, 1974.

Käsemann, E. "Ketzer und Zeuge." *ZThK* 48 (1951), pp. 292–311.

Kümmel, W. G. *The Theology of the New Testament*. Nashville: Abingdon, 1973.

Kysar, R. *John, the Maverick Gospel*. Atlanta: John Knox, 1976.

Ladd, G. E. "Eschatology," *ISBE* (1982). Volume 2. Pages 130–43.

_____. *The Pattern of New Testament Truth*. Grand Rapids: Eerdmans, 1968.

_____. *A Theology of the New Testament*. Grand Rapids: Eerdmans, 1974.

Law, R. *The Tests of Life*. 3d ed. Edinburgh: T. & T. Clark, 1914; Grand Rapids: Baker, 1968.

Lee, G. A. "Letters." *ISBE* (1986). Volume 3. Pages 107–8.

Lieu, J. *The Second and Third Epistles of John*. Edinburgh: T. & T. Clark, 1986.

_____. *The Theology of the Johannine Epistles*. Cambridge: Cambridge University, 1991.

Malatesta, E. *Interiority and Covenant*. Analecta Biblica 69. Rome: Biblical Institute, 1978.

Malherbe, A. J. "The Inhospitality of Diotrephes." In *God's Christ and His People*. Edited by J. Jervell and W. A. Meeks. Pages 222–32. Oslo: Universitet, 1977.

Malina, B. *Christian Origins and Cultural Anthropology*. Atlanta: John Knox, 1986.

Marshall, I. H. *Kept by the Power of God*. Minneapolis: Bethany House, 1975.

Martyn, J. L. *History and Theology in the Fourth Gospel*. Revised edition. Nashville: Abingdon, 1979.

Meeks, W. A. "The Man from Heaven in Johannine Sectarianism." *JBL* 91 (1972), pp. 44–72.

Morris, L. *The Biblical Doctrine of Judgment*. Grand Rapids: Eerdmans, 1960.

_____. *Jesus is the Christ: Studies in the Theology of John*. Grand Rapids: Eerdmans, 1989.

_____. *New Testament Theology*. Grand Rapids: Zondervan, 1986.

Neyrey, J. *An Ideology of Revolt: John's Christology in Social-Science Perspective*. Philadelphia: Fortress, 1988.

Painter, J. *John: Witness and Theologian*. London: SPCK, 1975.

_____. "The 'Opponents' in 1 John." *NTS* 32 (1986), pp. 48–71.

Pannenberg, W. *Jesus—God and Man*. Philadelphia: Westminster, 1968.

Perkins, P. *Love Commands in the New Testament*. New York: Paulist, 1982.

Rensberger, D. *Johannine Faith and Liberating Community*.Philadelphia: Westminster, 1988.

Reumann, J. *Variety and Unity in New Testament Thought*. New York: Oxford, 1991.

Richards, W. L. *The Classification of the Greek Manuscripts of the Johannine Epistles*. Society of Biblical Literature Dissertation Series 35. Missoula, Mont.: Scholars, 1977.

Robinson, J. A. T. *The Priority of John*. London: SCM, 1985.

Schaeffer, F. A. *The New Super Spirituality*. Downers Grove, Ill.: InterVarsity, 1972.

Schmithals, W. *Gnosticism in Corinth*. Nashville: Abingdon, 1971.

Schnackenburg, R. *The Gospel according to St. John*. Three volumes. Montreal: Herder/Palm, 1968; New York: Seabury/Crossroad, 1980, 1982.

Scholer, D. M. "Sins Within and Sins Without: An Interpretation of 1 John 5:16–17." In *Current Issues in Biblical Interpretation*. Edited by G. F. Hawthorne. Pages 230–46. Grand Rapids: Eerdmans, 1975.

Schweizer, E. *Church Order in the New Testament*. Studies in Biblical Theology, 32. London: SCM, 1961. Pages 117–30.
_____. *A Theological Introduction to the New Testament*.Nashville: Abingdon, 1991.

Scroggs, R. *Christology in Paul and John*. Philadelphia: Fortress, 1988.

Segovia, F. F. *The Farewell of the Word: The Johannine Call to Abide*. Minneapolis: Fortress, 1991.
_____. *Love Relationships in the Johannine Tradition*. Society of Biblical Literature Dissertation Series 58. Chico, Calif.: Scholars, 1982.

Smalley, S. S. *John: Evangelist and Interpreter*. Exeter: Paternoster, 1978.

Smith, D. M. *Johannine Christianity: Essays on its Setting, Sources, and Theology*. Columbia, S.C.: University of South Carolina, 1984.

_____. *John*. Proclamation Commentaries. 2d ed. Philadelphia: Fortress, 1986.

Stagg, F. "Orthodoxy and Orthopraxy in the Johannine Epistles." *RevExp* 67 (1970), pp. 423–32.

Taylor, V. *The Person of Christ in New Testament Teaching*. London: Macmillan, 1958.

Trites, A. A. *The New Testament Concept of Witness*. Cambridge: Cambridge University, 1977.

von Wahlde, U. C. *The Johannine Commandments: 1 John and the Struggle for the Johannine Tradition*. New York: Paulist, 1990.

_____. "The Theological Foundation of the Presbyter's Argument in 2 Jn (vv 4–6)." *ZNW* (1985), pp. 209–24.

Weiss, K. "Orthodoxie und Heterodoxie im 1. Johannesbrief." *ZNW* 58 (1967), pp. 247–55.

Wengst, K. *Häresie und Orthodoxie im Spiegel des ersten Johannesbriefes*. Gütersloh: Mohn, 1976.

Whitacre, R. *Johannine Polemic: The Role of Tradition and Theology*. Society of Biblical Literature Dissertation Series 67. Chico, Calif.: Scholars, 1982.

Wilson, J. "The Sociology of Schism." In *A Sociological Yearbook of Religion in Britain 4*. Edited by M. Hill. Pages 1–20. London: SCM, 1971.

Wohl, D. B. *Johannine Christianity in Conflict*. Society of Biblical Literature Dissertation Series 60. Chico, Calif.: Scholars, 1981.

Wright, G. E. *God Who Acts: Biblical Theology as Recital*. Studies in Biblical Theology 8. London: SCM, 1952.

Word Studies

Abba, R. "Name." *IDB* (1962). Volume 3. Pages 500–508.

Bietenhard, H., and F. F. Bruce. "Name." *NIDNTT* (1976). Volume 2. Pages 648–56.

Bornkamm, G. *"presbys, presbyteros, etc."* *TDNT* (1968). Volume 6. Pages 651–83.

Braumann, G. "Child." *NIDNTT* (1975). Volume 1. Pages 285–87.

Brown, C. "Child." *NIDNTT* (1975). Volume 1. Pages 283–85.

Bultmann, R. *"ginōskō."* *TDNT* (1964). Volume 1. Pages 689–719.

Coenen, L. "Bishop, Presbyter, Elder." *NIDNTT* (1975). Volume 1. Pages 188–201.

Coenen, L., and A. A. Trites. "Witness." *NIDNTT* (1978). Volume 3. Pages 1038–51.

Conzelmann, H. *"phōs."* *TDNT* (1974). Volume 9. Pages 310–58.

Delling, G. *"telos."* *TDNT* (1972). Volume 8. Pages 49–87.

Eichler, J. "Fellowship, Have, Share, Participate." *NIDNTT* (1975). Volume 1. Pages 635–39.

Foerster, W. *"sōzō, etc."* *TDNT* (1971). Volume 7. Pages 980–1012.

Guenther, J. "Brother." *NIDNTT* (1975). Volume 1. Pages 254–58.

Hahn, H.-C., and C. Brown. "Light." *NIDNTT* (1976). Volume 2. Pages 490–96.

Hanse, H. *"echō."* *TDNT* (1964). Volume 2. Pages 816–32.

Hawthorne, G. F. "Name." *ISBE* (1986). Volume 3. Pages 480–83.

Kauder, E. "Antichrist." *NIDNTT* (1975). Volume 1. Pages 124–26.

Kittel, G. *"abba."* *TDNT* (1964). Volume 1. Pages 5–6.

Klooster, F. H. "Judgment, Last." *ISBE* (1982). Volume 2. Pages 1162–63.

Laubach, F. "Blood." *NIDNTT* (1975). Volume 1. Pages 220–24.

Michaelis, W. *"mimeomai."* *TDNT* (1967). Volume 4. Pages 659–74.

Michel, O. *"homologeō, etc."* *TDNT* (1967). Volume 5. Pages 199–220.

_____. "Son of God." *NIDNTT* (1978). Volume 3. Pages 634–48.

_____. "Faith." *NIDNTT* (1975). Volume 1. Pages 602–3.

Oepke, A. *"pais."* *TDNT* (1967). Volume 5. Pages 636–54.

Peisker, C. H., and C. Brown. "Prophet." *NIDNTT* (1978). Volume 3. Pages 74–92.

Piper, O. "Child." *IDB* (1962). Volume 1. Page 558.

_____. "Life." *IDB* (1962). Volume 3. Pages 124–30.

de la Potterie, I. *La vérité dans Saint Jean.* Analecta Biblica 73–74. Two volumes. Rome: Biblical Institute, 1977.

Sasse, H. *"kosmos."* *TDNT* (1965). Volume 3. Pages 867–98.

Schneider, W. "Judgment." *NIDNTT* (1976). Volume 2. Pages 361–68.

von Soden, H. *"adelphos."* *TDNT* (1964). Volume 1. Pages 144–46.

Stein, R. H. "Entertain." *ISBE* (1982). Volume 2. Pages 105–7.

Thiselton, A. "Truth." *NIDNTT* (1978). Volume 3. Pages 889–94.

Thomson, J. E. H. "Antichrist." *ISBE* (1979). Volume 1. Pages 139–41.

Reference Works

Aland, K., M. Black, et al., eds. *The Greek New Testament*. 3d ed. Stuttgart: United Bible Societies, 1983.

Bauer, W., W. F. Arndt, F. W. Gingrich, and F. Danker, eds. *A Greek-English Lexicon of the New Testament and Other Early Christian Literature*. Chicago: University of Chicago, 1979.

Black, M., and H. H. Rowley. *Peake's Commentary on the Bible*. New York: Thomas Nelson, 1962.

Bromiley, G. W., ed. *The International Standard Bible Encyclopedia*. 4 volumes. Grand Rapids: Eerdmans, 1979–88.

Brown, C., ed. *The New International Dictionary of New Testament Theology*. 3 volumes. Translated, with additions and revisions, from *Theologisches Begriffslexikon zum Neuen Testament*. Edited by L. Coenen, E. Beyreuther, and H. Bietenhard. Grand Rapids: Zondervan, 1975–78.

Brown, R. E., et al., eds. *The Jerome Biblical Commentary*. Englewood Cliffs, N.J.: Prentice-Hall, 1968.

Buttrick, G. A., ed. *The Interpreter's Bible*. 12 volumes. Nashville: Abingdon, 1957.

_____, ed. *The Interpreter's Dictionary of the Bible*. 4 volumes. New York/Nashville: Abingdon, 1962.

Gaebelein, F., ed. *The Expositor's Bible Commentary*. 12 volumes. Grand Rapids: Zondervan, 1981.

Guthrie, D. *New Testament Introduction*. 3d edition. Downers Grove, Ill.: InterVarsity, 1970.

_____, et al., ed. *The New Bible Commentary: Revised*. Grand Rapids: Eerdmans, 1970.

Kittel, G., and G. Friedrich, eds. *Theological Dictionary of the New Testament*. 10 volumes. Translated by G. W. Bromiley. Grand Rapids: Eerdmans, 1964–76.

_____. *Theological Dictionary of the New Testament: Abridged in One Volume*. Edited and abridged by G. W. Bromiley. Grand Rapids: Eerdmans, 1985.

Kümmel, W. G. *Introduction to the New Testament*. Translated by H. C. Kee. Nashville: Abingdon, 1975.

Laymon, C. M., ed. *The Interpreter's One-Volume Commentary on the Bible*. Nashville: Abingdon, 1971.

Metzger, B. M. *A Textual Commentary on the Greek New Testament*. New York: United Bible Societies, 1971.

Nestle, E., K. Aland, et al., eds. *Novum Testamentum Graece*. 26th ed. Stuttgart: Deutsche Bibelstiftung, 1979.

The New Merriam-Webster Dictionary. Springfield, Mass.: Merriam-Webster, 1989.

Phillips, J. B. *The New Testament in Modern English*. Rev. ed. New York: Macmillan, 1972.

Vermes, G. *The Dead Sea Scrolls in English*. Baltimore: Penguin Books, 1975.

Wagner, G., ed. *An Exegetical Bibliography of the New Testament: John and 1, 2, 3 John*. Macon, Ga.: Mercer University, 1987.

Subject Index

Scripture Index